TECHNICAL REPORT

Near-Term Opportunities for Integrating Biomass into the U.S. Electricity Supply

Technical Considerations

David S. Ortiz • Aimee E. Curtright • Constantine Samaras • Aviva Litovitz • Nicholas Burger

Sponsored by the National Energy Technology Laboratory

Environment, Energy, and Economic Development

A RAND INFRASTRUCTURE, SAFETY, AND ENVIRONMENT PROGRAM

This research was sponsored by the National Energy Technology Laboratory and was conducted in the Environment, Energy, and Economic Development Program within RAND Infrastructure, Safety, and Environment.

Library of Congress Cataloging-in-Publication Data

Near-term opportunities for integrating biomass into the U.S. electricity supply : technical considerations / David S. Ortiz ... [et al.].
      p. cm.
  Includes bibliographical references.
  "TR-984."
  ISBN 978-0-8330-5835-5 (pbk. : alk. paper)
  1. Biomass energy—United States. 2. Electric power plants—United States—Fuel. 3. Electric power production—United States. I. Ortiz, David (David Santana).

   TP339.N43 2011
   333.95'39—dc23

                                                                                    2011027125

The RAND Corporation is a nonprofit institution that helps improve policy and decisionmaking through research and analysis. RAND's publications do not necessarily reflect the opinions of its research clients and sponsors.

RAND® is a registered trademark.

Published 2011 by the RAND Corporation
1776 Main Street, P.O. Box 2138, Santa Monica, CA 90407-2138
1200 South Hayes Street, Arlington, VA 22202-5050
4570 Fifth Avenue, Suite 600, Pittsburgh, PA 15213-2665
RAND URL: http://www.rand.org/
To order RAND documents or to obtain additional information, contact
Distribution Services: Telephone: (310) 451-7002;
Fax: (310) 451-6915; Email: order@rand.org

Preface

In light of potential regulatory limits on greenhouse-gas (GHG) emissions, requirements for greater use of renewable fuels, and higher prices for some conventional fossil resources, over the course of the next few decades, biomass is expected to become an increasingly important source of electricity, heat, and liquid fuel. One near-term option for using biomass to generate electricity is to cofire biomass in coal-fired electricity plants. So doing allows such plants to reduce GHG emissions and, in appropriate regulatory environments, to generate renewable-energy credits to recover costs.

The National Energy Technology Laboratory (NETL) asked the RAND Corporation to identify and quantify potential issues associated with cofiring biomass in existing facilities. This report focuses on two aspects of biomass use: plant-site modifications, changes in operations, and costs associated with cofiring biomass; and the logistical issues associated with delivering biomass to the plant. To ensure that our analysis builds on the existing experience base using biomass as a fuel for electricity generation, we conducted a series of interviews with plant owners and operators. To assist us in formulating the subsequent quantitative analysis, these interviews occurred at the beginning of the project.

The research and analysis reported here builds on prior work RAND has performed for NETL, particularly the following:

- "Incorporating Uncertainty Analysis into Life Cycle Estimates of Greenhouse Gas Emissions from Biomass Production," by David R. Johnson, Henry H. Willis, Aimee E. Curtright, Constantine Samaras, and Timothy Skone, *Biomass and Bioenergy*, Vol. 35, No. 7, July 2011, pp. 2619–2626
- *Calculating Uncertainty in Biomass Emissions Model, Version 1.0 (CUBE 1.0)*, by Aimee E. Curtright, Henry H. Willis, David R. Johnson, David S. Ortiz, Nicholas Burger, and Constantine Samaras, 2010 (see "Uncertainty in Biomass Greenhouse Gas Emissions," 2011)
- *Supplying Biomass to Power Plants: A Model of the Costs of Utilizing Agricultural Biomass in Cofired Power Plants*, by Tom LaTourrette, David S. Ortiz, Eileen Hlavka, Nicholas Burger, and Gary Cecchine, TR-876-DOE, 2011.

This report should be of interest to decisionmakers and analysts addressing issues associated with using biomass at existing coal-fired power plants. Because the analysis reports and is based on recent experience, it should be of interest to plant owners and operators interested in current and potential costs and other implications of using biomass as a fuel to generate electricity.

The RAND Environment, Energy, and Economic Development Program

This research was conducted in the Environment, Energy, and Economic Development Program (EEED) within RAND Infrastructure, Safety, and Environment (ISE). The mission of ISE is to improve the development, operation, use, and protection of society's essential physical assets and natural resources and to enhance the related social assets of safety and security of individuals in transit and in their workplaces and communities. The EEED research portfolio addresses environmental quality and regulation, energy resources and systems, water resources and systems, climate, natural hazards and disasters, and economic development—both domestically and internationally. EEED research is conducted for government, foundations, and the private sector.

Questions or comments about this report should be sent to the project leader, David Ortiz (David_Ortiz@rand.org). Information about EEED is available online (http://www.rand.org/ise/environ). Inquiries about EEED projects should be sent to the following address:

Keith Crane, Director
Environment, Energy, and Economic Development Program, ISE
RAND Corporation
1200 South Hayes Street
Arlington, VA 22202-5050
703-413-1100, x5520
Keith_Crane@rand.org

Contents

Figures

Tables

Summary

In light of potential regulatory limits on GHG emissions, mandates for renewable-energy use in emerging legislation, and potentially higher prices for some conventional fossil fuels, biomass could become an increasingly important source of fuel for generating electricity and heat and for manufacturing liquid fuels. Biomass energy resources are organic matter, typically trees or plants, grown and harvested for the purpose of producing energy. Examples of biomass resources include the uncollected tops and branches from forestry operations, agricultural residues, and crops specifically grown for the purpose of producing energy, such as switchgrass. In general, because plants convert carbon dioxide (CO_2) in the air into carbon-containing compounds that form the plant, the life-cycle GHG emissions of biomass are significantly less than those of fossil fuels.

In 2008, approximately 14 million tons of biomass were burned in dedicated or cofired facilities to generate approximately 28 billion kilowatt-hours (kWh) of electricity, 1.3 percent of total electricity generation in the United States (Energy Information Administration [EIA], 2009). If biomass is to significantly reduce GHG emissions that result from generating electricity, biomass use will need to increase substantially.

The U.S. Department of Energy's (DOE's) NETL requested that RAND characterize the technical and logistical constraints to using biomass, and potential solutions to overcome them, in the current U.S. energy system. RAND was asked to focus on plants that could easily use biomass resources, the technical issues associated with cofiring biomass, constraints that could arise in transporting and processing the biomass, and the conditions under which broader markets for biomass resources could develop.

This is the fourth study for NETL by RAND specifically focused on biomass resources. The first study analyzed biomass as a potential supplementary feedstock for the production of liquid fuels and supported a larger effort (NETL, 2009c). The second characterized the life-cycle GHG emissions from producing biomass (Curtright et al., 2010). The third study characterized the cost, quantity, and land used when producing biomass on agricultural lands for a single plant (LaTourrette et al., 2011).

Analytical Goals and Methodology

In this report, we posed four analytical questions:

- What are the technical constraints and costs of cofiring at the plant site? Biomass is a different fuel from coal and needs distinct handling and processing steps, requiring additional capital equipment and increasing operating expenses at the plant. The viability of biomass as a means of reducing GHG emissions from coal-fired power plants depends critically on these costs.

- What are the characteristics and costs of biomass supply systems, and what is their effect on delivered prices of biomass energy resources? In general, biomass is a low-density resource requiring a large area to supply commercial quantities of fuels. Are there opportunities for densifying biomass to reduce transportation costs and improve commercial viability?
- What GHG savings can cofiring provide and at what cost? Because the current motivation for using biomass resources to produce electricity is to reduce GHG emissions, a quantitative analysis of these emissions is needed.
- What are the current characteristics of markets for biomass energy resources, and what are likely paths to development? Under what conditions could this immature market develop to a more formal market with standard grades of biomass and more-formal supply contracts?

Because biomass has low levels of sulfur and is more reactive than coal, cofiring biomass can reduce the emissions of criteria pollutants from coal-fired power plants. The DOE carried out a number of cofire tests in collaboration with the Electric Power Research Institute (EPRI) demonstrating the viability of this approach (Tillman, 2001). In interviews, several generating companies were able to give us more-current insights into how they source biomass, plant-site requirements for cofiring and dedicated facilities, and the key factors underlying firm-level decisionmaking about using biomass. Using the information gleaned from these interviews, we formulated three distinct supply scenarios to analyze the costs of alternative approaches to sourcing biomass resources:

- biomass supplied from the local area, i.e., the contiguous area surrounding the plant
- biomass supplied from the local area augmented with densified biomass imported from another region
- densified biomass supplied entirely from a distant region.

The three supply scenarios differentiate themselves along the types of biomass supplied and the delivered cost of biomass. Table S.1 lists the results of this logistical analysis. To make the logistical analysis representative of current biomass sourcing and potential near-term alternatives, local biomass supplies are assumed to be clean greenwood.

Table S.1
Estimated Cost of Delivered Biomass for Three Logistical Scenarios

Scenario	Characteristics	Type(s) of Biomass	Cost of Delivered Biomass ($/GJ)	Cost of Delivered Biomass ($/metric ton)
1	Local sourcing of biomass	Woody biomass	2.1	40
2	Local sourcing, augmented with external deliveries via rail	Woody biomass and woody pellets	3.3	62
3	External deliveries via barge	Herbaceous pellets	6.9	120

NOTE: GJ = gigajoule (10^9 joules).

To determine the life-cycle GHG emissions from sourcing, processing, and burning biomass, we apply the Calculating Uncertainty in Biomass Emissions (CUBE) model (Curtright et al., 2010). By coupling the GHG analysis with the biomass costs derived for the supply scenarios and the plant-site costs, we are then able to determine the cost of avoiding a given amount of GHG emissions. Using information provided during the interviews, we then considered key factors in the development of biomass markets and the potential benefits of such markets.

Key Findings

Plant Operators' Experiences Cofiring Biomass

The Principal Challenge with Respect to Cofiring Biomass Is Maintaining a Consistent Fuel Supply. Plant operators reported that cofiring with biomass at up to 10 percent of total fuel energy had little effect on the performance of the boiler or on installed emission-control equipment. The lower energy content and increased moisture content of biomass relative to coal can result in a reduction in plant generating capacity, but plant operators did not cite this as a significant concern. These results are consistent with reported experience in Europe (Van Loo and Koppejan, 2008) and the United States (Tillman, 2001; Antares Group, 2009). However, most domestic experience to date concerning cofiring biomass with coal is recent, consisting of test fires or a year or two of cofiring. The potential effects that long-term cofiring (i.e., greater than five years) could have on plant components are still unknown.

One potential technical improvement that was identified, especially for boilers that burn pulverized coal (PC), is the development of a burner specifically designed to fire biomass or mixtures of biomass and coal. Biomass storage, handling, and processing can be challenging; plant operators reported that programs that facilitate the sharing of lessons learned and best practices could be a benefit.

The most significant concern cited by the majority of interviewees was the challenge of securing a consistent supply of biomass. Suppliers tend to be small, so plants find that it is necessary to maintain relationships with several dozen suppliers to meet the fuel requirements for the plant. We did speak with one aggregator who maintains a database of biomass fuel suppliers and will charge a premium to guarantee a consistent supply of biomass.

The Choice to Cofire Biomass Depends on a Confluence of Technical and Regulatory Factors. In the absence of regulation of GHG emissions, the decision to convert a plant to cofire depends more on regulatory and policy factors than on technical factors:

- The plant operator must be able to recover the additional costs of cofiring through renewable-energy credits (RECs) or increases in rates.
- The ability to burn biomass must be included in the existing air permit for the plant.

Surprisingly, we did not find that the type of boiler factored significantly into the decision about whether to cofire biomass with coal: Appropriate handling and processing methods have been devised and tested to allow biomass to be used with any type of boiler. It is the aggregate of the plant's technical characteristics, cost to implement, policy, and regulatory factors that currently lead plant operators to choose to cofire biomass with coal.

Plant-Site Costs of Cofiring

Cofiring Biomass Results in Increased Capital and Operating Costs and Lost Revenues.
We built a model to estimate the plant-site costs of cofiring biomass and coal at low cofire fractions (i.e., below approximately 10 percent biomass by energy content). At current prices for woody biomass (approximately $40 per dry metric ton), the additional costs associated with cofiring at 5 percent by energy are approximately $0.021 per kilowatt-hour. These costs include $0.007 per kilowatt-hour each for increased capital and nonfuel operating costs, $0.001 per kilowatt-hour for biomass fuel, and $0.005 per kilowatt-hour of lost revenue. The lost revenue is due to two factors: The plant is slightly less efficient when cofiring biomass, and the biomass requires additional parasitic electricity to process—electricity that could be sold. The costs rise linearly with the price of biomass, rising $0.006 per kilowatt-hour for each $10 increase in biomass prices: At prices for wood chips of $120 per dry metric ton, the cost of cofiring is an additional $0.069 per kilowatt-hour.

Densification of Biomass Does Not Result in Plant-Site Cost Savings. Because densified biomass (i.e., pellets) requires fewer plant-site modifications and can be commingled with coal, densification might result in significant plant-site cost savings over other biomass forms. As mentioned earlier, the additional costs of cofiring wood chips are $0.021 per kilowatt-hour at current prices of $40 per dry ton. Our analysis indicates that the delivered cost of herbaceous pellets would be $120 per dry metric ton. At that cost of biomass, the cost of cofiring at 5 percent is an additional $0.069 per kilowatt-hour.

Fixed-Price Renewable-Energy Credits Might Not Be an Effective Tool to Encourage Cofiring. Another interpretation of the cost of cofiring is the required price of a REC to recover costs associated with cofiring. For current woody biomass prices of $40 per dry metric ton, the implied price of a REC (at 5-percent cofiring) for a bus-bar electricity price of $0.0444 per kilowatt-hour is approximately $0.021 per kilowatt-hour. However, as the price of biomass rises, so does the required price of a REC. At biomass supply prices of $62 per dry metric ton, the implied price of a REC is $0.032 per kilowatt-hour, at $120 per dry metric ton, the implied price of a REC is $0.069 per kilowatt-hour. One of the plant operators we interviewed reported that he was able to receive a REC of $0.045 per kilowatt-hour, which covers costs of cofiring and associated revenue losses up to a biomass price of approximately $80 per dry metric ton. The implication of these results is that, because of the inherently varying nature of the costs, a fixed-price REC might not be an appropriate means to encourage cofiring and might be more applicable to other renewable-energy sources, such as wind, where most costs are fixed rather than variable.

Potential Biomass Demand and Logistics

The Appalachia and Northeast Regions Are Potential Biomass Importers, and the Pacific and Lake States Regions Are Potential Suppliers. Cofiring replaces a fraction of coal with biomass. If there were a widespread movement toward cofiring, regions in which a significant amount of the installed generating capacity is currently coal based could exhaust locally available resources. Conversely, a surplus of resources might exist in regions in which there was relatively little installed coal-fired electricity generating capacity. Our analysis indicates that the U.S. Department of Agriculture (USDA) Appalachia, Southern Plains, Northeast, and Mountain regions would likely exhaust local biomass resources under scenarios with significant development of cofiring, whereas the Pacific, Delta, Northern Plains, and Lake States regions could potentially be biomass suppliers.

Densification of Biomass Is Cost-Effective at Distances Greater Than 200 Miles. Densifying biomass adds between $16 and $34 per dry metric ton to the cost of biomass. However, pellets have a high bulk density and low moisture content and are easier to handle than other forms of biomass. As a result, the benefit of densification can be realized when transporting biomass long distances. Our analysis indicates that, when shipping by rail, the minimum distance at which the savings in transportation costs offsets pelletization costs is approximately 225 miles for wood chips and about 200 miles for herbaceous bales. When shipping by barge, the minimum distances are 230 miles for wood chips and 160 miles for bales. Although densification provides a cost savings over raw biomass at these transportation distances, additional transportation costs are still incurred. In our examples, these additional costs were $50 per dry metric ton for wood pellets transported from Minneapolis, Minnesota, to Pittsburgh, Pennsylvania, by rail and $15 per dry metric ton for herbaceous pellets transported from Paducah, Kentucky, to southern Ohio by barge.

Greenhouse-Gas Reductions from Cofiring

Cofiring Is a Cost-Effective Means of Reducing Greenhouse-Gas Emissions. The primary current motivation for cofiring biomass with coal is to reduce the life-cycle GHG emissions associated with producing electricity. We assess cofiring biomass at input-energy fractions of 2, 5, and 10 percent of total input energy because experience to date indicates that major plant modifications are not required to cofire biomass at or below these percentages. For the three supply scenarios that we considered, these results are summarized in Figure S.1; included in

Figure S.1
Cost of Abating Greenhouse Gases Through Cofiring Biomass with Coal

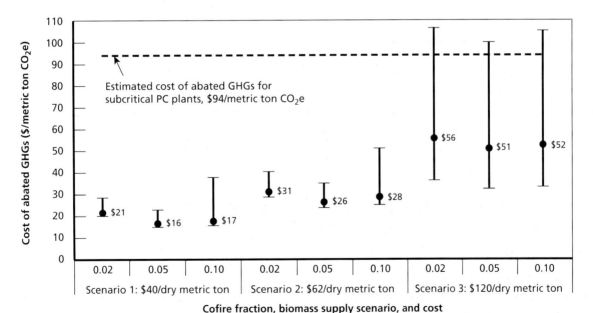

SOURCE: NETL (2010, Chapter Five and Appendixes B and E).
NOTE: $CO_2e = CO_2$ equivalent. Woody biomass is the source for scenarios 1 and 2, and herbaceous pellets are supplied in scenario 3. The price indicated on the figure represents the best estimate; error bars represent high and low estimates.
RAND *TR-984-S.1*

Figure S.1 is a reference line for the current estimated cost of abating a ton of CO_2 by carbon capture and storage (CCS) at a subcritical PC power plant (NETL, 2010).

Our analysis shows that the cost of abating GHG emissions is $21 per metric ton CO_2e at a cofire fraction of 2 percent and a biomass price of $40 per dry metric ton. The abatement costs drop as the cofire fraction increases: $16 per metric ton CO_2e for a cofire fraction of 5 percent. The cost of abating GHGs drops as the cofire fraction increases because it enables a higher utilization of the equipment installed to cofire biomass. The cost of abating GHGs rises for cofire fractions of 10 percent because additional electrical load is required to process the biomass, increasing processing costs. At a biomass supply cost of $120 per dry metric ton, approximately three times the current price of wood chips, the best estimate of the cost of abating GHGs is $51 per metric ton CO_2e when cofiring at 5 percent. These figures are compared with an estimated cost of abatement of $94 per metric ton CO_2e when retrofitting subcritical PC plants for carbon capture and sequestration (NETL, 2010). However, there is considerable uncertainty regarding the life-cycle GHG emissions of agricultural residues, resulting in estimated costs of abatement ranging from $33 to $100 per metric ton CO_2e.

Developing Biomass Markets

Biomass Markets for Electricity Generation Currently Cannot Support Densified Fuels. Currently, biomass energy markets in the United States comprise many small suppliers and are regionally diverse. Densified biomass could promote standardization and the integration of markets by (1) reducing plant-site costs for cofiring, (2) reducing transportation costs, and (3) increasing fuel flexibility and insulation from supply shocks. We found that propositions 1 and 2 are valid in certain circumstances and that 3 is questionable. It is true that biomass feed systems are less expensive for pellets than they are for raw biomass. For torrefied biomass, which is processed such that it has properties similar to those of coal, additional plant-site costs can be minimal. However, these differences in the costs of cofiring between densified and raw biomass are similar after taking into account the additional costs of producing a biomass pellet. Although transporting pellets long distances is less expensive than transporting raw biomass, the extra cost of manufacturing pellets results in a much higher total cost than that of using local raw biomass. Finally, the benefits of fuel flexibility do not exist in current biomass markets, which are characterized by an abundance of suppliers and an oversupply of biomass. In the absence of legislative requirements to use biomass, we expect such a situation to continue. If there were a requirement to use biomass, either as part of a state renewable portfolio standard or as a means of reducing life-cycle GHG emissions, that significantly increased delivered prices for local biomass, then pellets, and other densified forms of biomass, might become attractive.

Acknowledgments

First, we would like to thank all of the plant owners and operators whom we interviewed in carrying out this study. Of these, Jonathan Baylor and James O'Donnell at NRG Energy hosted us at their Dunkirk facility, provided key documentation regarding their plans for cofiring, and talked openly regarding their experiences. Greg Edwards, Norm Johnson, John Elder, Roy Byrd, David Leaf, and Conrad Francis of Dominion discussed their experiences and plans with us at length. Jordan Solomon and his team at Ecostrat provided significant insight regarding the potential for biomass integrators to resolve many of the supply challenges that are currently experienced. Additional people assisting us included Daniel McIntire, Paul Kramer, James Lefik, Thomas M. Nutter, Phil Wilhelm, Clyde E. Little, and Dan Dennis of Allegheny Energy (now FirstEnergy); Robert Grosjean and Hal Kruger of FirstEnergy; and Gus Cepero of Florida Crystals. Finally, we thank David O'Connor of the Electric Power Research Institute and Thomas Light of the RAND Corporation for their detailed and thoughtful reviews of the draft report.

We appreciate the work of the RAND team that maintains the CUBE model for assisting in the GHG analysis, especially David R. Johnson, who assisted in the development of the model of plant-site costs of cofiring. We would also like to thank NETL—in particular, Thomas J. Tarka, Timothy J. Skone, Robert M. Dilmore, and Michael Matuszewski for their feedback throughout the analytical process and to Maria Vargas and Kenneth C. Kern for their support of the work. As always, any errors and omissions are the responsibility of the authors.

Abbreviations

AMS	Agricultural Marketing Service
BCAP	Biomass Crop Assistance Program
BEA	Bureau of Economic Analysis
BNSF	Burlington Northern Santa Fe
Btu	British thermal unit
CARIA	Coosa-Alabama River Improvement Association
CCS	carbon capture and storage
CFB	circulating fluidized bed
CO	carbon monoxide
CO_2	carbon dioxide
CO_2e	carbon dioxide equivalent
CPI	consumer price index
CRP	Conservation Reserve Program
CUBE	Calculating Uncertainty in Biomass Emissions
CVBP	Chariton Valley Biomass Project
DEP	department of environmental protection
DOE	U.S. Department of Energy
EEED	Environment, Energy, and Economic Development Program
EIA	Energy Information Administration
EJ	exajoule (10^{18} joules)
EPA	U.S. Environmental Protection Agency
EPRI	Electric Power Research Institute
ERS	Economic Research Service

ESP	electrostatic precipitator
FB	fluidized bed
FGD	flue-gas desulfurization
GHG	greenhouse gas
GJ	gigajoule (10^9 joules)
GREET	Greenhouse Gases, Regulated Emissions, and Energy Use in Transportation
GW	gigawatt
GWh	gigawatt-hour
ha	hectare
HCl	hydrogen chloride
Hg	mercury
HHV	higher heating value
hp	Horsepower
IGCC	integrated gasification combined cycle
INL	Idaho National Laboratory
ISE	RAND Infrastructure, Safety, and Environment
ITC	investment tax credit
kWh	kilowatt-hour
LHV	lower heating value
MACT	maximum achievable control technology
MIT	Massachusetts Institute of Technology
mmBtu	million British thermal units (10^6 Btu)
MPB	mixed prairie biomass
MSW	municipal solid waste
MW	megawatt
MWe	megawatt electric
MWh	megawatt-hour
N_2O	nitrous oxide
NCC	National Coal Council
NERC	North American Electric Reliability Corporation

NETL	National Energy Technology Laboratory
NO_x	nitrogen oxides
NREL	National Renewable Energy Laboratory
NSR	New Source Review
O_3	ozone
O&M	operations and maintenance
ODE	overall decrease in efficiency
PC	pulverized coal
PJ	petajoule (10^{15} joules)
PM	particulate matter
$PM^{2.5}$	particulate matter smaller than 2.5 micrometers
PRB	Powder River Basin
PSD	Prevention of Significant Deterioration
PTC	production tax credit
quad	quadrillion British thermal units
R&D	research and development
RD&D	research, development, and demonstration
REC	renewable-energy credit
RPS	Renewable Portfolio Standard
SG	switchgrass
SNCR	selective noncatalytic reduction
SO_2	sulfur dioxide
SO_x	sulfur oxide
TDF	tire-derived fuel
T-fired	tangentially fired
TWh	terawatt-hour
USDA	U.S. Department of Agriculture

CHAPTER ONE

Introduction

In light of potential regulatory limits on greenhouse-gas (GHG) emissions, mandates for renewable-energy use in emerging legislation, and potentially higher prices for some conventional fossil fuels, biomass could become an increasingly important source of fuel for generating electricity and heat and for manufacturing liquid fuels. Biomass energy resources are organic matter, typically trees or plants, grown and harvested for the purpose of producing energy. Examples of biomass resources include the uncollected tops and branches from forestry operations, agricultural residues, and crops specifically grown for the purpose of producing energy, such as switchgrass. In general, because plants convert carbon dioxide (CO_2) in the air into carbon-containing compounds that form the plant, the life-cycle GHG emissions of biomass are significantly less than those of fossil fuels.

In 2008, approximately 14 million short tons, or 0.22 quadrillion British thermal units (Btu), of biomass were burned in dedicated or cofired facilities to generate approximately 28 billion kilowatt-hours (kWh) of electricity. This electricity accounted for 1.3 percent of U.S. electricity generation in that year (EIA, 2009). If biomass is to reduce GHG emissions that result from generating electricity, biomass use will need to increase substantially.

Effectively using biomass requires that energy facilities be built or modified and infrastructure constructed to transport and process biomass. A handful of dedicated and cofired plants in the United States currently use biomass to produce electricity. Many of these were part of an Electric Power Research Institute (EPRI)–U.S. Department of Energy (DOE) cooperative agreement to explore the effects of cofiring biomass with coal (Tillman, 2001).

Increasing the contribution of biomass to the U.S. energy supply will depend significantly on the availability and cost of biomass resources, policy requirements, community support for producing biomass energy resources, the technical capability to use effectively available resources, and the existence of appropriate infrastructure to gather, process, and deliver biomass. To address some of these uncertainties, this report quantifies the technical issues and recent experience associated with using biomass in dedicated and cofired facilities and identifies opportunities for research, development, and demonstration (RD&D) programs to encourage further use of biomass given an appropriate policy environment.

The DOE's National Energy Technology Laboratory (NETL) requested that RAND characterize the technical and logistical constraints to using biomass, and potential solutions to overcome them, in the current U.S. electric power system. RAND was asked to focus on plants that could easily use biomass resources, the technical issues associated with cofiring biomass, constraints that could arise in transporting and processing the biomass, and the conditions under which broader markets for biomass resources could develop.

1

This is the fourth study for NETL by RAND specifically focused on biomass resources. The first study analyzed biomass as a potential supplementary feedstock for the production of liquid fuels (NETL, 2009c). The second study characterized the life-cycle GHG emissions from producing biomass (Curtright et al., 2010). The third study characterized the cost, quantity, and land used when producing biomass on agricultural lands for a single plant (LaTourrette et al., 2011).

Background, Methodology, and Study Questions

Biomass offers a means for reducing emissions of GHGs and criteria pollutants from energy facilities. Since biomass is already being used for producing electricity and liquid fuels, our first task is to document the experience base regarding cofiring of biomass with coal. To carry out this task, we interviewed more than a dozen plant owners and operators with experience cofiring biomass with coal in electricity generating stations. The experiences of plant owners and operators are compared with findings from the literature (Van Loo and Koppejan, 2008; McGowan, 2009; Tillman, 2001).

Any effort to support the use of biomass should be consistent with the potential future scale of biomass use, both at the plant level and nationally. Among the key differences between biomass and coal are the scale and nature of the resource. Biomass energy resources grow throughout much of the country. But it is a relatively diffuse resource, yielding several tons of biomass per acre, which, in energy applications in the United States, has been collected and used locally. Coal, by contrast, is mined in specific areas and transported throughout the country, principally to generate electricity. The primary question underlying our second task therefore becomes, when growing and collecting biomass for energy use, under what conditions is it advantageous to transport it over long distances rather than use it exclusively locally? Observing the efficiency of the system for storing and transporting grain, the Idaho National Laboratory argues that a similar system based on densified biomass would be most advantageous to support a large-scale biomass industry (INL, 2009).

The market for biomass energy products in the United States is limited and geographically heterogeneous. There are no large-scale, commercial operations producing and providing biomass for energy purposes and, with few exceptions, no organized system for aggregating smaller-scale operations to deliver biomass products to end users (as exists for many agricultural commodities). Because these regional markets are generally underdeveloped, the supplies of biomass for energy are not well developed, and prices are depressed. Using the results of the plant-site and logistical analyses, we consider factors that could lead to the development of more-robust and efficient biomass energy markets supporting expanded production of electricity from biomass.

Finally, the acts of collecting forestry and agricultural residues and growing energy crops on a large scale will have environmental consequences. Some of these could be positive, such as reconstituting degraded lands by planting perennial grasses and improving ecosystem services. Others could be negative, such as contributing to soil erosion when insufficient residues are left on the ground, or inducing significant land-use changes. This report purposefully ignores these questions—not because they are not important but rather because we are concerned principally with initial applications of biomass resources; the scale of use proposed here is limited, as are environmental consequences. All should be included in a net-benefit analysis (e.g., Andrews, 2006; Hill et al., 2006).

Analytical Goals and Methodology

In this report, we pose four analytical questions:

- What are the technical constraints and costs of cofiring at the plant site? Biomass is a different fuel from coal and needs distinct handling and processing steps, requiring capital equipment and increasing operating expenses at the plant. The viability of biomass as a means of reducing GHG emissions from coal-fired power plants depends critically on these costs.
- What are the characteristics and costs of biomass supply systems, and what is their effect on delivered prices of biomass energy resources? In general, biomass is a low-density resource requiring a large area to supply commercial quantities of fuels. Are there opportunities for densifying biomass to reduce transportation costs and improve commercial viability?
- What GHG savings can cofiring provide and at what cost? Since the current motivation for using biomass resources to produce electricity is to reduce GHG emissions, a quantitative analysis of these emissions is needed.
- What are the current characteristics of markets for biomass energy resources, and what are likely paths to development? Under what conditions could this immature market develop to a more formal market with standard grades of biomass and more-formal supply contracts?

To begin answering these questions, we approached more than a dozen facilities with experience cofiring biomass and coal. Because biomass has low levels of sulfur and is more reactive than coal, cofiring biomass can reduce emissions of criteria pollutants from coal-fired power plants. Before 2001, the DOE carried out cofire tests in collaboration with EPRI demonstrating the viability of the approach (Tillman, 2001). Since that time, the electric power generating industry has consolidated; several of the plants that participated in that study have been purchased by other utilities. However, those generating companies that continued to operate cofired facilities were able to give us insights into how they source biomass, plant-site requirements for cofiring and dedicated facilities, and the key factors underlying firm-level decisionmaking about using biomass. For example, NRG Energy purchased the Dunkirk, New York, generating plant that had been part of the DOE cofire program in the 1990s. NRG is in the process of upgrading the biomass storage, handling, and processing systems at that plant. It is also considering opportunities for cofiring across its facilities. Other firms, such as Dominion and FirstEnergy, had experience burning biomass in their facilities and freely shared with us their experiences and how they came to decisions to use biomass.

Using the information learned from these interviews, we formulated a series of analytical tasks. Because of the significant diversity of biomass types and forms, boiler types, and biomass handling systems, we built an analytical tool to estimate the plant-site costs of cofiring. We formulated three distinct supply scenarios to analyze the costs of alternative approaches to sourcing biomass resources: (1) biomass supplied from the local area (i.e., the contiguous area surrounding the plant), (2) biomass supplied from the local area augmented with biomass imported from another region, and (3) biomass supplied entirely from a distant region. These scenarios are based on plausible biomass supply patterns derived from existing installed coal-fired power plant capacity and potential demands for biomass for cofiring with coal. To determine the life-cycle GHG emissions from sourcing, processing, and burning biomass, we apply the Calculating Uncertainty in Biomass Emissions (CUBE) model (Curtright et al., 2010). By coupling the GHG analysis with the biomass costs derived for the supply scenarios and the plant-site costs, we are then able to determine the cost of avoiding a given amount of GHGs. Using information provided during the interviews, we then considered key factors that would be needed to motivate the development of biomass markets, especially the potential benefits that might be brought by converting biomass to a standard form.

Regulatory Considerations

Though the scope of this analysis is technical, it is important to include a brief description of the policy environment to provide appropriate context. When conducting the interviews of plant owners and operators, we discovered that state and national policies are central to their decisionmaking process. In particular, the U.S. Environmental Protection Agency (EPA) is in the process of developing some rules regarding coal-fired power plants. Any coal-fired power plant owner considering cofiring with biomass would consider the relevance of these and other regulations in his or her decisionmaking process:

- National Emission Standards for Hazardous Air Pollutants for Utilities (EPA, 2011a). On March 16, 2011 (and updated May 3, 2011), EPA published a proposed rule regulating the emissions of mercury, heavy metals, acid gases, and toxic organic compounds, collectively referred to as hazardous air pollutants, from coal- and oil-fired electricity generating plants (EPA, 2011a). The proposed regulations limit the emissions of mercury and other air toxics. For new and existing coal-fired power plants, the proposed rule sets numerical limits on the amount of mercury, particulates (as a surrogate for other metals), and hydrogen chloride (HCl) (as a surrogate for acid gases). Toxic organic substances, such as dioxins, are formed from incomplete combustion of coal. As a response, the proposed rule establishes best work practices to ensure complete combustion and to reduce the emissions of these substances. The proposed rule is also known as the maximum achievable control technology (MACT) rule because the emission limits are set based on the average of the best-performing 12 percent of existing plants (North American Electric Reliability Corporation [NERC], 2010). Because there are no existing regulations of mercury from coal-fired power plants, the rule would affect essentially all coal-fired units in the United States, requiring investments in equipment to control emissions. Plant owners could choose to retire smaller and less economical units rather than invest in such controls. In the absence of requirements to use biomass, cofiring could be less attractive as a result of this rule and might occur only in the larger and more efficient units.
- The Cross-State Air Pollution Rule, which replaces the Clean Air Interstate Rule (EPA, 2011b). The purpose of the rule is to limit emissions of fine particulates and ozone (O_3) that can cross state lines, causing downwind pollution and problems maintaining stan-

dards for air quality.[1] The proposed rule applies to 27 states. Affected states are required to reduce annual emissions of SO_2 and nitrogen oxides (NO_x). Twenty states are required to reduce seasonal NO_x emissions that lead to the formation of ozone (EPA, 2010b). The strict emission controls can be met only with postcombustion flue-gas cleanup. NERC (2010) estimated that the rule would directly affect 163 gigawatts (GW) of coal-fired electricity generating capacity that does not have flue-gas desulfurization (FGD) systems installed and 180 GW of coal-fired electricity generating capacity that does not have postcombustion NO_x emission reduction installed. Biomass has inherently low levels of sulfur, and cofiring would reduce such emissions in proportion to the amount of biomass used at a plant. However, cofiring with biomass would be unlikely to result in reductions in SO_2 emissions sufficient to comply with the rule; new equipment would still be required, providing a disincentive to cofire with biomass.

- Prevention of Significant Deterioration and Title V Greenhouse Gas Tailoring Rule (a.k.a. the Tailoring Rule). Under this rule, issued in May 2010, EPA determined which facilities would be required to comply with regulations to reduce emissions of GHGs (EPA, 2010a). Notably, EPA did not exclude from its GHG-reduction permitting requirements those facilities that were combusting biomass. Biomass producers view the decision as a disincentive to use biomass for energy (Bravender, 2010). Our analysis regarding cofiring is consistent with the current language of the Tailoring Rule: We consider life-cycle GHG emissions that result from the cultivation, transportation, handling, and processing of biomass. However, without a regulatory guarantee of GHG reductions from biomass use, plant operators might hesitate to pursue cofiring as a means of achieving such reductions.

Outline of This Report

This report is structured as follows: Chapter Two presents the results of the plant operator interviews and key lessons that we carry forward in the technical analysis. Additional information regarding the plant operators, including descriptions of their firms and operating experience with biomass, appears in Appendix A. Chapters Three through Six present our analytical approach and results. Chapter Three presents the results regarding the plant-site costs of cofiring; documentation of the model supporting these results appears in Appendix B. An important consideration regarding the use of biomass to produce electricity is the potential national regional demand for biomass. In Chapter Four, we provide a coarse estimate of the potential demand for biomass and identify regions that are relatively biomass resource rich and poor with respect to currently installed coal-fired electricity capacity. Although a large-scale nationwide market for biomass energy does not exist in the United States, we hypothesize that the resource-rich regions are able to export biomass to meet potential demand in resource-poor regions. Using the regions identified in Chapter Four, in Chapter Five, we analyze the logistical costs of transporting biomass among regions, using a prototypical pulverized-coal (PC) plant cofiring biomass as the consumer. Chapter Six incorporates results from related RAND research regarding life-cycle GHG emissions of biomass, which permits the calculation of the

---

[1] O_3 is a reactive molecule of oxygen that can create health hazards when present above certain concentrations at ground level. Ambient concentrations of sulfur dioxide (SO_2) and nitrogen oxides (NO_x) are regulated under the 1997 and 2006 standards for fine particulates, i.e., particulate matter (PM) smaller than 2.5 micrometers ($PM_{2.5}$).

cost of reducing GHG emissions through cofiring biomass with coal. After presenting the analytical results, we consider some aspects of biomass markets. Chapter Seven identifies and discusses economic factors that could lead to the maturation of a market for biomass energy from its current heterogeneous and fragmented form into a more uniform system. Chapter Eight summarizes the conclusions of our analysis.

CHAPTER TWO

Cofiring Experience in the United States

Introduction

To gain an understanding of the most-immediate challenges faced by plants that will use biomass for electricity generation in the near term, we spoke with the designers and operators of facilities using or planning to use biomass. As biomass use for energy increases, facility staff members are learning what is required to make these plants operational, technically and economically, both from personal experience and from the experiences of their predecessors. Companies with successful experience cofiring at one site often apply their experience to the design and implementation of cofiring at additional sites. In addition to talking with current plant operators, we have also surveyed previous studies of biomass cofiring (Antares Group and Parsons Power, 1996; Wiltsee, 2000; Tillman, 2001; Alstom Power, 2008; Van Loo and Koppejan, 2008; Antares Group, 2009).

For this study, we interviewed individuals with detailed knowledge about the use of biomass in electricity generation from each of four major power-producing entities and an independent power producer that generates power for the company's own consumption. These interviews reflected experience at 11 different facilities in various stages of utilization or preparation to use biomass for commercial electricity generation, from early planning phases to full-scale commercial utilization. The major characteristics and specifications of these facilities are summarized in Table 2.1. The majority of these facilities are using or plan to use woody fuels, often local greenwood, at low cofire ratios (i.e., less than 10 percent), but some are using other feedstocks or are using biomass as almost 100 percent of their fuel. Biomass fuel acquisition and handling are reported to be the largest issues at most of the facilities. Herbaceous fuels are perceived to be—and have been shown to be—more problematic than woody ones. The facilities covered in this report span a range of sizes and boiler types, as well as levels of biomass fuel processing. The biomass handling and processing equipment and approach to biomass acquisition are highly site specific. Local and regional biomass supply conditions, state-level policy and regulatory environments, and technological and economic particulars of the plant all combine to influence the decision to use biomass.

This chapter begins with a brief discussion of how electricity is produced by burning coal or cofiring coal with biomass. The remainder of this chapter summarizes the general experiences of these facilities. The chapter is structured as a detailed case study of one facility, with additional information and insights from all of the other facilities whose representatives we interviewed included throughout the discussion. Appendix A contains additional information on all of these other facilities.

Table 2.1
Characteristics and Specifications of Facilities Included in This Study

Company (type of utility)	Facility (location)	Facility Specifications (capacity, boiler type)	Fuel Specifications (fuel type, % biomass, annual biomass use)	Handling (delivery, processing, storage, conveyance)	Combustion (dedicated versus commingling biomass burners, other details)	Emissions (controls, special issues, permitting)	Special Considerations (financial, policy, regulatory, technical)
Allegheny Energy (regulated and nonregulated)	Albright (W.Va.)	Unit 3 (of 3): 138 MW (of 286 MW) T-fired	Coal (Lower Freeport/eastern bituminous) and wood sawdust <10% by mass, ~4.7% by energy	Local via (moving-floor) trucks Storage in hopper (silo) Covered conveyers, moving floor	Commingled	Permitted up to 20% biomass; process took 9 months and required an NSR	Ran tests only Competitive biomass use (charcoal) became a supply problem
	Willow Island (W.Va.)	Unit 2 (of 2): 188 MW Cyclone	Coal and wood sawdust 5–6% by mass	Local fuel Moving floor	Commingled	Permitted up to 10% biomass but let permit lapse with nonuse of biomass	Local supply issues, sought alternative fuel source A previous switch to PRB coal reduced SO_x and eliminated the incentive to use biomass
Dominion (regulated utility)	Altavista (Va.)	63 MW Stoker fired	Coal and wood chips or dust (very fine) ~15% by mass	Local by truck No processing on-site Storage in 100-ton silo	Dedicated feed lines Coal at the bottom, dust blown in at top	Baghouse (particulates), SNCR (NO_x), dry scrubber (SO_x)	~250 suppliers in 44 counties, no contracts Pellet facility raised fuel price
	Pittsylvania (Va.)	80 MW (3 units) Stoker fired	~80:20 wood chips:dust 100% ~1 million tons	Local by truck 2 truck tippers ~40,000 tons fuel in open storage (~15 days) No processing on-site Conveyer belt fed, no redundancy	Not relevant; biomass only	Permit requires enclosed biomass processing, so not done on-site ESP (particulates), SNCR (NO_x)	Fly ash used for soil amendment
	Virginia City Hybrid Energy Center (Va.)	585 MW CFB	Coal (Va.) and wood chips Minimum 10%, up to 20%, by energy	Local by truck Minimal processing on-site Open storage, 10 days	Dedicated feed	SNCR (NO_x), dry spray scrubber (SO_x), baghouse (PM), activated carbon for Hg	Under construction PSD permit requires minimum biomass at 10%; if economic, within 8 years

Table 2.1—Continued

Company (type of utility)	Facility (location)	Facility Specifications (capacity, boiler type)	Fuel Specifications (fuel type, % biomass, annual biomass use)	Handling (delivery, processing, storage, conveyance)	Combustion (dedicated versus commingling biomass burners, other details)	Emissions (controls, special issues, permitting)	Special Considerations (financial, policy, regulatory, technical)
FirstEnergy (merchant generator)	Bay Shore (Oregon, Ohio)	Unit 1: 136 MWe; CFB Unit 3: 142 MWe; PC	Unit 1: Petroleum coke and biomass Unit 3: Coal and biomass 5% by mass	Rail delivery Minimal handling and processing	Commingled blend with coal	EPA permit: obtained an initial 6-month exemption for R&D	Initial testing complete in both units (with wood pellets) Potential issues, primarily in handling, were identified
	Burger (Shadyside, Ohio)	Units 4 and 5: 156 MW each on coal Both PC	Variety of engineered wood, greenwood, and torrefied wood products (and coal as needed) ~1 million tons	Barge delivery Indoor storage of engineered-wood products Both new and redesigned existing coal handling and milling equipment	Designed to handle up to 100% biomass Evaluating commingling of biomass with coal	Need to meet consent decree terms	Project has been cancelled
Florida Crystals (not a utility)	Okeelanta (Okeelanta, Fla.)	140 MW Stoker fired	Bagasse, wood chips (~50:50) ~100% ~1.5 million tons/year	Local via truck, average load is 23 tons 60 staff and 6 front-end loaders for fuel yard Conveyer-fed boiler	Not relevant; biomass only	Ash collector and ESP (particulates), urea injection (NO$_x$) Additional controls to limit opacity and CO	Integrated operation with sugar mill Corrosion problems; metallurgy upgraded
NRG (independent merchant generator)	Dunkirk (Dunkirk, N.Y.)	91 MW T-fired	PRB, greenwood ~10% by heat input 80,000 tons/year	Local via 25-ton truck trailers Choppers and hammer mills on-site, minimal processing 3–4 days Separate biomass stream, air and gravity fed	Separate feed, dedicated biomass burners	ESPs, baghouses Permitted for biomass use	PTC ($0.011/kWh) Increased rating with biomass because biomass feed system is independent of coal feed system Already permitted for biomass use

Table 2.1—Continued

Company (type of utility)	Facility (location)	Facility Specifications (capacity, boiler type)	Fuel Specifications (fuel type, % biomass, annual biomass use)	Handling (delivery, processing, storage, conveyance)	Combustion (dedicated versus commingling biomass burners, other details)	Emissions (controls, special issues, permitting)	Special Considerations (financial, policy, regulatory, technical)
NRG, continued	Montville Generating Station (Uncasville, Conn.)	Unit 5: 82 MW	~100% Presently oil and natural gas	In planning	In planning	In planning	Planning phase, operations planned for early 2012
	Big Cajun II (New Roads, La.)	Units 1–3: 1,700 MW	PRB with option for SG or sorghum	Biomass grown on-site	In planning	In planning	Planning/exploratory phase

NOTE: MW = megawatt. T-fired = tangentially fired. NSR = New Source Review and resulting permit, as required by the Clean Air Act of 1977. PRB = Powder River Basin, referring to the subbituminous coal from that source. ESP = electrostatic precipitator. SNCR = selective noncatalytic reduction. CFB = circulating fluidized bed. Hg = mercury. PSD = Prevention of Significant Deterioration. MWe = megawatt electric. R&D = research and development. CO = carbon monoxide. PTC = production tax credit.

Producing Electricity from Coal and Biomass

The principal differences between a plant that fires only coal and a plant that is modified to cofire coal and biomass are facilities and equipment for storing, processing, and feeding biomass to the furnace. Once the coal and biomass are fed into the furnace, the process of producing steam to drive a turbine and generator are the same.

Biomass can be delivered to the power plant in several forms. Wood can be delivered in the form of logs, chips, or sawdust. Switchgrass (SG) or corn residue would typically be delivered as bales but could be chopped and packed into loaves. Alternatively, the biomass could be delivered as fuel pellets, which are uniform in shape and physical properties. Another option is to use torrefied biomass. Torrefaction is a process that converts the biomass into a charcoal-like substance. In the United States, there is no experience at a commercial scale using torrefied biomass, so we do not consider it in this study. There is some experience in Europe (Van Loo and Koppejan, 2008).

Because biomass is supplied locally, delivery occurs most often by truck. Most coal-fired power plants have access to rail, which would also be a delivery option, especially if the biomass were to be delivered from a long distance.

Once received, special facilities and processes store and process the biomass. To satisfy the plant's demand for biomass between deliveries, some storage is required. It is possible to store raw biomass—logs, chips, or bales—outside, but, because there is a risk of degradation due to exposure to the elements (and freezing), it is most common to provide covered storage. Covered storage is required for biomass pellets, which would turn into mush if exposed to water.

The biomass must be processed into a form compatible with the existing boiler. Stoker-fired boilers have the widest range of potential fuel specifications, and, often, relatively unprocessed woodchips of the appropriate size can be mixed with coal and fed into the boiler using a common conveyer belt. For other boilers, the biomass must be processed into particles such that they can be fed into the boiler using equipment originally designed for coal. Alternatively, the biomass can be fed into the boiler using dedicated equipment. Processing typically entails drying the biomass and grinding it in a hammer mill until it reaches the proper size specification. Having preprocessed biomass simplifies any plant modifications because the processed biomass can be mixed with coal and ground in existing coal mills used to prepare coal for feeding to and burning in the furnace. Conveyance of the processed biomass and coal to the boiler occurs pneumatically for PC boilers.

General Information on the Companies and Their Facilities

The experience of NRG—in particular, the conversion to commercial biomass use at its Dunkirk facility—illustrates many of the key lessons and observations of other operators with whom we spoke and is consistent with the literature. As such, this chapter is structured around this case study. The experiences of other facilities are also included herein, either as supporting or contrasting examples, in the context of the corresponding section of the NRG case study. Appendix A provides further details on the other facilities we included in this study. This chapter also contains some supplemental literature-based and nonattributed information.

Allegheny Energy

Allegheny Energy has two facilities with cofiring experience in West Virginia, the Albright and Willow Island sites, which have tested for cofiring in the past. Both facilities have been cofired at modest levels (approximately 10 percent and 5 percent, respectively) with minimal technical difficulties but are presently not using biomass.

Dominion

Dominion has three biomass facilities in Virginia: the dedicated biomass Pittsylvania Station facility, the Altavista Station cofired facility, and the future Virginia City Hybrid Energy Center cofired facility. Biomass supply concerns and plant technical issues have been minimal, although biomass costs, especially relative to natural gas, have recently become a concern at the Altavista facility.

FirstEnergy

FirstEnergy tested biomass cofiring at two locations, the R. E. Burger facility and the Bay Shore facility. In 2009, FirstEnergy announced plans to repower units 4 and 5 at the R. E. Burger facility to be able to combust up to 100 percent biomass. In November 2010, FirstEnergy announced that it would cancel the project. Since the time the R. E. Burger biomass repowering project was announced, market prices for electricity had fallen significantly, and expected market prices no longer support a plant repowered to combust biomass. The Bay Shore facility conducted cofire testing with wood pellets at a 5-percent (by mass) cofire ratio, and the R. E. Burger facility conducted cofire testing with wood pellets at a 20-percent (by mass) cofire ratio.

Florida Crystals

Florida Crystals is a sugar producer that operates its own electricity generation facility that runs on nearly 100 percent chipped wood and sugarcane waste (bagasse). Use of bagasse has presented some technical challenges compared with other facilities that have utilized only woody biomass fuels.

NRG Energy

NRG is looking at the potential for biomass utilization across its entire multistate portfolio of facilities. The Dunkirk facility was the first site selected for biomass cofiring. This facility was originally the site of a DOE/EPRI biomass utilization test project (Antares Group and Parsons Power, 1996; Tillman, 2001). NRG acquired the facility after the initial DOE testing was completed. NRG has done subsequent test firings using this original configuration. Many of the system components, as originally designed, are not ideal for the greenwood chips that NRG has utilized in its tests and plans to continue to use; the original DOE tests used waste wood, generally a relatively dry biomass fuel, rather than greenwood chips. Consequently, NRG is reconfiguring the Dunkirk facility for commercial biomass use. The planned adaptations at Dunkirk, primarily intended to enable better handling of a range of woods with a variety of moisture contents, will require additional capital investments. Regardless of the actual cofire ratios that are used in practice, the up-front costs are fixed.

Precombustion Biomass Considerations

Biomass Fuel Selection

Most facilities whose representatives we interviewed for this study make use of local, green, woody biomass fuels, but there were some notable exceptions. In all cases, the biomass type and form—generally, sawdust, chips, or pellets—have been dictated primarily by site-specific considerations and the local price and availability of fuels. Although moisture content of the biomass affected operating capacity, none of the individuals interviewed cited high moisture content of biomass as a major practical concern as long as it was below 50 percent.[1] Facilities fell into two broad categories in terms of cofire ratios: low (less than 10 percent by energy) or majority (almost 100 percent) biomass use.

NRG's Dunkirk facility has been using coal from the PRB since 2006 and plans to cofire a range of greenwood chips to satisfy New York's requirements.[2] Ideally, it would use 30- to 35-percent moisture-content biomass, but it has successfully burned fuel with up to 50 percent moisture content.[3] To allow flexibility in fuel use and to minimize supply problems and the resulting potential for increased costs, NRG has purposely not designed to narrow fuel specifications. As such, it has tested a range of wood types and moisture contents, all with reasonable success, including dried woods and greenwoods, hardwoods and softwoods. Many biomass types, such as agricultural wastes, are not being considered. Firing greenwood poses some additional challenges, including requirements for additional power to operate the transport system and grinders, but also has advantages, including relative ease of permitting and minimal ash problems.

NRG views the use of engineered-wood pellets or other densified products as prohibitively expensive—Dunkirk staff estimated prices of $150–200 per ton—and notes that, from the perspective of its facility and location, the additional cost for the engineered product yields unnecessary or even undesirable processing.[4] Given its ability to source nearby biomass, the trade-off between the higher handling and shipping costs of greenwood versus the extra expense of a densified, dried, engineered product favors the greenwood. Similar arguments have thus far precluded consideration of biomass fuels, which are partially combusted in a process known as torrefaction, creating essentially charcoal. Torrefied biomass has properties similar to those of coal and would not require the special handling and processing of raw biomass. Pellets can also create a potential fire hazard as coal and wood pellets are commingled and ground in a conventional coal mill, due to different grind index behavior and material dropout. NRG would like to consider biomass explicitly planted for energy use, such as willow, but this option

---

[1]   This 50 percent figure is consistent with the literature, where higher moisture levels have been noted to be problematic for feeding systems and to lead to high CO emissions (Wiltsee, 2000).

[2]   In the state of New York, only untreated and uncontaminated woods can be burned to meet the renewable portfolio standard. This is true in many states and localities, where, even if the use of waste-wood fuels is not strictly forbidden, it can complicate permitting and become overly burdensome.

[3]   At 50 percent moisture, it can still splinter wood successfully; wetter wood becomes pulpy and could potentially gum up the mills.

[4]   The processing would be nonbeneficial and therefore undesirable, for example, in the case of a PC boiler, in which the fuel needs to be reground before use. Such processing overkill is not an issue for stoker-type furnaces.

presently appears to be too expensive.[5] In terms of agricultural residue utilization, NRG has conducted laboratory test burns with 100-percent corn stover with favorable results but is concerned with the potential ash characteristics that can result from the lowering of the ash fusion (i.e., melting) temperature when cofiring stover with coal.

Most other facilities whose representatives we interviewed for this study have made (or plan to make) similar woody fuel selections due to access to sufficient supplies of locally produced greenwood residues. For example, Dominion's Pittsylvania facility uses wood chips for most of its 100-percent biomass fuel, with moisture content averaging around 50 percent, with the balance made up of sawdust. Other facilities located in wooded regions also have had access to mill residues in the form of sawdust and have been able to take advantage of this relatively dry fuel. For example, Allegheny Energy's Willow Island facility used 5- to 6-percent (by mass) cofire ratios with sawdust at moisture contents of approximately 30 percent. The other Allegheny Energy facility whose representative we interviewed, Albright, used a 10-percent-by-mass cofire ratio of sawdust. Both of these facilities were originally coal-fired plants and were subsequently modified for sawdust use. Dominion's Altavista Station was originally designed and built to use 15 percent sawdust (by mass) from a neighboring furniture plant and continued to source sawdust from other locations, mostly very fine sander dust, after the furniture plant shut down. Dominion's Virginia City Hybrid Energy Center, now under construction, plans to make use of a combination of forest residues and sawdust from the large local woodshed and wood-product industry.

Although agricultural residues are being considered as biomass fuels by several companies, including NRG (which, as noted earlier, has done some combustion testing with corn stover), we were able to identify only one facility that is presently using herbaceous, rather than woody, fuels. Florida Crystals uses nearly 100 percent biomass for its operations at a ratio of approximately 50:50 herbaceous to woody biomass. As in other examples, this choice of fuel is entirely dictated by local availability. As a sugar producer, the facility has ample supplies of sugarcane waste, called bagasse. The balance of its fuel consists of yard trimmings and construction waste wood.

The only company whose representative we interviewed that had looked at a more diverse, nonlocal fuel supply was FirstEnergy. Although it conducted cofire testing at its Bay Shore facility with wood pellets, it had considered a range of options for the R. E. Burger facility. Prior to cancellation of the repowering project, the biomass fuels that FirstEnergy had selected included a variety of pellets, greenwood chips, and torrefied wood products. The need for more biomass than is locally available necessitated this fuel-sourcing approach, and access to relatively inexpensive barge fuel transportation at the R. E. Burger facility enabled a broad geographic range of sourcing to be considered. Although utilization of a broad range of fuel types and forms was the exception to the rule among the facilities covered in this study, there is literature precedent for designing facilities to accept a range of biomass fuels (Van Loo and Koppejan, 2008).

According to our interviews, local woody biomass would seem to be the first choice of fuel for cofiring or dedicated biomass combustion. Alternatives to this fuel choice become attractive only in the absence of sufficient quantities of local woody fuel, such as in the case of

---

[5]   It estimates that closed-loop products, such as switchgrass, cost approximately $5–6 per million Btu (mmBtu) versus $3–4 per mmBtu for wood residues, where relative crop density seems to account for a large part of the cost difference. NRG is exploring the possibility of using switchgrass and sorghum at another one of its facilities, the Big Cajun in Louisiana.

the FirstEnergy R. E. Burger facility, or in the presence of a readily available alternative, such as in the case of the Florida Crystals facility.

Biomass Fuel Acquisition, Receiving, Preprocessing, and Storage

As was the case for biomass fuel selection, the specific approach to fuel acquisition and receiving is dictated by local conditions for the specific facility. Frequently, facility staff acquire biomass from several to dozens of small-scale biomass suppliers on a relatively informal, noncontractual basis; although some have considered the use of aggregators, none had engaged such a service at the time of our interviews. Preprocessing depends on the form of biomass received and the facility's characteristics and is generally minimal if performed at all. Storage solutions are varied in terms of size and level of protection from the elements and are primarily dependent on fuel type and form, cofire ratios, and climate.

NRG's fuel sourcing occurs from within approximately 50 miles of the Dunkirk facility, an area that is highly forested and where there is not much competition for thinnings and timber-industry residues. By its estimates, truck transportation of wood fuel farther than 100 miles does not make economic sense. Sourcing fuel from a distance of 100 to 300 miles by barge and greater than 300 miles by rail might be cost-effective. However, NRG has thus far not explored any of these options due to the adequacy of the local resource base.

Nevertheless, guaranteeing a supply of wood is one of its most difficult problems. Long-term contracts are not an option because the inherently small-scale suppliers are unable or unwilling to enter into such contracts. NRG feels that having a contract would be meaningless anyway because such small suppliers would have no means to pay penalties associated with breaking a contract. If wood prices were to drastically change, contracts would likely be broken. Therefore, these relationships need to be managed on a day-to-day basis. NRG is likely to look to an aggregator to manage its fuel supply once it is up and running commercially. One way to build a stronger relationship with a supplier would be to invest in capital—e.g., to purchase and lease a chipper to a timber company—and create an interdependency. In the past, NRG has lent chippers to biomass producers to achieve some minor economies of scale and help smooth out the boom-and-bust market for suppliers.

Wood will be delivered to NRG's Dunkirk facility through a simple receiving bay at the facility in 25-ton truck trailers, with 80,000 tons of greenwood consumed per year. The truck tipper it is installing will cost about $340,000, and, when the electrical and foundation work and supporting equipment are added, it anticipates costs of about $1 million. For initial preprocessing prior to storage, it presently has an oversized hog that produces 2-inch chips.[6] However, approximately one-third of the product could be handled with less size reduction, and so another chipper is being acquired.

The Dunkirk facility currently has capacity for three to four days of storage on-site, assuming a 10-percent cofire ratio. NRG would like to upgrade to allow five to seven days of storage, but the facility has space constraints, partly due to its location on Lake Erie. Additionally, the fuel flexibility of cofiring relative to dedicated biomass use means that additional coal can always be used as a stopgap, so, in reality, one to two days of storage is sufficient for this facility. Purchase of roundwood (stored offsite) when prices are low could also make up for some gaps in supply, especially in winter. With the present storage system, NRG has had some

---

[6]   A hogger is a machine that converts logs to wood chunks or large chips.

problems with freezing of the high-moisture-content biomass and is therefore relocating the storage space to above the building where wood milling occurs to take advantage of building heat to create a semi–climate-controlled environment for fuel storage.

As in the Dunkirk example, nearly all facilities included in this study were making use or planning to make use of local biomass fuels (i.e., sources within a 100-mile radius of the plant), and all of these local fuels were being transported by truck. For example, Dominion's Pittsylvania Station acquires 92 percent of its biomass fuels from within a 100-mile radius. Dominion considers the approximately 200-mile distance separating its three facilities sufficient to place them all well outside of their respective woodsheds. Similarly, Florida Crystals' farthest suppliers of biomass fuel are about 100 miles away. At this distance, transportation is the largest contributor to total fuel costs. FirstEnergy's facilities were the exception to this local-only fuel approach. FirstEnergy had planned to make use of rail and barge to import nonlocal fuels.

As was the case for NRG, despite the existence of sufficient supplies from local woodsheds, fuel acquisition was frequently cited as one of the greatest concerns for the various facilities. None of the facilities had contracts for biomass supply, long term or otherwise. For example, Florida Crystals noted that maintaining an adequate, high-quality fuel supply was always a challenge. All of the facilities whose representatives we interviewed that depended on sawdust have had supply problems due to competition for sawdust from other users or other economic pressures. For example, the Albright facility saw prices of sawdust increase due to competition from a local charcoal facility. The increase in price contributed to Albright's decision not to continue cofiring. The sawdust-only facility owned by Dominion, the Altavista Station, was planning to go to "cold reserve" status as of the writing of this report, in part due to competition from gas-fired generating plants that benefited from lower prices for natural gas. On the other hand, Dominion had not experienced any supply issues with nonsawdust fuels and did not anticipate problems in the near term. Despite these concerns, none of the facilities whose representatives we interviewed had made use of external biomass aggregators.

The logistics of receiving can be quite complex, particularly at facilities with high levels of biomass use. For example, Dominion's Pittsylvania Station uses approximately 1 million tons of biomass annually. An average of 135 trucks with biomass arrive each day with an average load of 25 tons.[7] As a biomass-only facility, it has approximately 15 days of on-site storage. The local climate enables outdoor storage, but the facility must derate during rainy periods due to the high moisture content of the fuel. Similarly, Florida Crystals uses 1.5 million tons of biomass annually and receives approximately 100 trucks per day with an average load of about 23 tons. The Virginia City Hybrid Energy Center initially plans to receive biomass five days per week, with 10-hour shifts, and will have two truck tippers on-site. Its eventual 20 percent cofire target would require 125 tons per hour, or 80 to 156 trucks per day arriving over two 12-hour shifts staffed with a bulldozer operator. Eventually, it will need a 24-hour drop-off system. It has sufficient space initially for ten days of biomass storage on-site but could expand this to 15 days.

The approach to biomass receiving and storage is also necessarily site specific due to considerations of biomass type and form, amount of biomass required, and local climate conditions and space constraints. Details regarding the various facilities' storage capabilities and approaches are given in Appendix A.

---

[7] It takes approximately 13 minutes to unload a truck, so its maximum capacity is 311 truckloads per day.

Biomass Fuel Handling, Processing, and Feeding

Biomass handling was often cited as one of the biggest technical considerations for the facilities whose representatives we interviewed for this study and often results in the most-significant plant modifications. Due to the lower energy density of biomass relative to coal, handling systems used for coal might not allow sufficient biomass throughput to maintain the facility capacity, and the significantly different physical properties of the two fuels could necessitate modifications. The form of biomass being used determines the details of the modifications. The final technical solutions are often achieved only after many iterations and trial and error.

Although the boiler type influences the level of biomass processing required (e.g., a PC boiler might require more–finely processed fuel than a stoker-fired boiler would), the combustion process is relatively forgiving of particle size and homogeneity.[8] A few facilities have opted to do some or all of their own biomass processing to maximize fuel flexibility, while others worked to minimize on-site biomass processing and the resulting logistical concerns and equipment requirements. None of the facilities was predrying its biomass fuels on site at the time of our interviews. Feeding approaches ranged from pneumatic tubes to conveyer belts to bucket elevators to moving-floor conveyers, largely dictated by the fuel form.

The original test configuration at NRG's Dunkirk facility utilizes a machine moving-floor conveyer unloader, a bucket elevator, and an air sweep for grinding and feeding the material to the boiler. Power for the biomass processing and handling is supplied from the main power line from the plant, parasitically drawing power that would otherwise be exported to the grid.[9] There are two hammer mills along the feeding system.[10] After the first, the biomass is screened and moved to a bunker from which it can be used on demand.[11] The second hammer mill takes the fuel size to 0.125 inch or less.[12] The configuration and sizing of the original equipment is not ideal, and the chippers and hammer mills are choke points.

The Dunkirk facility has four individual biomass feeds per boiler. As originally designed, the biomass feeding system uses ambient air and requires 1.8 lb of air to convey 1 lb of biomass.[13] The biomass enters at the topmost port and is conveyed by ambient air. This supply system is specified to move 10 tons of biomass per hour, but NRG has been able to operate it reliably only at 8 tons per hour because the system was designed for dry wood rather than the greenwood that NRG intends to continue to source; the available power source cannot sustain a feed rate of 10 tons per hour. There is some long-term concern that the hammers might wear

---

[8]   A few rules of thumb have been noted in the literature (Wiltsee, 2000). For example, stoker and cyclone boilers can readily accept 2-inch chips, but PC burners would require a grate to effectively burn chips of this size. CFB and PC boilers handle pulverized pellets or sawdust well and, as a result, require minimal modifications with these fuel types. Bubbling bed systems handle biomass well in general but have higher parasitic loads than do other boiler types.

[9]   The parasitic load for processing is approximately 10 percent of power produced by biomass for woody biomass.

[10]   A hammer mill is a machine that grinds material by means of quickly rotating hammers within a drum. A screen lines the drum so that only material of the desired size is able to exit the mill.

[11]   The screening process allows fuel between 0.625 inches and 2 inches to pass.

[12]   The grinders were originally designed for granite, and the manufacturer will not guarantee 0.125 inch or less unless the wood has 20 percent moisture or less. However, NRG has found that, although it might not be achieving 0.125 inch, the system is adequately handling the biomass as processed. The new hammer mills will have hydraulic backs that open for easier maintenance.

[13]   This is the specification for coal, but it is stoichiometrically lean for biomass.

unevenly because of the present feeding system and that, if the hammers strike metal, sparking could be a risk.

The original Dunkirk system design was constructed in the absence of experience and, in NRG's opinion, is not well suited to the choices that have since been made at the plant. The new system design has some similarities with the original, but there will also be improvements. For example, the redesign is being developed specifically to deal with larger amounts of biomass, allowing up to 20 tons per hour through the addition of a second processing train. It will also be better tailored to chipped greenwood; for example, NRG will not utilize the bucket elevators in the original design, which are arguably better suited to finely ground biomass fuel. Additional improvements include better climate proofing of fuel storage and upgrading the power supply to the mills.[14] NRG also plans to store the processed biomass in an elevated holding bin and use a combination of flue-gas recirculation and gravity to carry the biomass to the boiler. Moving away from the use of ambient air for feeding to make better use of gravity, pneumatic tubes, and flue gas will achieve better efficiencies, improve the boiler performance, and take advantage of waste heat to dry the fuel. NRG is considering modifying the pneumatic transport system to the individual burners to a small-diameter pipe, thus reducing the amount of tramp air that is associated with the larger piping while maintaining adequate transport velocity and allowing the boiler wind-box secondary air registers to better manage combustion properties. Less air use in the redesigned feeding system should also reduce NO_x emissions.

As was the case for NRG, optimization of handling, processing, and feeding has generally been reported to be a trial-and-error process at most of the facilities. Although only minimal modifications, such as installation of a hopper and blower, and minor operational issues were reported at the Albright facility, initial feeder clogging did require valve changes and feeding-screw adjustments. Virtually the only facility changes at the Willow Island facility were related to handling, but, in retrospect, facility staff would not recommend the approach they took due to unforeseen problems—namely, that the moving-floor conveyer they selected requires relatively hard-to-find moving-floor dump trucks for the purpose of the tests. Few broad generalizations can be made with respect to handling and processing, but all users of sawdust fuel cited the need to "keep the fuel moving" and, to maintain safety, to remove sparking sources.

There are often a number of trade-offs among the costs of a given fuel type and form and the specific handling needs of the fuel. For example, less expensive greenwood fuels might require more-expensive and complex handling but are able to be stored under a range of conditions. Engineered-wood products (e.g., pellets) require much less processing and can be handled with relative ease but must be stored in a dry environment. Dominion's approach at all of its biomass facilities has been to contract out as much of the trucking, processing, and handling of the biomass fuels as possible. For quality control, prescreening for undesirable and oversized fuel is performed at the Pittsylvania facility. The Virginia City facility plans to specify biomass energy content and moisture levels to within a required range. In contrast, Florida Crystals expends considerable effort handling and processing diverse biomass feedstocks on-site. Florida Crystals has a set of contracts for the operation of the delivery trucks. The plant employs 60 people to cover three shifts in the fuel yard for mixing the various biomass fuel streams with rollers and to operate six front-end loaders to manage fuel piles and feed the boil-

---

[14] The mills presently have a power rating up to 200 horsepower (hp) each, and they are looking to upgrade to 500 hp each.

ers. FirstEnergy had planned to accept a range of fuels but had to ensure that the fuels were stored and handled appropriately.

Considerations for Combustion of Biomass

Technical Concerns with Biomass Combustion

In contrast to the relative complexity of biomass acquisition and handling, the combustion experience of the facilities whose representatives we interviewed for this study has been relatively straightforward and not particularly problematic. This is especially true in the cofire examples but was also the case for dedicated biomass facilities using only woody fuels. Derating, or purposefully reducing plant electricity output, seems to be the primary technical concern across the facilities. In general, specific combustion issues can vary depending on the type of coal and biomass used.[15] It is difficult to know what will happen in practice until a cofire fuel combination and configuration are tested at a given facility. Even with a more mature cofire industry, plant-specific adaptations and considerations might always be necessary. Nevertheless, the relative lack of combustion issues at the various facilities and their specific approaches to minor biomass-use modifications are instructive.

In their experience, the NRG staff at the Dunkirk facility have seen very few adverse effects as a result of biomass combustion, especially compared with the challenges faced in biomass acquisition and handling. Dunkirk's experience has admittedly been limited in duration and was not for commercial production, but, given its use of unadulterated wood products at modest cofire ratios, the virtual absence of problems with boiler and turbine operations is somewhat expected. NRG expressed the opinion that this would bear out at commercial scale and over a much longer duration of cofiring. It also noted that the boiler would be able to handle even much higher cofire ratios than it was planning to utilize.

The Dunkirk boiler has a dedicated set of biomass burners rather than using a commingled coal/biomass fuel. Accordingly, the two fuels have separate dedicated feed lines to their respective entry points to the boiler. This minimizes handling complications associated with mixing the fuels and allows better control of combustion. As noted, using waste heat to predry the biomass is under consideration, which would improve boiler efficiency.

Thus far, NRG has seen no product dropout in the bottom ash and burning embers in the fly ash at the Dunkirk Facility. Neither corrosion nor ash accumulation has been observed. Presumably because of the additional air required to move the biomass in the handling system, loss on ignition—a measure of noncombustible matter entering the boiler—has actually decreased, and the overall efficiency has increased accordingly.

The other facilities whose representatives we interviewed for this study represent a range of boiler types and have designed the biomass feed both for separate feeds and dedicated biomass combustion and for commingling of biomass and coal. All reported virtually no adverse impacts associated with biomass use apart from derating, as discussed elsewhere in this chapter. The notable exception to this was the experience of Florida Crystals. Although the plant was originally designed for dedicated biomass combustion, operations have been a learning

---

[15] For example, certain biomass/coal combinations can yield problematic eutectic ash, as noted by NRG. The literature also notes that fouling and slagging can be more severe with biomass and coal than when either is fired individually due to the alkali content of the wood interacting with sulfur in the coal (Wiltsee, 2000).

process. For example, ash alkalinity has been a problem.[16] Within a few years of operation, the plant had to upgrade the metallurgy in the boiler, especially the superheater, to reduce corrosion. This is consistent with literature recommending stainless steel to minimize corrosion issues when burning this type of biomass (Wiltsee, 2000). Ash characteristics have also sometimes varied at the Florida Crystals facility as a result of the mix of biomass fuels, so waste handling can be a challenge.

The principal negative impact of biomass use across the facilities is the potential derating associated with the lower heat and higher moisture content of biomass compared to coal. This drawback was noted by most of the facilities but not cited as a major concern by anyone interviewed. Conversely, at one facility, it was noted that a switch to a lower-rank coal (e.g., substituting PRB for bituminous coal), coupled with any limitations in the existing coal processing and handling system, could itself force a derating of a plant. In a case like this, building in additional biomass-handling capabilities could actually increase the capacity of a facility that has some boiler margin by adding fuel throughput relative to the bituminous coal–only system.

Biomass Emissions, Emission Controls, and Waste

In general, emissions of SO_x and NO_x have been observed to decrease or remain unchanged with biomass use. Emission-control processes have accordingly been minimally affected by biomass combustion and have generally not been modified. Waste disposal has not differed significantly from coal-only combustion for woody cofiring applications.

The pollution-control equipment at NRG's Dunkirk facility has not been adversely affected by up to 10 percent cofire over the range of moisture levels and wood types tested. This includes ESPs, which remove particles by charging them, and baghouses, which filter particulate emissions, although the latter could theoretically be damaged by incomplete combustion of biomass. Although increased NO_x levels with biomass use is a concern due to the already low levels obtained with PRB compared with other coals, during testing, the clustering of the dedicated biomass burners at the top enabled the facility to maintain neutral NO_x levels relative to dedicated PRB coal combustion.[17] Flue-gas recirculation could alleviate this concern entirely or, ideally, could enable even lower NO_x levels than with PRB alone. CO emissions, however, were observed to increase with biomass use. Additionally, flue-gas volume increased as a result of the additional moisture in the fuel.[18] At higher cofire ratios, one might expect problems with emission-control equipment, but operators do not anticipate any adverse issues at planned cofire levels.

None of the other facilities whose representatives we interviewed reported emission increases or problems with emission controls as a result of biomass use. In fact, the R. E. Burger facility is repowering for biomass use in response to a consent decree that requires it to lower sulfur oxide (SO_x), NO_x, and PM emissions; switching from coal to biomass is one way to achieve the required limits.

---

[16] The literature has specifically noted chlorine in agricultural residues to be a potential corrosion problem (Wiltsee, 2000; Van Loo and Koppejan, 2008).

[17] The switch to PRB coal enabled the operators at the Dunkirk facility to reduce emissions to 0.15 lb NO_x/mmBtu. The wood burner is now the top of four burners rather than in the middle as originally configured.

[18] From its observations, NRG estimates that 100-percent biomass use would be expected to result in an 18-percent increase in flue-gas volume.

The Dunkirk facility presently puts its fly ash in a nearby landfill site and plans to continue to do so. The facility is unconcerned with the effects that using biomass could have on the composition of fly ash. Other facilities cofiring with coal have similarly disposed of their waste. However, coal-fired power plants that sell their flyash as an amendment to concrete might not be able to do so when cofiring. Fly ash sold for use in concrete should satisfy ASTM International Standard C618, which currently specifies that only fly ash from coal combustion could be used, regardless of whether the cofired fly ash satisfies the material specification. For example, the Chariton Valley Biomass Project (CVBP) tested its fly ash and determined that it did meet the performance specification (Antares Group, 2009) and argued that the ASTM standard should be a performance standard such that its fly ash would qualify. A plant that currently sells fly ash for use in concrete would need to factor in the lost revenues that could result from cofiring with biomass. Biomass-only plants have another option: The Pittsylvania Station, for example, has been able to make use of its biomass-only fly ash as a soil supplement for local farms. As noted earlier, NRG has concerns with the undesirable characteristics of ash obtained when mixing herbaceous fuels and coal.

Economic, Regulatory, and Policy Issues

Economic, regulatory, and policy issues, including permitting, have, in general, been of great concern to facilities using biomass. Technical and logistical issues aside, these issues have generally been the primary motivations or potential deal breakers for the use of biomass. Please refer to Chapter One for a discussion of some regulatory issues related to coming EPA regulations of hazardous air pollutants; SO_2, NO_x, and O_3; and permitting requirements for GHG emissions.

In response to anticipated future economic and policy changes, NRG has conducted scenario planning across all of its assets; biomass utilization is just one part of this portfolio-wide planning.[19] NRG has dedicated two staff members to systematically work to identify the best coal plants for biomass development across its portfolio of facilities from both a technical and economic perspective. For NRG, key drivers for decisions on conversion are the availability of an ample fuel supply and state or local regulatory systems that would provide a financial incentive to use biomass, such as Renewable Portfolio Standards (RPSs).[20] Under some regulatory systems, utilities located in jurisdictions with RPSs could purchase RECs from other utilities that have better access to supplies of renewable energy rather than generate their own renewable energy.[21] The decision to utilize biomass, therefore, is driven by regulations that vary from state to state and based on site-specific considerations. Here, we outline the many factors that NRG highlighted as potential drivers, then describe the most-important factors in NRG's own decisionmaking process.

[19] Much of this planning is related to anticipated regulation of emissions of CO_2. NRG also intends to add wind, solar thermal, and nuclear assets.

[20] An RPS mandates that utilities generate a specified share of the electricity they sell from renewables or obtain renewable-energy credits (RECs) from a market to meet their obligation.

[21] Two primary facilities were identified in this portfolio-wide search: the Dunkirk plant and the Montville, Connecticut, plant, which will repower to 100 percent biomass. Other opportunities exist for coal-fired power plants in Texas and Delaware. NRG is also looking at plasma arc gasification.

NRG notes that cost is a major disincentive to use biomass at power plants. NRG estimates that the total cost to build a new 50 MW facility for biomass would be approximately $200 million, or approximately $4,000 per kilowatt.[22] Repowering an existing solid fuel–fired power plant to biomass use could run half to two-thirds the cost of a new facility. In general, there is no mechanism for independent power producers to recover the cost of capital to retrofit for biomass use. In theory, a regulated utility could recover its capital investments from ratepayers.

Although many states have RPSs, there are only two areas of the United States that have markets for RECs: California and a group of states in New England. However, biomass is not plentiful enough in either location to provide a major source of demand for meeting renewable mandates. Utilities in the New England region could purchase renewable energy from other regions in the form of a REC. However, the current market price for RECs for New England utilities is too low for generators to invest in a new or refurbished biomass generating plant.[23]

PTCs, subsidies provided by the federal government for power generated from renewable resources, offer another source of revenue for generators contemplating investing in biomass generating plants. However, the federal government has not made these permanent, nor are they high enough to cover the costs of a biomass-fueled facility.[24] The federal government also has provided investment tax credits (ITCs) to add inventory in renewable energy. However, access to ITCs has been restrictive and has not applied to systems cofiring with forestry residues. This is because forestry residues are considered open-loop biomass energy resources: A closed-loop biomass energy resource would be a dedicated energy crop, such as SG. In the absence of a charge for emissions of CO_2, there are few financial incentives for merchant generators to use biomass. Assuming that the government imposes a charge for emissions of CO_2, NRG estimates that a market price of about $23 per metric ton CO_2 would be needed to motivate investment in new technology at facilities and spur the development of additional feedstocks and feedstock markets.[25]

NRG notes that, even once a decision to retrofit has been made, it is not clear how often a biomass facility would be operated. If utilities receive a substantial PTC or REC, a utility would want to use biomass as much as possible. However, in some instances, a utility might cofire a facility only during certain periods; for example, plants operating at reduced capacity at night might tip the balance in favor of using less or no biomass. Biomass prices are likely to rise during certain seasons or during a year of drought, making biomass less economical to use and making higher cofire ratios less attractive.

Financing biomass power production can be a challenge. NRG notes that a bank or other financier is likely to require a facility to guarantee access to five to six times its annual biomass

---

[22] Repowering to cofire biomass might require less of an investment: FirstEnergy estimated that the cost to repower its Burger facility was about $200 million or $700 per kilowatt. Most of this investment would be used for handling, processing, combusting, and storage upgrades and changes.

[23] Because of a relatively high demand for renewables and a relative scarcity of renewable generation, the Northeast region of the country has a fairly robust REC market that can enable reasonable recovery of costs for biomass use.

[24] The federal government has provided generators that use open-loop biomass generating systems a PTC of $0.011 per kilowatt-hour for ten years, and generators using closed-loop biomass generating systems with a PTC of $0.021 per kilowatt-hour. A certificate is required to receive the open-loop credit. The agency that previously provided certification no longer exists. Consequently, only a few plants, such as the Dunkirk facility, receive the open-loop PTC.

[25] NRG's estimate was that approximately $25 per short ton of CO_2 would be required, absent other incentives, such as RECs.

needs within its local woodshed (i.e., within 100 miles or less) to obtain financing. Consequently, it is unlikely that a bank would provide financing for a cofired facility if there were already an existing cofired power plant in the same woodshed. A facility owner could choose to self-finance, but, as the demand rises, biomass prices will presumably rise, too. Liquid-fuel facilities are at a particular disadvantage because they require such a large amount of biomass, even for a relatively small facility (i.e., 1 million tons per year for approximately 3,500 barrels per day.) To date, NRG has self-financed its biomass initiatives and made its own considerations concerning the adequacy of fuel supplies.

NRG notes that, because of the many financial barriers and the lack of financial incentives, the decision to use biomass is currently driven entirely by existing or anticipated future regulations or potential legal actions. NRG notes that some states might be more willing to subsidize or mandate biomass cofiring than they would other renewables if biomass were a more plentiful and economic resource than other renewables within the state. In this manner, the state government would hope to keep the economic benefits of mandating the use of renewable resources to generate electricity within the individual state. Some regulations mandating the use of renewables could discourage the use of biomass at power plants.[26] For example, RPS programs can be very strict and can vary greatly from state to state in terms of what constitutes renewable energy, complicating decisionmaking for a company that, like NRG, provides power to multiple states. Individual states could, as Connecticut has, require a certification by a state agency that the forest products were harvested sustainably or, as New York has, simply not consider biomass to have a carbon benefit relative to coal. Even if allowable, there can be restrictions on the absolute amount of biomass used; for example, Virginia currently sets an annual statewide maximum of 1.5 million tons of woody biomass for energy use, presumably as a means of conservation.

In some instances, using biomass reduces other pollutants. However, biomass does not contribute to reducing emissions of CO. If a generating plant faces caps on CO, cofiring with biomass would not contribute to helping to meet it because biomass does not emit less CO per kilowatt of electricity generated than coal. NRG also notes that any changes at a facility that would trigger an NSR for an aging coal plant without modern emission equipment will be unlikely to be considered for conversion to cofiring biomass.

NRG found that, after weighing all these factors, only its Dunkirk plant was, at that time, an attractive candidate for cofiring biomass. The area around the plant provides a sufficient local biomass fuel supply. The plant is certified to collect a federal site-specific PTC. NRG knew from DOE tests that the boiler could accommodate biomass without apparent difficulty. Dunkirk already had air permits in place. These factors combined to make the Dunkirk site the best candidate for initial biomass use within NRG's portfolio of plants.

Economics determine whether biomass is used, regardless of technical and logistical feasibility. Allegheny Energy's Albright facility opted to discontinue biomass use in 2002 in part due to the high price and lack of availability of the sawdust it had previously used in cofire testing. However, Allegheny Energy is presently looking into the possibility of using sawdust again at this time. The existence of cost-effective technical solutions to reducing emissions of criteria pollutants has removed much of the financial motivation for biomass use. Dominion is expecting that the RECs received for biomass use at the Virginia City Hybrid facility will

---

[26] NRG notes that, because the agency formerly responsible for certification of PTC or RPS eligibility for biomass cofiring is closed, the number of facilities that can take advantage of biomass use through these mechanisms is limited.

make biomass fuel cost-effective at that site. However, the facility air permits require biomass use only under the condition that it is in the interest of ratepayers, so unexpectedly high biomass costs would result in discontinuation or reduction of biomass use. FirstEnergy's fuel-selection process, based on existing plant equipment, transportation and related unloading options, and plant location, is driven by the effect that these factors could have on the cost of the delivered biomass. The company's original decision to use biomass at the R. E. Burger facility was based on the relative costs of the various technical solutions for meeting the consent decree's requirements and the expected power market price forecasts at the time. As noted earlier, in November 2010, FirstEnergy canceled the project after the market prices for electricity had fallen significantly, and expected market prices no longer supported repowering of units 4 and 5 at the R. E. Burger facility.

Many facilities whose representatives we interviewed for this study noted the complexity of the permitting process as a potential barrier to using biomass. Dominion staff from both the Pittsylvania and Altavista facilities cited the requirement to have appropriate air permits as the biggest issue in their experience with biomass use. Dominion also expects this to be the biggest problem faced at its new hybrid energy facility, where its permit is contingent on biomass use at specified percentages on a defined timetable.[27] Allegheny Energy's Albright facility underwent a nine-month iterative permitting process, working to set biomass cofire ratios to appropriate levels and alleviate concerns regarding the potential for increased emissions of PM with biomass use. Despite having gone through the permitting process for biomass cofire testing, the Willow Island facility decided to allow its permit to lapse and to discontinue biomass use. A switch to low-sulfur coal meant that one of the primary advantages Willow Island saw in biomass use—namely, lower emissions of SO_x—was no longer necessary to comply with emission requirements.

Key Concerns

The biomass-utilization staff at NRG flagged a number of issues that they felt that, if addressed, could encourage more-widespread use of biomass for cofire applications in the United States. On the technical side, they noted a lack of a centralized knowledge source about experiences with cofiring biomass. For example, although there is significant past experience on cofiring and knowledge of the requirements and pitfalls of cofiring biomass in a conventional boiler, it is hard to access this information because of a lack of a central repository of knowledge.[28] Although there are many issues that are site specific, such as the precise facility caps on emissions of CO and NO_x, biomass-specific ash characteristics, and local fuel supply issues, a general database and treatment of cofiring would be useful to new facilities interested in making the conversion.

---

[27] However, as noted, Dominion's biomass requirements would be reduced or eliminated in the case of "significant ratepayer impact."

[28] This is especially true of the accumulated experience of facilities in California in the 1980s and 1990s. For example, NRG is aware of a firm using a 4-inch transport line—which is able to use one-quarter of the air and transport biomass, at the same velocity, that their own biomass transport line uses—but they have been unable to obtain further details on the design.

Additionally, there are some potential research areas relevant to biomass utilization in which the DOE could add value. There are no commercially available biomass-specific burners for use in cofiring applications. Currently, facilities using biomass are adapting coal burners, but they do not know whether this technology is ideal. Research that could inform the development of such burners might examine, for example, what the optimal configuration of a burner for wood cofiring would look like. NRG speculates that it might be appropriate to modify the air-to-fuel ratio to less than 1.6 lb of air per 1 lb of fuel but does not know for sure what the trade-offs would be in the absence of systematic research in this area; a report by EPRI addresses the topic (EPRI, 2010).

In the economic, policy, and regulatory arenas, there are also unanswered questions, and the current frameworks are not ideal. For example, for companies making investment decisions about biomass conversion, it is not clear how issues of supply security trade off against issues of increases in capital investment. What are the relative value and risk of a system designed for a specific biomass type versus one that has some flexibility? More broadly, where is the greatest value of biomass use, and who will pay more for the resource, power or biofuel companies? In terms of policy, if there is a desire to encourage the use of biomass, there needs to be an economic mechanism to recover capital investments and operational costs. In the absence of a national policy regarding GHGs, a national RPS would help decisionmaking and remove state-to-state differences and complications.

The top concerns of other facilities included securing and coordinating biomass supply, technical and logistical issues of biomass handling, and regulatory complications resulting from biomass use. Additionally, some facility staff provided insights into specific technical and

---

Text Box 2.1
Specific Questions and Concerns for Biomass Facility Staff

Technical

Biomass handling and processing
  Improved technology for chippers specific to biomass combustion applications.

Combustion research
  Optimal furnace volume for cofiring relative to dedicated biomass operations; the best strategy for design and modification for cofiring is not known.
  The interactions of biomass ash chemistry and boiler materials with biomass use; the factors that contribute to corrosion are not all known, so the boiler and cladding material are not optimized.
  Front-fired boilers for biomass
  Ways to increase durability of cofiring equipment
  Combustion optimization (e.g., how to ensure sufficient pellet and chip suspension for full combustion)
  Burner configuration optimization for cofiring, presently based on experience with coal, but, for example, optimal air-to-fuel ratios are unknown

Policy

Biomass supply
  Ways to provide incentives to agriculture to produce a biomass product that meets energy-industry needs (e.g., a fast-growing crop with desirable chemistry); need a reliable fuel that allows NO_x and SO_2 to be kept at acceptable levels, has appropriate alkalinity and silica content, and will not compete with the food supply

General
  A national policy regarding GHGs or renewables would help generators serving more than one state make decisions. In particular, biomass energy advocates have expressed concern that the current EPA decision not to exclude biomass from GHG permitting requirements will stifle development of the industry (Bravender, 2010).

policy needs and concerns, listed in Text Box 2.1. Although it was agreed that technical barriers are not preventing biomass cofiring or dedicated biomass combustion today, it is clear that company and facility staff feel that there is still room for technical improvements and optimization in some areas related to using biomass for electricity production.

Summary

The interviews with facility staff summarized in this chapter were intended to identify the near-term technical and logistical issues for biomass utilization for electricity production in existing coal-fired power plants. This summary is therefore based on the actual experiences of the individuals who have worked to implement such transitions in real facilities. Though significant uncertainties regarding best practices for cofiring biomass and long-term implications remain, some generalizations can be made:

- Biomass fuel selection and acquisition are major concerns for biomass use. Finding an adequate, economical fuel supply is essential. Most facilities choose to obtain fuel from several vendors without the help of aggregators and prefer to do so locally (i.e., within approximately 100 miles). At distances beyond 100 miles, transportation by truck becomes a significant contributor to cost. Competitive uses of local biomass resources— for example, for the production of retail charcoal briquettes—could limit supply and increase acquisition costs. Herbaceous fuels are not commonly used or, as yet, are not frequently considered.

- Storage, processing, and handling can be problematic and are site specific. The amount of storage capacity and the type of storage range broadly depending on the cofire ratio, biomass type and form, climate, and available space at the site. Handling and processing equipment is often the largest expense, and the most significant technical complication, in a retrofit for biomass use. This is due to differences in methods and equipment from those in coal handling. Biomass might clog equipment designed for processing and feeding coal. Many capital costs are fixed and are, up to a point, relatively independent of the amount of biomass used at the facility. Handling and processing solutions are generally site specific and have required trial and error to reach an acceptable solution.

- In general, technical problems with combustion have been minimal. Cocombustion of biomass and coal has posed few challenges: Facilities we surveyed have successfully cofired at biomass-to-coal ratios of 10 percent (by energy) with greenwood of moisture content of up to 50 percent. Dedicated biomass facilities have also experienced few technical problems with combustion. Plant operators often assign dedicated burners or regions of the furnace for biomass firing. Some boilers types—such as stoker boilers—might be able to burn a wide range of biomass sizes, but, in general, plant operators have not had significant challenges cofiring with fluidized-bed (FB) or PC boilers. Solutions are specific to the site and the type and quantities of biomass used. Users have observed minimal effects on boilers, especially from cofiring. The principal drawback to cofiring biomass is the potential for minor derating due to the inherently lower energy content and higher moisture content of biomass. Biomass fuel generally burns well and, for woody biomass, with virtually no corrosion issues. Herbaceous fuels can be problematic for emissions (e.g., NO_x, PM), and corrosion has occurred in dedicated facilities. Some emissions of pollutants decrease, especially SO_x. Emission-control equipment is generally not adversely affected, especially when using woody biomass.

- Economic, regulatory, and policy considerations drive operators' decisions to use biomass. Biomass is generally more expensive than coal, but prices vary regionally. The availability of RECs in some states and federal PTCs to offset the costs of conversion are key drivers for the use of biomass. Differences across states in the use of RECs are a major factor in driving decisions by generators to use or not use biomass. However, RECs and PTCs frequently do not cover the additional capital and operating costs of using biomass. Putting a price on emissions of CO_2 would have a strong effect on decisions to use biomass. Permitting is a potential issue concerning the use of biomass. If modifications that were needed to burn biomass in a plant trigger an NSR, interviewees were unanimous in stating that they would not have proceeded with the investment. Though not discussed in interviews, the potential for biomass to complicate compliance with other regulations would also be an impediment to its use. In short, generators will choose to cofire with biomass if local supply conditions are favorable, there are economic incentives to use biomass, and the plant does not face technical, logistical, and regulatory constraints.

Key Findings

Key findings from this portion of the study are the following:

- Although cofiring with biomass is technologically mature and commercially available, operational experience is not widely shared. The knowledge base regarding cofiring resides primarily within the firms that have the actual experience. This presents a potential opportunity for information sharing on the part of the DOE, which could serve as a central repository for information on experience with biomass use.

- There is little long-term operational experience with cofiring biomass with coal in the United States. As a result, plant-site considerations, such as long-term effects on operations and maintenance (O&M), are not well understood. Long-term adequacy of fuel supplies and logistical systems are potential problems. A potential role for the DOE would be to participate in longer-term—i.e., three or more years—demonstration projects that would provide experience in these areas, possibly building on European experience.

- The majority of the limited experience to date has been with greenwood. Herbaceous biomass resources are potentially significant, but they are significantly different fuels from clean greenwood. They produce more ash and have higher–alkali metal content, both of which can contribute to fireside corrosion at plants. The DOE could facilitate additional long-term tests of alternative biomass energy resources to develop a base of experience on which commercial operations could grow.

- Existing equipment is suboptimal for biomass and coal cofiring applications. Commercially available equipment specific to biomass could generate appreciable improvements in efficiency by, for example, improving burners or fuel-feeding systems for specific use in cofire applications. The DOE has a potential research role in this area.

- In the absence of national regulations on emissions of GHGs, the decision to cofire biomass will be confined to areas where state policies encourage the use of biomass. Within these areas, decisions to modify a facility to cofire biomass will depend on several site-specific technical, economic, and policy factors. These include the technical feasibility and costs of cofiring for the specific facility, which are influenced by factors ranging from the boiler type and age, to the site-specific ability to accommodate storage and handling equipment, to the availability of sufficient biomass in the local area. The facility will also need to be able to cover the higher costs of biomass through rates, PTCs, RECs, or other policy measures. The decision to cofire using biomass also depends on whether the appropriate air-quality permits are in hand or readily available.

Biomass Utilization Decision Process

Text Box 2.2 lists the factors that determine the decision to cofire biomass at a specific plant. The first row lists factors that would be required to motivate a plant owner to pursue biomass use at a given facility. With the exception of these first mandates for biomass use, it is unlikely that any single factor will determine whether a facility is appropriate for conversion to biomass use. A company is more likely to want to identify several strong factors for a specific facility and, if appropriate, compare factors across several plants. In most cases, a combination of site-specific factors will be required to choose to use biomass.

Text Box 2.2
Factors Contributing to Biomass Utilization Decision Based on Interviews with Plant Owners and Operators

Mandates for Biomass Use
Legal or legislative requirement
Biomass-specific RPS; limited alternative renewables and nonspecific RPS

Strong Factors for Biomass Use
Policy and regulatory
    An RPS in which biomass electricity generation qualifies
    Need to reduce criteria pollutants
    Previously obtained permits for biomass use

Technical
    Scheduled plant upgrades or modifications, especially in handling equipment, regardless of biomass use
    Site-specific advantages (e.g., previous experience with cofire testing)

Economic
    Abundant, inexpensive biomass resources in vicinity of plant
    PTCs, ITCs, RECs
    Ability to regain lost capacity due to a refiring with a lower-rank coal (in cases in which biomass is fed into the boiler separately)

Additional Considerations for Biomass Use
Technical and economic
    Age and size of facility (i.e., older, smaller facilities might be most appropriate from the perspective of biomass supply but might be unfavorable when considering anticipated EPA regulations of electricity generators)
    Boiler type
    Characteristics relative to those of all facilities company wide

Logistical
    In the absence of local biomass, access to inexpensive transport options (i.e., rail and barge)
    Sufficient space for biomass handling equipment or storage

---

CHAPTER THREE

Plant-Site Costs of Cofiring

This chapter derives plant-site costs of cofiring, using a model that the research team developed (Appendix B), and provides estimates of the potential costs of cofiring biomass with coal at the plant site. Cost estimates include capital expenses for biomass handling and processing equipment and plant modifications, in addition to the cost of receiving, handling, processing, and firing biomass. We also provide estimates of net changes in GHG emissions from replacing coal with biomass. This part of the analysis incorporates estimates from the CUBE model (Curtright et al., 2010) for the life-cycle GHG emissions of the cofired biomass, which are then compared to the life-cycle GHG emissions that would result from firing coal only. The CUBE model is a tool built by RAND for NETL to estimate the life-cycle GHG emissions of cultivating, transporting, and processing biomass energy resources. It includes a wide range of potential biomass feedstocks and provides regional estimates of life-cycle GHG emissions.

Summary of Model of Plant-Site Costs of Cofiring

We constructed a model of the plant-site costs of cofiring biomass with coal. The model includes capital charges for biomass-specific equipment; operational charges associated with cofiring biomass, including biomass storage, handling, and processing; and the effects of plant-site implications of cofiring biomass with coal, most principally the additional electric load required to process the biomass, and the decrease in plant efficiency that results from cofiring with biomass. Appendix B fully documents the model of plant-site costs of cofiring biomass with coal.

Model Inputs and Outputs

Table 3.1 lists the model inputs, ranges, and default parameters of the model of the plant-site costs of cofiring. We make several assumptions to facilitate the analysis. Please see Appendix B for a complete list of the assumptions that we made in building the model of plant cofiring costs.

Estimating the Costs of Cofiring

By considering the direct costs associated with capital recovery, O&M, and biomass fuels and comparing those costs with the amount of electricity attributed to the biomass fuel, the model disaggregates the costs of producing electricity from biomass. This is the specific cost of repowering to fire biomass. It takes the inputs, either default inputs as listed in Table 3.1 or user-specified inputs, then calculates and tabulates these cost components. We assume that

Table 3.1
Parameters and Default Values of Model of Plant-Site Costs of Cofiring

Parameter	Value
Boiler rated capacity	100 MW
Boiler type	Stoker, FB, PC
Boiler capacity factor	85 percent
Type of coal	Subbituminous (default), bituminous
Coal energy content	17.4 mmBtu/ton for subbituminous coal; 23.9 mmBtu/ton for bituminous coal; both are as fired energy contents
Plant heat rate	11,000–13,000 Btu/kWh for stoker boilers; 9,800–13,000 Btu/kWh for FB boilers; and 9,300–12,400 Btu/kWh for PC boilers. The effective heat rate changes as the amount of biomass increases.
Cofire fraction	0.02; 0.05 (default); 0.10
Biomass storage capacity	3–7 days, depending on biomass type
Price of coal	$1.9/GJ ($34/metric ton)
Price of biomass	$2/GJ, variable
Plant cofire capacity	Constant fuel heat input (default), constant fuel mass input
Bus-bar price of electricity	$44.4/MWh
Capital charge rate	6.41%
Economic life of capital investments	30 years
Capital cost contingency factor	25%
Type of biomass	Wood chunks, wood chips, sawdust, bales, pellets
Biomass moisture content	See Table 3.2
Biomass energy content	See Table 3.2
Life-cycle GHG emissions of biomass	See Appendix E
Biomass processing line	Separate: new (default) and modified; commingled
Subsidy for cofiring biomass	$0/MWh
Include additional parasitic load in calculation of total costs?	Yes
Biomass moisture content	See Table 3.2

NOTE: MWh = megawatt-hour. GJ = gigajoule. The bus-bar price of electricity is the price received for the electricity as the electricity leaves the power plant. The capital charge rate is the average for the electricity generating sector, per Crane et al. (2011).

the coal-fired power plant being modified is fully depreciated, so capital costs are only those associated with making investments to facilitate receiving, storing, handling, and processing the biomass. O&M costs are estimated separately for coal and for biomass. For coal, O&M costs are estimated using industry-standard cost-estimating parameters. For biomass, O&M and labor costs are calculated, as are the costs of the parasitic electricity required to process the biomass to a form required by the boiler. This is especially important for cases in which the cofiring occurs in a PC boiler.

Prior experience with cofiring showed decreased boiler efficiencies when cofiring with biomass. The model also estimates the decrease in gross electricity production that typically results from replacing coal with biomass and estimates net electricity production available for dispatch to the grid, assuming full capacity utilization. Often, a plant that is cofiring will produce less electricity than a plant operating on coal alone. This decrease is due to the reduced efficiency when cofiring biomass and to the additional parasitic load required to process the biomass into a form appropriate for feeding into a boiler. As a result, the plant will forfeit revenue from electricity sales when it chooses to cofire biomass, but this is dependent on the plant configuration and how it is operated, as a plant could operate below full capacity. From the perspective of the plant operator, the cost of cofiring includes the additional equipment, operating, and fuel costs associated with cofiring biomass and the lost revenue from the reduced production of electricity.

Results

Base-Case Input Parameters and Assumptions

Our base energy facility is a 100-MW capacity boiler. (Please see Appendix B for a complete list of the assumptions that we made in building the model of plant cofiring costs.) We assume that the operator of the boiler wishes to cofire wood chips at a cofire fraction of 5 percent by energy, holding the heat input to the plant constant. We assume that the capacity factor of the plant is 85 percent, representing baseload supply, although many older coal-fired facilities that would be good candidates for cofiring have lower capacity factors. We assume that the coal plant is fully depreciated, so that there are no capital expenses associated with operating the plant prior to the installation of equipment for handling and processing biomass. We also assume that the delivered price of subbituminous coal is $1.9 per GJ ($2 per mmBtu, $34 per short ton) at the plant gate. The results regarding the costs of electricity do not depend significantly on whether the coal is bituminous or subbituminous. All costs are in 2010 dollars. The results also depend on the moisture content and energy content of the biomass. Table 3.2 lists our assumed moisture and energy content parameters.

Table 3.3 lists the cost components associated with repowering our base-case plant to cofire biomass. The capital costs of electricity apportioned to biomass associated with repowering are $0.007 per kilowatt-hour, and the nonfuel operating costs associated with repower-

Table 3.2
Moisture Content and Energy Content of Biomass Feedstocks

Biomass	Moisture Content (%)	Energy Content, Dry Mass Basis (GJ/dry metric ton)
Woody biomass, chunks	35	19.0
Woody biomass, chips	35	19.0
Woody biomass, sawdust	20	19.0
Herbaceous biomass, bales	15	17.0
Mixed biomass, pellets	5	17.4

SOURCE: Oak Ridge National Laboratory (ORNL) (2010).

Table 3.3
Cost Components for Repowering to Cofire Biomass

Price of Biomass ($/dry metric ton wood chips)	Capital Costs ($/kWh)	Operating Costs ($/kWh)	Biomass Fuel Costs ($/kWh)	Cost of Using Biomass ($/kWh)
38	0.007	0.012	0.023	0.041
57	0.007	0.012	0.034	0.053
76	0.007	0.012	0.045	0.064
95	0.007	0.012	0.057	0.076
114	0.007	0.012	0.068	0.087
133	0.007	0.012	0.079	0.098
152	0.007	0.012	0.091	0.110
171	0.007	0.012	0.102	0.121
190	0.007	0.012	0.113	0.132

NOTE: The results shown are for a PC boiler repowering to cofire wood chips at a 5-percent cofire fraction using a new processing line to prepare the wood chips for cofiring.

ing are $0.012 per kilowatt-hour. The price of biomass is an independent variable. The cost of repowering is $0.041 per kilowatt-hour at a price of wood chips of $38 per dry metric ton ($2 per gigajoule, $2.1 per mmBtu, $34 per dry short ton). The cost of repowering rises $0.006 per kilowatt-hour for each $10 increase in the price of wood chips.

The capital and operating costs of repowering to cofire biomass depend on the type of biomass being cofired and the cofire fraction. As discussed in Chapter Two, although wood chips are the most common fuel today, other biomass fuels include bales of corn residue and engineered fuel pellets. In general, the costs of cofiring bales will be higher than the cost of cofiring wood chips because the bales require additional equipment and operating steps to prepare for cofiring; conversely, pellets have lower cofiring costs because they are easier to prepare for cofiring. Additionally, the amount of biomass that is cofired depends on the cofire fraction. At higher cofire fractions, per–kilowatt-hour capital costs of repowering decrease because additional electricity from biomass is produced, allowing for greater cost recovery. Figure 3.1 illustrates these results for a PC boiler.

Operating costs are constant on a per–kilowatt-hour basis and are $0.012 per kilowatt-hour for wood chips, $0.013 per kilowatt-hour for bales, and $0.009 per kilowatt-hour for pellets. Capital costs decline from $0.016 per kilowatt-hour for wood chips at a cofire fraction of 2 percent to $0.003 per kilowatt-hour at a cofire fraction of 10 percent. The results for bales and pellets are similar, with bales having higher capital costs.

Total Cost of Firing Biomass and Prices for Renewable-Electricity Credits
When cofiring biomass in a plant that is operating close to capacity, it is often necessary to derate the plant because of the lower heat content of the biomass fuel. In these instances, the plant produces less electricity and forgoes revenues that it would otherwise receive when firing with coal only. The biomass displaces coal, which reduces operating costs associated with coal, at the expense of the additional operational costs of using biomass. The sum of changes in

Figure 3.1
Capital and Operating Costs of Cofiring Biomass

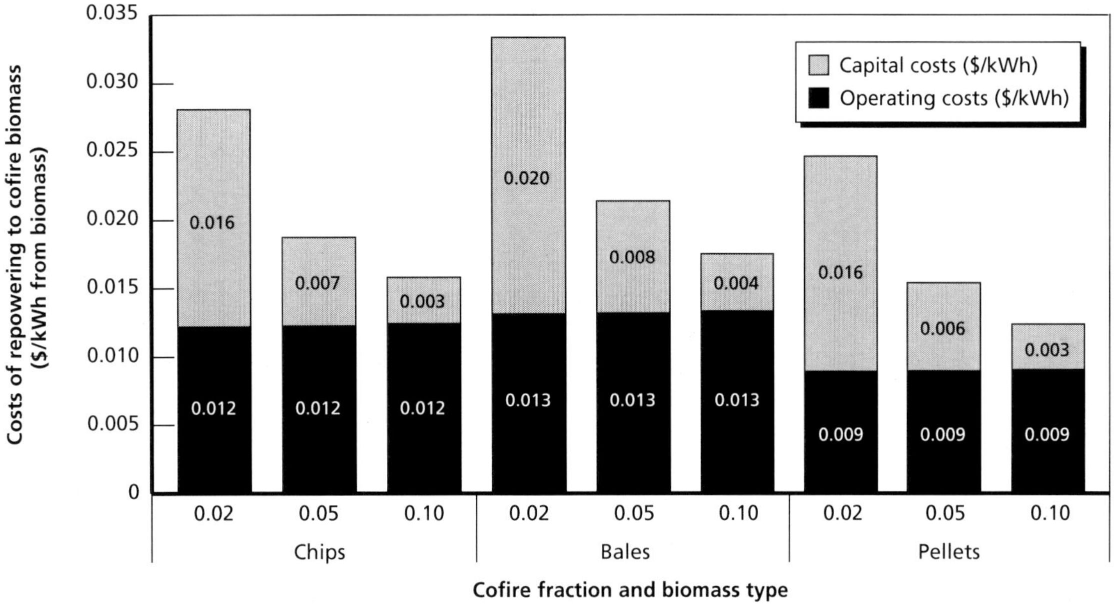

NOTE: The results shown are for a PC boiler repowering to cofire biomass using a new processing line to prepare the biomass for cofiring.
RAND *TR-984-3.1*

plant-site costs for fuel, operating costs, capital costs, and forgone revenues from lost electricity sales are the total costs to the plant of firing biomass.

Our simplified analysis does not take into account several factors that could slightly shift the costs of cofiring. For example, coal-fired power plants often do not operate at full capacity. Such a plant would be able to avoid derating by increasing the power produced when cofiring. Alternatively, many coal-fired power plants sell their fly ash as an amendment to portland cement. As discussed earlier, ash from cofiring does not currently meet the ASTM specifications, so any plant considering cofiring with biomass would have to factor into its decision-making the forgone revenues from fly-ash sales.

If the plant operator is to seek a REC to offset plant-site costs of cofiring, then it is these total changes in plant profits that must be offset. We define the implied price of a REC to be the ratio of the difference in profits (revenues less costs) when firing coal only and cofiring with biomass and the amount of electricity (in kilowatt-hours) produced by the biomass (the total electricity produced times the cofire fraction).

To determine these total costs, we begin by presenting the costs of producing electricity from coal. To review, we assume a 100-MW PC boiler firing subbituminous coal. The plant is fully depreciated, so capital expenses are zero. We assume coal to have a delivered cost of $1.90 per gigajoule ($2 per mmBtu, $34 per short ton), which is consistent with current costs. Table 3.4 details the cost components.

Cofiring decreases plant performance. When cofiring, there is typically a decrease in the plant's efficiency. In the case of cofiring wood chips, the decrease is due to the increased water content of the biomass fuel. The plant efficiency when firing coal only is 33.45 percent, and the plant efficiency when cofiring wood chips at 5 percent is 33.34 percent. This difference is

Table 3.4
Costs Associated with Producing Electricity from Coal

Cost of Fuel ($/kWh)	Capital Costs ($/kWh)	Operating Costs ($/kWh)	Cost of Electricity ($/kWh)
0.0204	0.000	0.0054	0.0258

notable but, in practice, would be difficult to measure in the field. Additionally, grinding and processing the biomass incur an additional parasitic load, which reduces the amount of electricity available for sale. For wood chips with a moisture content of 35 percent, the parasitic load is an additional 53 kWh per dry metric ton of biomass. These figures can be used to derive the annual plant output resulting from cofiring biomass, which is presented in Table 3.5.

Next, we calculate the additional fuel and operating costs associated with biomass cofiring. By assumption, the heat input to the plant is constant, so we apportion the biomass energy to be 5 percent of the energy in the coal-only case. The fuel costs for coal and biomass are then calculated and compared with the cost when cofiring only with coal. It is then possible to calculate the change in fuel costs and the additional costs of cofiring per kilowatt-hour of electricity. The example presented in Table 3.6 is for a biomass price of $2.0 per gigajoule ($2.1 per mmBtu, $38 per dry metric ton, $34 per dry short ton), which is the current price of wood chips cited in our interviews with plant owners and operators. It is likely that delivered prices of biomass would be higher, especially if more owners and operators were to cofire. The series of calculations presented in Table 3.6 needs to be repeated for different costs of delivered biomass.

The final cost factor to determine is the change in operating costs when cofiring biomass with coal. The model presented in Appendix B estimates the operating costs of coal to be $0.502 per gigajoule ($5.30 per mmBtu) of coal and $1.08 per gigajoule ($1.14 per mmBtu) of wood chips. Using these figures, we are able to calculate the change in operating costs using the energy contributions for coal and biomass estimated in Table 3.6. As in Table 3.6, the

Table 3.5
Annual Electricity Production and Value from Coal-Only and Biomass Cofiring

Item	Value
Electricity produced from coal (million kWh)	744.6
Electricity produced from cofiring (million kWh)	742.1
Additional parasitic load (million kWh)	1.7
Electricity sales from firing with coal ($ million)	33.06
Change in electricity for sale (million kWh)	(4.2)
Electricity produced from biomass (million kWh)	37.1
Net electricity produced from biomass (million kWh)	35.4
Change in electricity sales ($ thousand)	(186.4)
Change in electricity sales ($/kWh from biomass)	(0.0053)

NOTE: Values are for a 100-MW PC boiler operating at a capacity factor of 85 percent and cofiring wood chips at a cofire fraction, by energy, of 5 percent.

Table 3.6
Fuel Energy and Costs for Coal-Only and Biomass Cofiring

Item	Value for Coal	Value for Biomass
Total heat input, coal-only firing (million GJ/year)	8.01	
Cost of fuel, coal-only firing ($ million/year)	15.2	
Total heat input cofiring (million GJ/year)	7.61	0.401
Cost of fuel, cofiring ($ million/year)	14.4	$0.801
Additional fuel cost ($/year)	41,800	
Additional fuel cost ($/kWh from biomass)	0.0012	

NOTE: Values are for a 100-MW PC boiler operating at a capacity factor of 85 percent and cofiring wood chips at a cofire fraction, by energy, of 5 percent.

operating costs for coal and biomass are estimated separately, summed, and compared with the coal-only costs. Table 3.7 presents these results.

Using the costs for coal-only and biomass cofiring listed in Tables 3.5 through 3.7, it is possible to tabulate the total costs of cofiring. These are listed in Table 3.8. We treat the price of biomass as an independent variable.

The total costs of cofiring are $0.02 per kilowatt-hour when wood chips are $38 per dry metric ton ($2 per gigajoule, $2.1 per mmBtu, $34 per dry metric ton). On an energy basis, this price for wood chips is 5-percent greater than the price of coal, so incremental fuel costs are minimal ($0.001 per kilowatt-hour).

The change in operating costs, capital costs, and lost sales revenue vary according to the type of biomass, the cofire fraction, and the site-specific issues associated with the power station, such as equipment margins, original fuel, and environmental costs. As was the case when we considered isolated costs of biomass cofiring, when compared with wood chips, bales have higher capital and operating costs, and pellets have lower capital and operating costs. The effect of cofire fraction varies. As before, at higher cofire fractions, per–kilowatt-hour capital costs of cofiring decrease. However, as the cofire fraction increases, revenues from electricity sales decrease as compared with coal. Figure 3.2 illustrates these results.

Costs per kilowatt-hour of electricity from biomass decrease as the cofire fraction increases. The capital costs per kilowatt-hour are the same as in the biomass-only case because the plant is

Table 3.7
Operating Costs for Coal-Only and Biomass Cofiring

Item	Value for Coal	Value for Biomass
Variable operating cost for coal ($/GJ)	0.502	
Variable operating cost for biomass ($/GJ)		1.08
Operating cost, coal ($ million/year)	4.02	
Operating cost, cofiring ($ million/year)	3.82	0.433
Additional operating cost ($/year)	232,000	
Additional operating cost ($/kWh from biomass)	0.0066	

Table 3.8
Total Costs of Cofiring Biomass with Coal

Price of Biomass ($/dry metric ton wood chips)	Change in Fuel Costs ($/kWh)	Capital Costs ($/kWh)	Change in Operating Costs ($/kWh)	Change in Revenue from Electricity Sales ($/kWh)	Total Costs of Cofiring ($/kWh)
38	0.001	0.007	0.007	−0.005	0.020
57	0.013	0.007	0.007	−0.005	0.031
76	0.024	0.007	0.007	−0.005	0.042
95	0.035	0.007	0.007	−0.005	0.054
114	0.047	0.007	0.007	−0.005	0.065
133	0.058	0.007	0.007	−0.005	0.076
152	0.069	0.007	0.007	−0.005	0.088
171	0.081	0.007	0.007	−0.005	0.099
190	0.092	0.007	0.007	−0.005	0.110

NOTE: The results shown are for a PC boiler repowering to cofire wood chips at a 5-percent cofire fraction and using a new processing line to prepare the wood chips for cofiring.

Figure 3.2
Incremental Nonfuel Costs of Cofiring Biomass with Coal

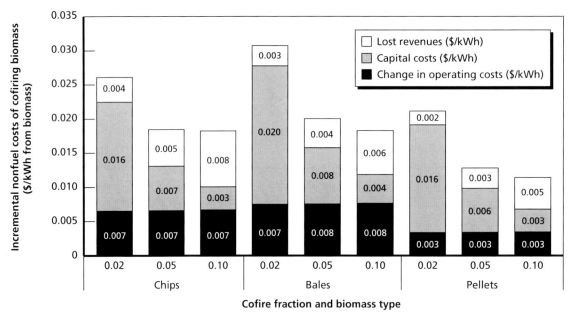

NOTE: The results shown are for a PC boiler repowering to cofire biomass using a new processing line to prepare the biomass for cofiring.
RAND *TR-984-3.2*

assumed to be fully depreciated. The change in operating costs is $0.007 per kilowatt-hour for wood chips, $0.008 per kilowatt-hour for bales, and $0.003 per kilowatt-hour for pellets. The lost revenues that result from cofiring are $0.004 per kilowatt-hour for wood chips at a cofire fraction of 2 percent and increase to $0.008 per kilowatt-hour at a cofire fraction of 10 percent.

Lost revenues are smaller for bales ($0.006 per kilowatt-hour at a cofire fraction of 10 percent) and even smaller for pellets ($0.005 per kilowatt-hour at a cofire fraction of 10 percent). This is largely a result of the water content of wood chips (35 percent) as compared with bales (15 percent) or pellets (5 percent).

CHAPTER FOUR

Near-Term Potential Demand for Biomass for Cofiring Applications

Introduction

This chapter describes current biomass use and estimates the potential near-term demand for biomass. The method employed begins by compiling current demand for biomass energy resources and coal use for generating electricity at the state level. Currently, biomass use for electricity in the industrial, electric power, commercial, and residential sectors comprises 1.3 percent of total generation, but, because a large share of biomass is used for industrial energy, biomass use in the electric power sector comprises only about 0.6 percent of generation. Parametrically, we increase the amount of biomass used to produce electricity to 1 percent, 2 percent, and 5 percent of coal input energy, with 1 percent and 2 percent representing near-term expansion of cofiring. We aggregate the state-level results into U.S. Department of Agriculture (USDA) regions, which represent regions of biomass production. Using published estimates of current biomass production and availability, we determine the potential near-term regional demand for biomass and the regional disparities. State-level summaries are included in Appendix C.

Methodology and Data for Estimating Potential Biomass Demand

Current Biomass Energy Use

Biomass provided about 4.1 exajoules (EJ; 1 EJ = 10^{18} joules; 4.1 EJ = 0.9 quadrillion BTU, or *quads*) of energy in the United States in 2008. About half of total biomass energy (2.15 EJ) was from wood and wood-derived fuels; about 36 percent was from corn ethanol and other biofuels (1.5 EJ); and the remainder was from biomass wastes (0.46 EJ) (EIA, 2009). Assuming an energy value of 19 GJ per dry metric ton for woody biomass, the 2.15 EJ of wood and derived fuels used in 2008 has a mass of approximately 113 million dry metric tons (125 million dry tons). Figure 4.1 displays U.S. biomass energy use by fuel type for 2003–2008, the latest year for which detailed data are available.

EIA aggregates energy-use and emission data across sectors of the economy—industrial, residential, transportation, commercial, and electric power. Slightly more than half (2.1 of the 4.1 EJ) of 2008 biomass energy was used in heat, combined heat and power, or on-site generation at industrial sites for the heat and electricity needed for industrial processes, such as paper and ethanol production. Biomass use in the transportation sector (0.9 EJ) was predominantly corn ethanol blended into motor gasoline. Residential biomass use (0.5 EJ) is solely wood and wood-derived fuels for home heating, while commercial biomass use (0.1 EJ) is predominantly

Figure 4.1
Total U.S. Biomass Energy Use by Fuel Type

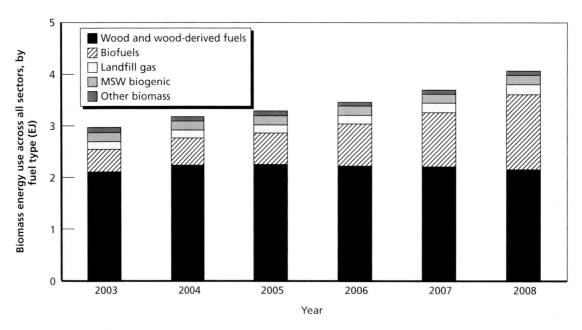

SOURCE: EIA (2010c).
NOTE: MSW = municipal solid waste. Total biomass energy use in 2008 was about 4.1 EJ.
RAND *TR-984-4.1*

woody fuels and MSW. The electric power sector, which sells electricity or electricity and heat primarily to the public, used about 0.45 EJ of biomass energy in 2008. About 44 percent of biomass use in the electric power sector was from woody biomass, with biogenic MSW and landfill gas comprising the bulk of the remainder (EIA, 2009). Figure 4.2 displays the total U.S. biomass uses for energy, classified by sector and fuel type for 2008; it is the latest year for which detailed data are available.

Biomass use for power generation comprises (1) woody biomass fuels, including solid and liquid wood and wood waste, and (2) waste biomass fuels, such as landfill gas, biogenic MSW (paper, food, textiles, yard trimmings), and other biomass (sludge waste, agricultural by-products, other products). In 2008, biomass generated about 55.9 terawatt-hours (TWh) and accounted for 1.3 percent of total net electricity generation (EIA, 2009). Biomass also provided about 0.6 EJ of useful thermal output in combined heat and power plants across all sectors. Biomass use for electric power has remained relatively constant from 2003 to 2008, yet, due to the considerable increase in wind power generation, the share of biomass generation in nonhydro renewable generation fell from about 67 percent to 45 percent over the same period (EIA, 2009). Figure 4.3 illustrates these trends.

Industrial paper, paper goods, and, to a lesser extent, lumber production have historically utilized wood wastes and black liquor (a waste from wood pulp processing) to generate heat and electric power. In 2008, biomass contributed about 28.5 TWh in the industrial sector and 1.6 TWh in the commercial sector from these sources (EIA, 2009) and generated approximately 25.8 TWh in the electric power sector, the sector relevant for this study. Of these 25.8 TWh, 10.9 TWh were generated from wood and wood-derived fuels, while 14.9 TWh were generated from biomass wastes (EIA, 2009). About 0.01 EJ of wood fuels and 0.008 EJ

Figure 4.2
Total U.S. Biomass Energy Use by Sector and Fuel Type

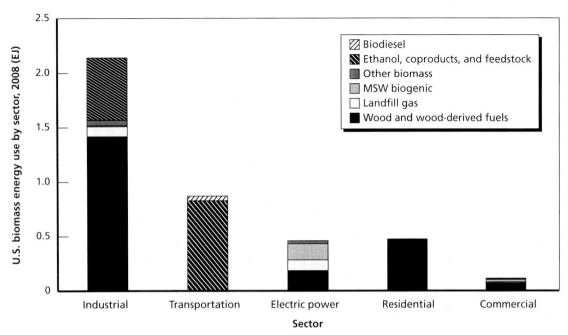

SOURCE: EIA (2010c).

RAND TR-984-4.2

Figure 4.3
Biomass Comprises About 45 percent of Nonhydro Renewable Generation

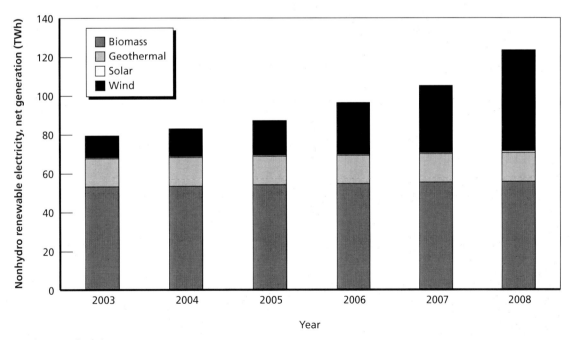

SOURCE: EIA (2009).

RAND TR-984-4.3

of biomass waste fuels also generated heat at combined heat and power plants in the electricity sector. Figure 4.4 illustrates biomass generation by fuel from 2003 to 2008. The "other biomass" category includes agricultural by-products and wastes and was a relatively small contributor to total biomass generation of electricity (EIA, 2010c). Wood and wood-derived fuels are the dominant current source of biomass energy for producing electricity.

Existing cofiring capacity includes power plants in the electric power and industrial sectors. Expanded near-term biomass use in the electric power sector will likely be through cofiring at existing coal-fired power plants. In 2007, 62 power plants reported having a total generating capacity of about 5 GW capable of cofiring biomass and coal. Appendix C lists the individual power plants and boiler types (EIA, 2010c).

Figure 4.4
Biomass Generation and Fuels Used in the Electric Power Sector

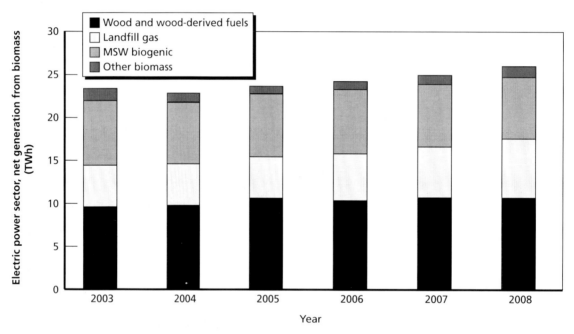

SOURCE: EIA (2010c).
RAND *TR-984-4.4*

Near-Term Potential Demand for Biomass Energy Resources for Cofiring

This section estimates the near-term potential demand for biomass for the purpose of cofiring with coal to produce electricity. It is estimated by state and aggregated to the USDA region level. We use estimates by the Energy Information Agency (EIA) for 2008 for coal demand, average energy content of delivered coal by state, and coal-fired net generation in the electric power sector in each state (EIA, 2010a, 2010d). These estimates are summarized in Appendix C. Table 4.1 and Figure 4.5 present the demand for coal to be used for electric power production by region; Alaska and Hawaii are omitted because they do not operate in traditional U.S. regional energy and fuel markets. Displacing 1 and 2 percent of the energy of coal demanded with biomass provides insight into potential biomass that could be needed for

Table 4.1
2008 Electric Power Sector Coal Demand and Generation Scenarios

Region	Electricity Generated by Coal (TWh)	Coal Used to Generate Electricity (million metric tons)	Coal Energy Used to Generate Electricity (EJ)	1% of Coal Input Energy (EJ)	2% of Coal Input Energy (EJ)
Appalachia	345	141	3.9	0.04	0.08
Corn Belt	463	229	5.2	0.05	0.10
Delta	67	37	0.75	<0.01	0.01
Lake States	143	77	1.7	0.02	0.03
Mountain	214	109	2.4	0.02	0.05
Northeast	197	84	2.2	0.02	0.04
Northern Plains	89	58	1.1	0.01	0.02
Pacific	15	9	0.19	<0.01	<0.01
Southeast	267	110	2.9	0.03	0.6
Southern Plains	184	115	2.1	0.02	0.04
Total	1,984	969	22.4	0.22	0.45

SOURCES: EIA (2010a, 2010d).

NOTE: Figures might not sum, due to rounding. USDA production regions are as follows: Appalachia (Kentucky, North Carolina, Tennessee, Virginia, and West Virginia); Corn Belt (Illinois, Indiana, Iowa, Missouri, and Ohio); Delta (Arkansas, Louisiana, and Mississippi); Lake States (Michigan, Minnesota, and Wisconsin); Mountain (Arizona, Colorado, Idaho, Montana, Nevada, New Mexico, Utah, and Wyoming); Northeast (Connecticut, Delaware, Maine, Maryland, Massachusetts, New Hampshire, New Jersey, New York, Pennsylvania, Rhode Island, and Vermont); Northern Plains (Kansas, Nebraska, North Dakota, and South Dakota); Pacific (California, Oregon, and Washington); Southeast (Alabama, Florida, Georgia, and South Carolina); and Southern Plains (Oklahoma and Texas). Alaska, Hawaii, Puerto Rico, and the Pacific Basin are not included in any USDA production region (Economic Research Service [ERS], 2008).

near-term cofiring by region; this 1–2 percent would likely be met by several plants in a region cofiring at fractions of 5–10 percent.

Near-term biomass supplies for cofiring will likely be sourced from lowest-cost biomass, typically residues. These include forest residues from logging operations and thinnings, primary mill residues from manufacturing plants utilizing wood, secondary mill residues from woodworking operations, and agricultural residues. One estimate of potential U.S. biomass residues was completed by the National Renewable Energy Laboratory (NREL) using 2007 data and a methodology described in an earlier assessment (Milbrandt, 2005). Using county-level data from the NREL assessment, we aggregate potential demand for biomass into each of the ten USDA regions and compare demand with the available quantities of biomass residues in 2007 (see Table 4.2). The 300-million-dry-metric-ton estimate used here includes solely forest, mill, and crop residues. It does not include the 61 million to 84 million dry metric tons of dedicated energy crops that could potentially be grown on Conservation Reserve Program (CRP) farmland (Milbrandt, 2005). Additionally, since there are no existing coal-fired power plants in Rhode Island or Vermont, these states will not demand biomass for cofiring but might provide biomass supply to the Northeast USDA region.

Figure 4.5
Regional Coal Energy Demanded for Electric Power Production in 2008

SOURCE: EIA (2010d).
RAND *TR-984-4.5*

Table 4.2
Potential Biomass Energy from Forest, Mill, and Crop Residues per Year

Region	Forest Residues (million dry metric tons)	Primary and Secondary Mill Residues (million dry metric tons)	Crop Residues (million dry metric tons)	Total Residues (million dry metric tons)
Appalachia	12.2	8.9	6.1	27.3
Corn Belt	4.1	2.4	66.4	72.9
Delta	12.7	11.4	10.0	34.1
Lake States	7.6	4.1	20.1	31.7
Mountain	1.5	4.1	6.3	11.9
Northeast	6.7	3.6	3.0	13.3
Northern Plains	0.3	0.3	35.9	36.5
Pacific	8.0	15.3	3.9	27.3
Southeast	14.0	13.3	4.6	31.8
Southern Plains	2.9	4.0	7.3	14.2
Total	70.0	67.5	163.5	301.0

SOURCE: Milbrandt (2005).

NOTE: Figures might not sum, due to rounding.

The energy content of biomass varies depending on the type of biomass and its moisture content. Table 4.3 and Figure 4.6 show an estimate of the potential biomass energy available from forest, mill, and crop residues (Appendix C presents further detail at the state level).

In the near term, biomass use for cofiring is likely to occur locally, to minimize transportation, storage, and processing costs. Yet, in regions where supply and demand are not aligned, biomass might have to be traded across regions. From the estimates of potential near-term coal demand and biomass supply presented earlier, three types of regions emerge. First, there are regions with both high biomass supplies and high coal demand, which include the Corn Belt and Southeast regions. If coal-fired power plants in these regions develop cofiring capacity, local biomass supplies to fuel them are likely to be sufficient. These supplies could be existing resources, such as corn stover, or they could be new supplies developed explicitly for biomass energy use, such as SG. Because of the large biomass resources in these two regions, some biomass could be exported if sufficient local demand does not develop. Second, there are regions that have high biomass supplies but low coal demand, including the Pacific, Delta, Northern Plains, and Lake States regions. Although some cofiring capacity might develop to use these resources, these regions have the capacity to export biomass to relatively resource-poor regions. Finally, there are regions with high coal demand but without sufficient local biomass resources to meet a large fraction of potential demand for cofiring. These include the Appalachia, Southern Plains, Northeast, and Mountain regions. If considerable biomass demand for cofiring develops in these regions, they might need to import biomass from other areas. Figure 4.7 shows the percentage of available biomass residues in each region that would be required to substitute for 1, 2, 5, and 10 percent of the coal used in that region to generate electric power. Figure 4.8 depicts potential biomass exports from areas with high biomass availability to areas

Table 4.3
2008 Potential Biomass Energy from Forest, Mill, and Crop Residues

Region	Energy Available from Forest and Mill Residues (EJ/year)	Energy Available from Crop Residues (EJ/year)	Total Biomass Energy Available (EJ/year)
Appalachia	0.40	0.10	0.51
Corn Belt	0.12	1.1	1.2
Delta	0.46	0.17	0.63
Lake States	0.22	0.34	0.56
Mountain	0.11	0.11	0.21
Northeast	0.20	0.05	0.25
Northern Plains	0.01	0.61	0.62
Pacific	0.44	0.07	0.51
Southeast	0.52	0.08	0.60
Southern Plains	0.13	0.12	0.26
Total	2.61	2.78	5.38

SOURCE: Milbrandt (2005).
NOTE: Figures might not sum, due to rounding.

Figure 4.6
Total Biomass Residue Potential Availability by Region

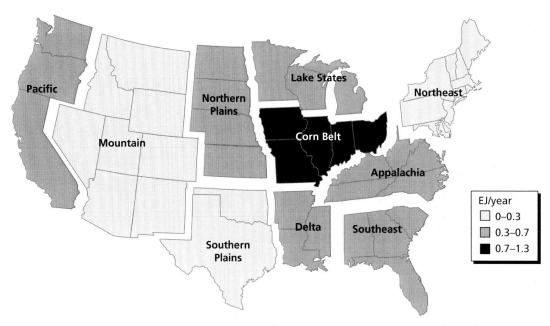

SOURCE: Milbrandt (2005).
NOTE: Includes crop, forest, and primary and secondary mill residues.
RAND *TR-984-4.6*

Figure 4.7
Potential Biomass Importing and Exporting Regions, Based on Availability and Coal Demand

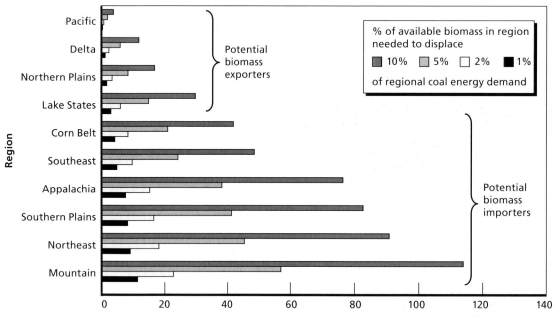

RAND *TR-984-4.7*

Figure 4.8
**Potential for High Biomass Regions to Export to Regions with High Coal Demand and
Low Biomass Resources**

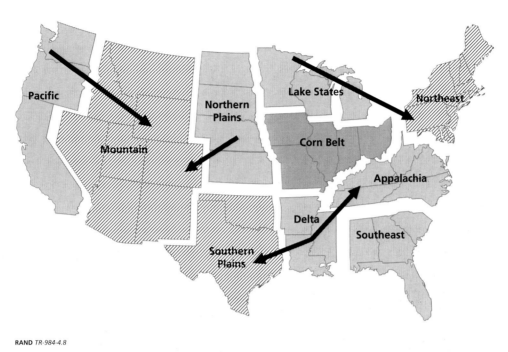

with potential high demand for biomass to be cofired with coal but with limited biomass resources. The following chapter considers the cost implications of several supply scenarios.

Near-Term Potential Supply Constraints

The near-term 300 million metric ton supply of biomass residues is a national estimate. Individual power plant owners, however, are subject to the conditions of the local biomass market, either through direct negotiations with local suppliers or through a supply aggregator. The local availability and price also depends on the local demand and number of users. Wood fuel requirements for a dedicated 100 MW biomass-fired power plant are about 1.0 million to 1.2 million metric tons per year. A typical economical collection area in western Pennsylvania encompassing a two-hour driving distance currently will yield about 0.5 million metric tons per year (Solomon, 2010). If several cofiring power plants had overlapping local supply areas, they would compete for biomass, pushing up local biomass prices (LaTourrette et al., 2011). A detailed market assessment of local resources, demands, and pricing would be required for specific power plants considering biomass cofiring as a long-term strategy.

CHAPTER FIVE

Logistical Considerations

Introduction

This chapter examines the costs of handling, transporting, storing, and processing biomass from the farm gate to the energy facility. It characterizes the costs, employing three principal scenarios for supplying biomass to an energy facility: (1) biomass supplied from the local region (the current scenario for plant operators we interviewed), (2) biomass supplied from the local region and from a more distant region by long-haul transport, and (3) all biomass supplied from a distant region by long-haul transport. Each scenario considers several variants. The analysis quantifies the cost and GHG trade-offs among the alternative processing and transportation options. The methodology is applied to U.S. regions with significant differences in their near-term supply of biomass and near-term demands. For example, the Pacific region is able to produce a significant quantity of forestry residues but has relatively few coal-fired power plants. Therefore, this region could export biomass in the form of chips, chunks, or pellets to the Mountain region, incurring additional transportation costs. Several cases throughout the United States are identified and characterized.

Costs of Handling, Processing, and Transporting Biomass

Logistical costs for biomass apply to all costs associated with transporting biomass from the field to the energy facility. These costs fall into four general categories: loading and unloading biomass, including transshipment of biomass from truck to rail or barge; transportation; storing biomass; and processing and densifying to facilitate handling, storage, and firing. Appendix D documents the data and methods that we used to estimate the logistical costs of biomass.

Loading and Unloading Biomass

Every loading and unloading operation imposes a cost. We assume that biomass is loaded onto an appropriate truck at the farm (for herbaceous biomass) or at the collection site (for woody biomass). The loading and unloading processes, equipment, and costs differ for the two major biomass types, as described in this section.

For herbaceous biomass, such as corn stover or SG, we assume the biomass to be baled and stacked at the roadside as part of harvesting. We assume woody biomass to be chipped remotely and blown into a trailer designed to carry chips. Costs for loading are taken from Mahmudi and Flynn (2006) and adjusted for moisture content of 15 percent for herbaceous

Table 5.1
Loading and Unloading Costs for Biomass on Truck

Biomass Type	Moisture Content (%)	Loading and Unloading Cost ($/dry metric ton)
Herbaceous biomass (bales)	15	5.90
Woody biomass (wood chips)	35	4.80
Densified biomass (pellets)	5	2.74

SOURCES: Mahmudi and Flynn (2006); Edwards and Johanns (2011).
NOTE: Costs are reported in 2010 dollars.

biomass and 35 percent for woody biomass. We assume that the cost of loading and unloading pellets is comparable to that of grain and apply published custom rates for loading grain.

The loading and unloading costs for rail are those associated with capital and labor at a transshipment facility (assuming that, initially, all biomass has to be collected by truck) and at the energy facility. Mahmudi and Flynn (2006, Table 2) estimate these costs, which we modify as detailed in Appendix D. The resulting cost estimates appear in Table 5.2.

Transportation

Transportation costs refers to the variable cost for moving a good and is expressed in terms of mass distance (ton-miles). Transportation costs include capital recovery and depreciation of equipment, maintenance, fuel and lubricants, and labor. Truck transport costs for herbaceous biomass are derived from Mahmudi and Flynn (2006), from Solomon (2010) for wood chips, and from Edwards and Johanns (2011) for pellets (see Appendix D). Key drivers of transportation costs for biomass are bulk density and moisture content: Pellets are both denser and drier than either bales or wood chips. Table 5.3 lists these rates.

To estimate the distance-variable cost of transporting biomass by rail, we use published rates for transporting bales, wood chips, and grain on the Burlington Northern Santa Fe (BNSF) and CSX lines. As described in Appendix D, we choose routes greater than 600 miles and select carload rates that apply to unit trains using carrier-owned cars. Two rates are identified. We estimate car capacity by using nominal bulk density parameters as listed in the *Biomass Energy Data Book* (ORNL, 2010) applied to standard rail cars (CSX, undated [a]). Derived nominal distance-variable costs for transporting biomass by rail are listed in Table 5.4. The two derived rates are listed as a range, which is not necessarily inclusive of all possible rates.

Table 5.2
Loading and Unloading Costs for Biomass on Rail

Biomass Type	Moisture Content (%)	Loading and Unloading Cost ($/dry metric ton)
Herbaceous biomass (bales)	15	4.65
Woody biomass (wood chips)	35	2.68
Densified biomass (pellets)	5	1.83

SOURCES: Mahmudi and Flynn (2006); Edwards and Johanns (2011).
NOTE: Costs are reported in 2010 dollars.

Table 5.3
Distance-Variable Cost for Truck Transport of Biomass

Biomass Type	Moisture Content (%)	Distance-Variable Cost ($/dry ton-mile)
Herbaceous biomass (bales)	15	0.09
Woody biomass (wood chips)	35	0.07
Densified biomass (pellets)	5	0.04

SOURCES: Mahmudi and Flynn (2006); Solomon (2010); Edwards and Johanns (2011).
NOTE: Costs are reported in 2010 dollars.

Table 5.4
Distance-Variable Cost for Transporting Biomass by Rail Freight

Biomass Type	Moisture Content	Distance-Variable Cost Range ($/dry ton-mile)
Herbaceous biomass (bales)	15	0.05–0.07
Woody biomass (wood chips)	35	0.07–0.09
Densified biomass (pellets)	5	0.02–0.02

SOURCES: CSX (undated [a], undated [b]); BNSF Railroad (undated).
NOTE: Costs are reported in 2010 dollars. Figures are reported to two significant figures.

Storage Requirements and Costs

Because herbaceous biomass is harvested annually or semiannually, it has to be stored, often for extended periods of time (Leesley, 2009). The cost of storage is the sum of the costs of building and operating the storage barn and loading and unloading the bales from the flatbed trailer. We estimate the cost of storage based on the experience of the CVBP (Antares Group, 2009). As detailed in Appendix D, we estimate the cost of storing herbaceous biomass, including loading and unloading, capital, O&M, and land costs for the storage facility, to be $18 per dry metric ton. This cost estimate apportions costs equally to all biomass passing through the facility. The cost of stacking the bales in the storage shed is $0.77 per dry metric ton.

Densification Costs

We base our estimate of the costs of producing biomass pellets on Mani et al. (2006). We build four cases to cover alternative configurations, including drying and ash removal. Details of the method appear in Appendix D. The four cases estimate production costs of pellets from (1) herbaceous biomass without active drying, (2) herbaceous biomass with ash removal, (3) woody biomass with natural gas–fired drying, and (4) woody biomass with wood-fired drying. The final cost estimates, on a mass and energy basis, are listed in Table 5.5.

We did not consider the potential of densifying biomass at the farm, allowing both local and long-distance transportation to reap the benefit of reduced costs (see, for example, Idaho National Laboratory [INL], 2009). In the near term, the ability of smaller, mobile systems to demonstrate significant cost reduction is unlikely because (1) biomass production is dispersed over a large area, so any single processing site will be able to supply only a relatively small amount of biomass before the mobile densification system needs to be moved to a new loca-

Table 5.5
Estimated Densification Costs for Biomass

Case	Densification Cost ($/dry metric ton)	Densification Cost ($/GJ)
Herbaceous biomass, without drying	16	0.96
Herbaceous biomass, without drying, with ash removal	22	1.2
Woody biomass, with natural gas–fired drying	34	1.8
Woody biomass, with biomass-fired drying	31	1.6

SOURCES: Mani et al. (2006); ORNL (2010); Bureau of Economic Analysis (BEA) (2010).

NOTE: Costs are reported in 2010 dollars. Figures are reported to two significant figures. Costs do not include the biomass feedstock, which is assumed to be $4.00/GJ.

tion, and (2) because of their relatively small capacity, such systems tend to be less efficient and require more labor inputs per unit of product than would a centralized system.

Biomass Sourcing Scenarios

The logistical cost components described in the previous section show up as costs when applied to particular scenarios for sourcing biomass. In this section, we develop three generic scenarios for sourcing biomass. The power plant locations and biomass supply areas were selected to be broadly representative of logistical conditions, with each having access to truck, barge, and rail delivery routes. Together, the scenarios represent the major characteristics of biomass logistics; the sensitivity of the results to different transportation modes, shipping distances, handling costs, and other parameters is discussed in Appendix D. The first scenario represents the standard method by which biomass is sourced today—namely, a plant acquires biomass from the local area. The second scenario modifies the first by supplementing local biomass with biomass sourced from an external supply area. The third scenario represents a situation in which the plant does not have access to a reliable biomass supply locally and must source all of its biomass from an external supply area. When the plant sources biomass from an external supply area, densification of the biomass has the potential to reduce costs of delivered biomass by improving long-distance transportation efficiency; this is explored in both of the external-supply scenarios. For all scenarios, we derive the marginal cost of supply and the life-cycle GHG emissions associated with producing and transporting the biomass to the plant.

Scenario 1: Local Supply of Biomass Energy

In scenario 1, all biomass required for cofiring is produced in the local supply area, bounded approximately by a two-hour driving distance around the plant (see Figure 5.1). Power plants will traditionally secure their own biomass from local contractors or might pay a premium to a third-party aggregator to arrange biomass delivery and mitigate some of the associated risks. Since nearly all existing cofiring operations utilize woody biomass residues, the first scenario illustrates the costs and trade-offs associated with cofiring local woody biomass delivered by truck. We chose a representative power plant in western Pennsylvania to highlight insights from a local biomass supply market.

**Figure 5.1
Scenario 1, Local Woody Biomass
Cofiring in Western Pennsylvania**

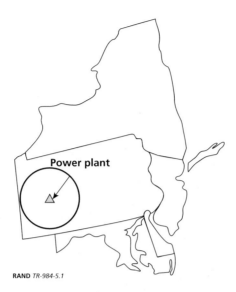

Power plant

RAND *TR-984-5.1*

Using the assumptions outlined in Appendix D, the delivered cost of local woody biomass is $40 per dry metric ton or $2.1 per gigajoule, as shown in Table 5.6.

The marginal cost of biomass in a local supply market scenario is captured by the cost of expanding the distances traveled to secure additional supply or by growing biomass on more-expensive land closer to the plant. For local biomass collection, we assume the trucking freight distance to be 93 miles, or about a two-hour drive (see Appendix D). As trucking distance increases, the total cost of truck freight transportation increases, thereby increasing delivered biomass costs. At a distance of 93 miles, the cost of transportation is approximately $17 per dry metric ton. This cost increases rapidly as distances increase (see Figure 5.2), indicating that trucking is not a viable mode for long-haul transport of biomass. Because herbaceous bales have higher truck transport costs than wood chips do, the decision to expand the collection area for herbaceous bales will increase costs more than expanding the collection area for wood chips.

**Table 5.6
Costs for Local Woody Biomass, Scenario 1**

Cost Category	Cost
Biomass feedstock cost ($/dry metric ton)	18
Local handling ($/dry metric ton)	2.4
Local transportation ($/dry metric ton)	17
Total delivered cost ($/dry metric ton)	40
Total delivered cost ($/GJ)	2.10

Figure 5.2
Impact of Trucking Shipping Distance on Truck Freight Costs for Wood Chips and Bales

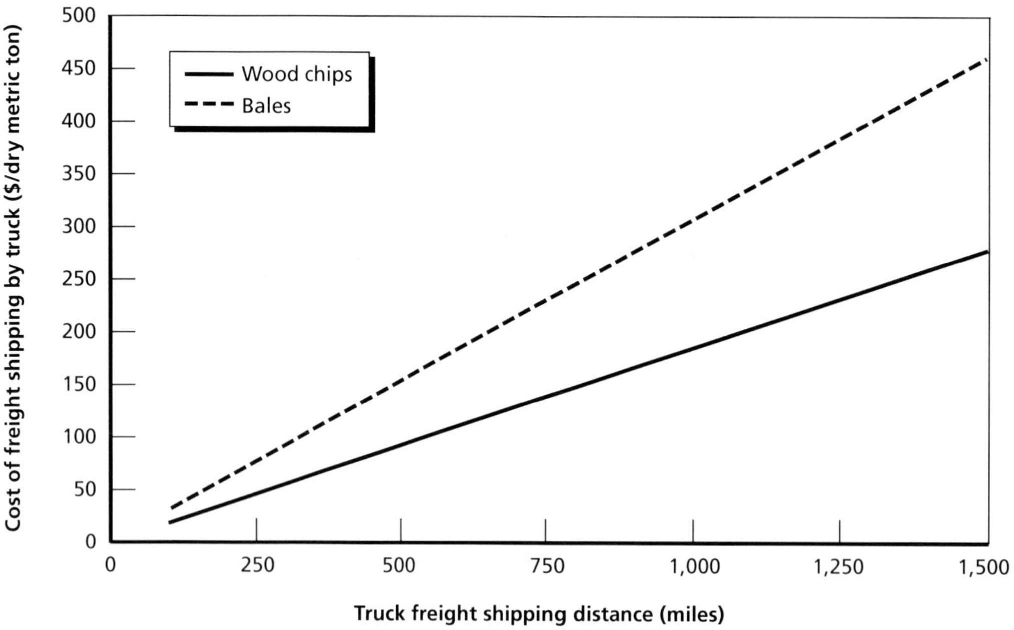

RAND *TR-984-5.2*

Scenario 2: Local and External Supply of Biomass Energy

In scenario 2, 75 percent of biomass required for cofiring is produced in the local supply area of western Pennsylvania and 25 percent is imported from another region (see Figure 5.3). As discussed in Chapter Four, regions that are likely to export biomass for cofiring applications are those that have abundant biomass supplies, lower cofiring opportunities, and adequate established transportation infrastructure. The Lake States region (Michigan, Minnesota, and Wisconsin) exhibits favorable attributes for biomass exporting. This region is assumed to be the external supply region in scenario 2. Long-haul transportation is assumed to be rail, but inland waterway could be substituted, potentially at slightly reduced expense.

The marginal cost of biomass in a mixed local and external supply market scenario is represented by the cost of expanding the local distances traveled to secure additional supply or of utilizing an external supply source. As discussed earlier, the cost of local woody biomass is about $40 per dry metric ton. Using the assumptions outlined in Appendix D, the delivered cost of external woody biomass chips is $240 per dry metric ton, and the delivered cost of external woody biomass pellets is $130 per dry metric ton, as shown in Table 5.7.

Using wood pellets instead of wood chips is more cost-effective when sourcing woody biomass from the Lake States for cofiring in the Northeast. The additional handling and densification costs of wood pellets add about $31 to the price per dry metric ton of woody biomass, excluding the long-haul freight transportation costs. The cost of densification is offset by reduced rail freight charges for pellets when transportation distances are more than 225 miles for wood chips, and about 200 miles for herbaceous bales, as shown in Figure 5.4. These distances are approximately the distance from Pittsburgh, Pennsylvania, to Harrisburg, Pennsyl-

Figure 5.3
Scenario 2, Local Biomass Cofiring in Western Pennsylvania with External Supply from the Lake States

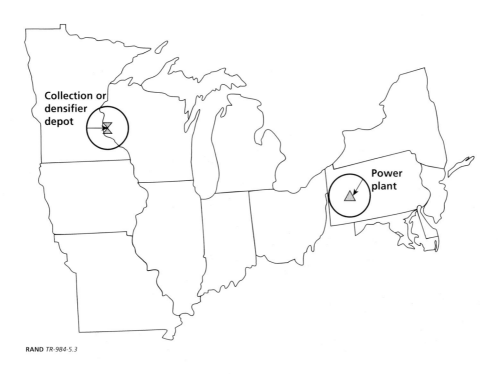

RAND *TR-984-5.3*

Table 5.7
Costs for Local and External Woody Biomass, Scenario 2

Cost Category	Cost for Wood Chips	Cost for Wood Pellets
Biomass feedstock cost ($/dry metric ton)	18	18
Local handling ($/dry metric ton)	1.3	0.44
External handling ($/dry metric ton)	8.5	11
External collection truck transportation ($/dry metric ton)	17	17
Densification ($/dry metric ton)	—	31
Subtotal prior to long-haul transportation ($/dry metric ton)	45	78
Long-haul rail transportation ($/dry metric ton)	190	50
Total delivered cost for external biomass ($/dry metric ton)	240	130
Total delivered cost for external biomass ($/GJ)	12	6.7
Blended delivered cost for local and external biomass ($/dry metric ton)	90	62
Blended delivered cost for local and external biomass ($/GJ)	4.6	3.3

vania. When we use a blended cost of 75 percent local and 25 percent external biomass, the result is a delivered cost of wood pellets of $62 per dry metric ton.

Figure 5.4
Rail Freight Cost Savings Realized by Utilizing Pellets

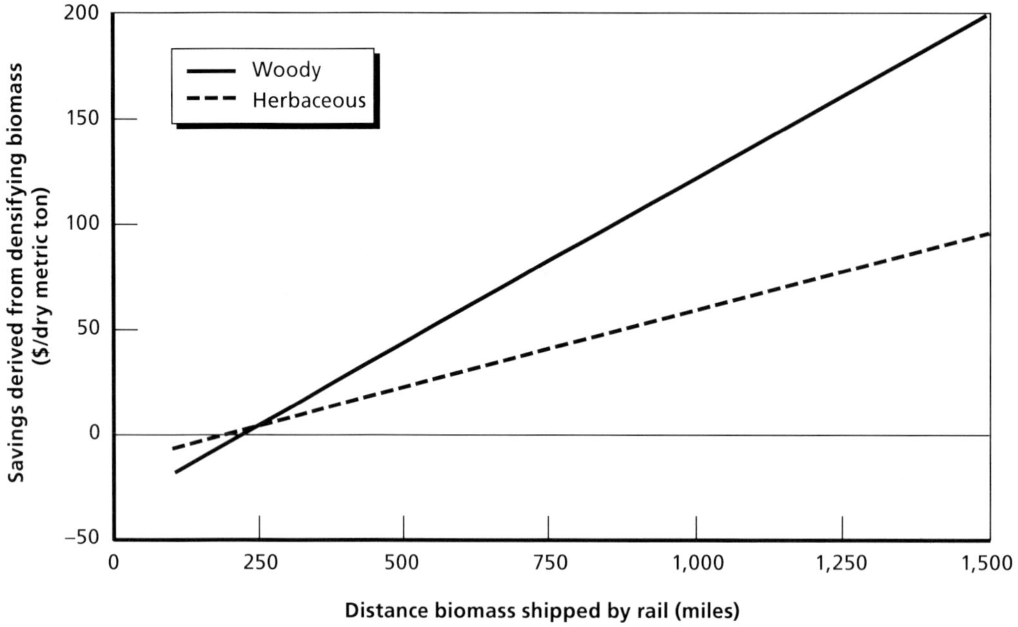

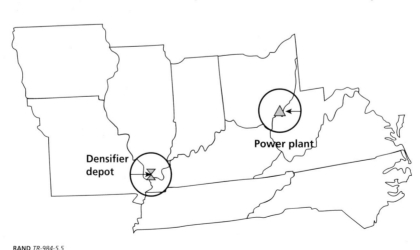

RAND *TR-984-5.4*

Scenario 3: External Supply of Biomass Energy

For scenario 3, we demonstrate the effects of a commoditized biomass market in which all biomass is sourced from one or more dedicated central processing facilities (see Figure 5.5). A representative coal-fired power plant along the Ohio River in southern Ohio is chosen to illustrate this scenario. This power plant would accept densified biomass from inland barges and could also accept biomass from rail or truck. The supply area of southern Illinois was chosen due to its abundant biomass resources and access to the inland waterway system. The supply area could include the Corn Belt region and portions of the Appalachia region.

Figure 5.5
Scenario 3, Commoditized Cofiring Market in the Ohio River Valley

RAND *TR-984-5.5*

Utilizing herbaceous pellets instead of bales is more cost-effective when sourcing herbaceous biomass from the Corn Belt for cofiring in the Ohio River Valley (see Table 5.8). The additional handling and densification costs of pellets add about $16 per metric ton to the cost of herbaceous biomass, excluding the long-haul freight transportation costs. The cost of densification is offset by reduced barge freight charges for pellets when transportation distances are more than 230 miles for wood chips and above 160 miles for herbaceous bales, as shown in Figure 5.6.

Table 5.8
Costs for External Herbaceous Biomass

Cost Category	Cost for Bales	Cost for Herbaceous Pellets
Biomass feedstock cost ($/dry metric ton)	26	26
Local handling ($/dry metric ton)	2.3	0.44
External handling ($/dry metric ton)	12	14
External collection truck transportation ($/dry metric ton)	29	29
External storage ($/dry metric ton)	18	18
Densification ($/dry metric ton)	0.00	16
Subtotal prior to long-haul transportation ($/dry metric ton)	87	100
Long-haul barge transportation ($/dry metric ton)	76	15
Total delivered cost ($/dry metric ton)	160	120
Total delivered cost ($/GJ)	9.6	7.0

Figure 5.6
Barge Freight Cost Savings by Utilizing Pellets

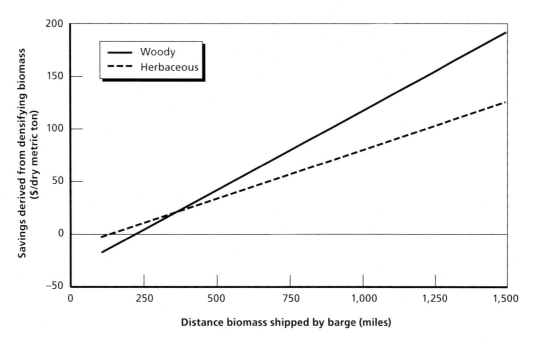

RAND TR-984-5.6

CHAPTER SIX

Reductions in Life-Cycle Greenhouse-Gas Emissions from Cofiring with Biomass

Introduction

At the time of the initial DOE biomass cofiring demonstration program in the 1990s, the primary motivation for cofiring biomass with coal at electricity generating plants was to reduce criteria pollutant emissions (Tillman, 2001). Widespread switching to lower-sulfur coals, as well as the installation of pollution controls, has obviated the initial motivation for cofiring. Currently, the primary motivation for cofiring biomass with coal at electricity generating plants is to reduce GHG emissions.

In light of this objective, in this chapter, we estimate the potential reductions in GHG emissions that would result from cofiring with biomass at 5 percent by input energy. Appendix E describes these calculations and underlying assumptions in detail. Our estimates of GHG emissions correspond to those expected from providing biomass for cofired facilities in accordance with the supply scenarios described in Chapter Four and delivered according to the logistical scenarios described in Chapter Five. Estimates are based on life-cycle emissions of GHGs. Under these assumptions, we estimate the range of costs of carbon abatement for the four scenarios.

Estimating Greenhouse-Gas Emissions from Cofiring

Net life-cycle GHG emissions of a given fuel feedstock include all of those associated with producing, transporting, and processing the fuel and with the emissions from burning the fuel. GHG emissions associated with cofiring with biomass include emissions attributed to both coal and biomass. Biomass generally produces significantly fewer life-cycle GHG emissions than coal does. Utilizing biomass instead of coal could therefore reduce the life-cycle GHG emissions associated with producing electricity. The questions are by how much and at what cost compared with coal.

We used the RAND/NETL CUBE model to estimate production emissions for biomass feedstocks. CUBE 1.0 was made publicly available in March 2010 (Curtright et al., 2010); our analysis is based on CUBE 2.0, which is expected to be released in late 2011. Production emissions for biomass feedstocks vary widely depending on the choice of feedstock and the geographic region and prior land use where the biomass is grown. Even if the biomass is a coproduct or a residue, such as corn stover or forest residues, choices regarding how to allocate GHG emissions between the residue and the primary product affect net GHGs. In some cases—for example, if a forest is cleared and burned to make way for biomass energy production—the loss of carbon from the soil and trees can result in life-cycle GHG emissions for the farmed biomass that are greater than those of coal. It could potentially require averaging GHG savings over many subsequent years of biomass production on this same land to offset these initial high net positive emissions (Fargione et al., 2008). Appendix E provides the details of the calculations and assumptions that underlie the values associated with the scenarios in this analysis. Transportation and processing emissions were estimated consistently with the supply and logistics scenarios in Chapters Four and Five, respectively, and are described in detail in Appendix E. The avoided coal emissions, as well as changes in emissions at the cofire facility as a result of biomass use, were included in these estimates. Figure 6.1 summarizes the net values derived from the various scenarios in this study for each of the fuels that the plant uses. Note that the wide ranges in the estimates for herbaceous pellets derive primarily from the land-use change emissions, and uncertainty thereof, that result from withdrawing residue that would otherwise be left on the soil (see Table 6.1).

Implications of Biomass Life-Cycle Greenhouse-Gas Emissions of Cofiring

The results presented in Figure 6.1 can be compared with the life-cycle GHG emissions that would result from using coal to determine the costs of reducing GHG emissions through cofiring.

We first calculate the net reductions in GHG emissions for each of the four scenarios. We then divide the net reductions in emissions by the additional costs associated with using biomass to generate electricity in that plant. The result is a cost per ton of GHG emissions abated, as illustrated in Figure 6.2.

Figure 6.1
Change in Greenhouse-Gas Emissions Using Biomass Relative to Subbituminous Coal

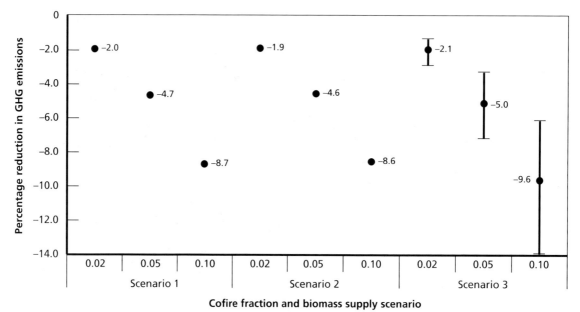

SOURCE: Plant Site Cost Model results (Chapter 3 and Appendix B) and Appendix E.
RAND *TR-984-6.1*

Table 6.1
Feedstock-Related Greenhouse-Gas Emissions of Biomass and
Subbituminous Coal

Scenario	Type of Fuel	Net Biomass Fuel Emissions, kg CO_2e/GJ (from Table E.9 in Appendix E)		
		Low	Mid	High
1	Wood chips	2.76	3.58	5.16
2	Wood chips and wood pellets	7.33	8.14	9.69
3	Herbaceous pellets	−44.4	3.97	44.8
	Subbituminous coal		125	

NOTE: CO_2e = CO_2 equivalent.

Figure 6.2
Cost of Abating Greenhouse Gases Through Cofiring Biomass with Coal

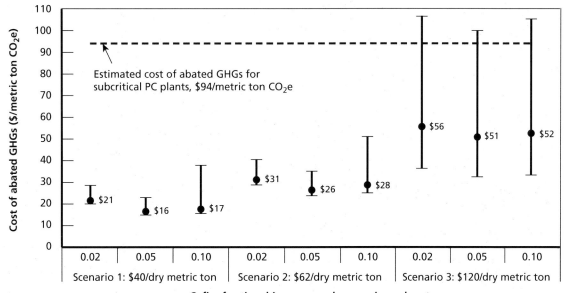

SOURCE: NETL (2010).
NOTE: Results compare the midlevel for PC boilers firing subbituminous coal. The supply scenarios are described in Chapter Five.
RAND TR-984-6.2

The cost of abating GHG emissions through cofiring depends on the price of biomass and the cofire fraction. The prices for biomass were derived in Chapter Five for three distinct supply scenarios. At a cofire fraction of 2 percent, the best estimate for the cost of abating GHG emissions is $21 per metric ton CO_2e for scenario 1, $31 per metric ton CO_2e for scenario 2, and $56 per metric ton CO_2e for scenario 3. The cost of abating GHG falls for a cofire fraction of 5 percent but rises slightly for a cofire fraction of 10 percent. This increase in costs of abating GHG emissions at higher cofire fractions is due to the increase in lost revenues resulting from the additional processing load, as discussed in Chapter Three. Recall that operators of the

Dunkirk generating station estimated a price of about \$20 per metric ton CO_2e to motivate cofiring. Ignoring site-specific costs, our results indicate that this criterion might be satisfied at prices of biomass below \$40 per dry metric ton (\$2.1 per gigajoule).

Biomass cofiring is an alternative to carbon capture and storage (CCS). In CCS, the CO_2 is captured from the flue gas and compressed for pipeline transport and permanent storage (NETL, 2010). In Figure 6.2, the reference line indicates the current estimated cost per ton abated for subcritical PC plants employing CCS, \$94 per metric ton CO_2e (NETL, 2010). We see that, for our three supply scenarios, our most likely cost of abating GHGs never rises above this estimate. Only for the case of herbaceous pellets does the high cost estimate rise above this value for abating GHGs from PC plants, and the best-estimate values are well below it. This result implies that, in a carbon-constrained world, cofiring would be an attractive option for reducing GHG emissions when compared with CCS at today's costs. This result holds for the relatively expensive biomass–pellets transported over long distances, except at the high end of the cost estimates.

Although the cost per ton of reducing GHG emissions is more attractive with cofiring than with CCS, the total number of tons of GHG emissions avoided is relatively small. Systems for CCS typically remove 80 to 90 percent of CO_2 from flue-gas streams, reducing life-cycle GHG emissions by a similar percentage. As indicated in Figure 6.1, cofiring subbituminous coal and wood chips at 10 percent results in GHG reductions of 8.7 percent because so much of the electricity is still generated by coal.

CHAPTER SEVEN

Factors Influencing the Development of Biomass Markets

Introduction

Existing markets for biomass as fuel are small and regionally specific, largely because biomass is a marginal fuel compared with coal. Biomass production varies across and within regions, with small clusters of grass-based production in the Midwest, forestry residues collected in the Northeast and Southeast, and some woody biomass cultivation in the West and Northeast. Mill residues available for fuel use are concentrated in the southern and southeastern states; residue use for off-site energy production, approximately 37 million tons in 2007, constitutes roughly half the total mill residue production (ORNL, 2010). Pelletized biomass, whether wood based or using other feedstocks, is produced primarily in the northeastern, Pacific, and mountain states, totaling 667,000 tons in 2004–2005 (ORNL, 2010). In general, producers within these regions tend to be small.

Purchasers of biomass are generally few, small, and isolated. In most cases, biomass purchasers will contract with small suppliers. Buyers typically do not compete with other bioenergy firms. This gives purchasers monopsony power, which would be expected to suppress prices and reduce incentives for additional production. The result is that the markets for biomass energy resources are not integrated either nationally or regionally.[1] Among the dedicated and cofiring plants that we surveyed (see Table 2.1 in Chapter Two), annual biomass demand is typically hundreds of thousands, or even a million, tons. However, many large-scale facilities use biomass only in a demonstration or test capacity. In some cases, those experiments have not led to long-term, consistent biomass use. For example, the CVBP culminated in a long-term test burn in 2008 and has not operated as such since (Antares Group, 2009).

This chapter considers market and economic factors that would support the development of more-robust regional markets for biomass. It begins with a discussion of the current limitations affecting the development of biomass energy markets, including price, technological considerations, and information exchange among producers and purchasers. The next section examines how densifying biomass—making it a more uniform and easily shipped product—might help biomass energy markets develop. The chapter closes with a discussion of events that might lead to the maturation of biomass energy markets from their current small-scale and heterogeneous form to larger, more homogeneous ones.

---

[1] A thin market exists when there are few buyers and sellers of a good and is characterized by volatile prices.

Limiting Factors for Biomass Markets

The limited scale and scope of biomass markets in the United States can be attributed to factors that include price, high production and delivery costs, technology, and information constraints. We review each of these factors in this section.

Biomass Prices and Production Costs

Anecdotal data suggest that mill residues in the Appalachia region, when available, have been purchased for as little as $22–28 per green metric ton (i.e., including the moisture content) delivered, or approximately $1.8–$2.2 per gigajoule (at an assumed 35-percent moisture content), which is competitive with the price of coal. However, these prices for delivered biomass are neither consistently nor widely available. For example, one of the plant operators we interviewed indicated that mill residues were becoming scarcer and more expensive because of the recent opening of a commercial charcoal-briquette plant that competed with their own plant. Higher prices reduced plant demand. However, because residues are a by-product, in this instance, they do not result in increased production—that is determined by demand for lumber, the primary product.

Prices for mill residues in the Appalachia region are not indicative of costs of other types of biomass. Costs of these types of biomass include the costs of collecting and transporting them. The logistical analysis presented in Chapter Four shows that it costs approximately $18 per metric ton to deliver wood chips or sawdust 100 miles. When the biomass is farmed, costs must include the opportunity cost of the land on which it is planted. A recent analysis for NETL concluded that delivered costs for biomass produced on agricultural lands are a minimum of $80 per green metric ton ($4.0 per gigajoule) to produce, collect, store, and deliver to an energy facility, with the cost increasing as plant demand grows (LaTourrette et al., 2011). The result is that, on an equivalent energy basis, most biomass in most regions is more expensive than coal.

In addition, prospective purchasers of biomass by-products are currently at the mercy of the supply of the primary product. The availability of mill residues and, to a lesser degree, forestry residues depends on the demand for paper and wood products. Some plant operators are finding it difficult to acquire sufficient mill residues because of production cutbacks in the lumber industry.

High biomass prices relative to coal prices discourage electric power generators from substituting biomass for coal. Prices for fossil fuels, such as coal, are lower than they should be if they do not fully account for the environmental costs they impose (Tharakan et al., 2005). The U.S. federal government does not currently impose a charge on GHG emissions that reflect the costs these emissions impose on the environment. If such a levy were to be imposed, electricity generated from coal would be more expensive than it currently is.

Policy proposals designed to encourage biomass use generally propose making biomass more cost-competitive by imposing a charge on fossil fuels. Some states offer RECs for producing electricity from biomass, effectively subsidizing lower-carbon fuels. California and the northeastern states have introduced regulations along these lines. Policies, such as a cap-and-trade system or a tax on emissions of CO_2, would explicitly raise the cost of fossil energy, making biomass more competitive.

However, the life-cycle GHG emissions of producing electricity from biomass might not always be less than those of coal. Our analysis of GHG emissions as documented in Curtright et al. (2010) indicates that the life-cycle GHG emissions that result from producing or collecting biomass, transporting, storing, and processing it, and finally burning it to produce energy vary significantly according to the type of biomass and the assumptions that are made about the land used for producing biomass. Moreover, converting land to produce biomass for energy can result in significant releases or gains in soil organic carbon depending on the prior land use and what biomass energy sources are to be produced. For example, growing a mixture of native prairie grasses on degraded lands can result in gains in soil carbon, whereas clearing a forest for the purpose of supplying biomass can result in releases in soil carbon (Tilman, Hill, and Lehman, 2006; Searchinger et al., 2008; Fargione et al., 2008).

Technological Constraints on Biomass Production

An alternative approach to making biomass more competitive with fossil fuels is to reduce unit production costs. One approach is to develop and apply technology to reduce the cost factors for biomass energy resources. For farmed biomass resources, such as SG or short-rotation woody crops, improving yields is the most effective way to reduce overall unit costs because many agricultural inputs and activities, such as preparing the soil, fertilizing, and harvesting biomass, are more or less fixed. In general, biomass energy crops can be grown using standard farm practices and equipment; however, these processes are optimized for food production rather than bioenergy production. Specialized equipment might be able to improve the efficiency of energy-crop production and the collection of forestry residues. Similarly, integrated roundwood and residue collection in forestry operations can improve the efficiency with which forestry residues are collected, lowering production costs.

Many cost factors are not necessarily amenable to reductions in costs. The most important of these is the cost of agricultural land for the production of biomass crops and stumpage fees for the collection of forestry residues. If demand for biomass increases significantly, both land costs and stumpage fees are likely to rise. Transporting, storing, and processing biomass depends on established methods that are already relatively efficient. Handling systems in Europe are more automated than those in the United States, but these come at the expense of increased capital and maintenance costs. Nor is densification of biomass likely to achieve significant benefits: The analysis in Chapter Five indicates that, at rail transportation distances above several hundred miles, the benefits associated with increased bulk density of densified biomass can realize savings over undensified biomass. But at relatively short—and, today, common—distances, the benefits of densified biomass do not outweigh the additional production costs.

Burning raw biomass in an energy facility requires that the plant be purpose built or modified to accommodate biomass fuels, most principally in the handling, processing, and feed systems. Our analysis in Chapter Three focused on the specific modifications required at a plant to accommodate a certain type of biomass—wood chips versus bales, for example. The requirements for processing at the plant depend on both the type of biomass and the boiler type; stoker boilers can accept the widest range of biomass sizes, and PC boilers the narrowest. Our interviews with plant operators indicate that, in cofiring applications, the combustion processes have been very robust. Moreover, our analysis suggests that the difference in costs of producing electricity among alternative plant configurations, biomass types, processing line choices, and boiler types are relatively small. If a plant is located in an area in which a wide range of potential biomass types are available, then investing in equipment to accommodate these varied biomass types might be advantageous. Such plants have been built in Europe (Van Loo and Koppejan, 2008).

Asymmetric Information

If biomass consumers lack information on potential supply or if creditors do not accurately estimate investment risks due to limited knowledge of the biomass industry, then, in the absence of a regulatory requirement to use biomass, biomass markets are unlikely to develop as rapidly as they otherwise would (Rösch and Kaltschmitt, 1999; Trømborg et al., 2008). As discussed in Chapter Two, the developer of a biomass energy project might be required to demonstrate that the supply area in the vicinity of the project is able to supply five to six times annual demand. The reason for this crude risk-management method is that there is little experience with large-scale biomass-powered energy and long-term risks of supply shortfalls. The result is that financing for biomass energy projects is constrained for independent power producers and might be difficult to justify for other owner-operators.

Biomass is not traded on national or regionally integrated markets. A plant seeking biomass advertises to a network of suppliers a price that it is willing to pay for biomass meeting certain parameters—i.e., "clean greenwood." The buyer sets a price, and small-scale providers respond. There are emerging exceptions: Ecostrat, a biofuel purchaser and reseller, offers to its customers a "biomass credit swap." Ecostrat has developed a detailed database of U.S. biomass fuel providers, their production volumes, and their capacities. A purchaser of the biomass credit swap pays Ecostrat a fee to guarantee a consistent supply of biomass. Using its database, Ecostrat manages the network of suppliers and organizes deliveries to the plant. According to Ecostrat, if a plant has purchased the "biomass credit swap," it is able to improve its financing terms, making development available to independent firms and not only those capable of self-financing (Solomon, 2010). Because biomass suppliers are guaranteed a consistent price and demand for biomass energy, they are able to make investments in equipment to improve production efficiency and volumes.

Plants that cofire biomass might not benefit as much from the services of biomass aggregators as dedicated biomass facilities can. As noted in Chapter Two, a plant cofiring biomass is always able to fire 100 percent coal if the price of biomass rises or the availability of biomass becomes constrained.

The Potential for Processing to Facilitate Biomass Market Expansion

Currently, biomass energy markets are local and specialized. Biomass comes in many shapes and forms (e.g., bales of grasses or agricultural residue, wood chunks or chips, pellets, construction wastes). Each biomass type has different physical properties, energy and moisture content ranges, and ash characteristics, factors that can also vary within a particular type of biomass (McKendry, 2002). Some biomass consumers have found it advantageous to be able to accept a range of biomass (Van Loo and Koppejan, 2008). Biomass densification allows these heterogeneous products to be combined into a product with predictable physical and chemical characteristics, facilitating dedicated combustion and cofiring with coal. For example, the Show Me Energy Cooperative produces a mixed biomass pellet to tight specifications (Flick, 2009).

Pellets facilitate many activities at the plant site. Biomass pellets are uniform in size and moisture content. As a result, they can be handled easily and commingled with coal and processed in existing coal mills. But because pellets are hydroscopic, they must be stored in specialized silos, similar to those for storing grain.

An indirect potential benefit of densification is that it might reduce supply risks and infrastructure costs to both producers and consumers. Pellet producers might mix biomass types, reducing their dependence on any single feedstock and minimizing risks of shortfalls or price increases for specific inputs. A recent analysis by INL explored the technical potential of a commoditized biomass supply chain (INL, 2009). Economically, a biomass user is able to reduce the risks of correlated supply failures of local biomass resources if it supplements its local supply with pellets. This insurance comes at a cost, however: As shown in Chapter Five, the costs of pelletization add substantially to the costs of local production, delivery, and storage—namely, approximately $1.6 per gigajoule ($1.7 per mmBtu; $28 per dry short ton).

Even without widespread pelletization, the quality of biomass fuel can be controlled. Plant operators with whom we spoke indicated that they source "clean greenwood," free of dirt and other debris and freshly harvested. The Show Me Energy Cooperative tests the moisture content of all incoming biomass and pays on an energy basis. The cooperative has introduced steps to ensure the quality of the biomass in the production, harvesting, and delivery processes (Van Loo and Koppejan, 2008).

Another potential benefit to densifying biomass is that long-distance transportation becomes feasible because of the high bulk density and uniform size of pellets. The analysis in Chapter Five assumed that pellets could be transported in covered grain hoppers, which have rail tariffs significantly below those for wood chips or bales. In general, pelletizing can permit cost-effective biomass transport over longer distances, such as by rail or ship (Wahlund et al., 2004; Mahmudi and Flynn, 2006). As discussed earlier, however, the transportation cost savings associated with densification are relatively limited, given that most products are not currently transported over long distances.

Although there are benefits to processing, there is no clear indication that densified biomass will become a dominant product. We estimate that pelletizing biomass increases costs by $16 to $34 per dry metric ton ($0.96–1.80 per gigajoule). For pelletizing to be economically viable, the benefits with respect to plant-site costs, transportation cost, and fuel supply need to outweigh the additional fuel cost. The analysis in Chapter Three indicates that using pellets as a fuel does not have significant benefits—at the plant—over other forms of biomass, even when compared on an equal-cost basis. The result is that the cost of pellets delivered begins at $99 per dry metric ton ($5.7 per gigajoule), as compared to local delivered biomass prices beginning at $38 per dry metric ton ($1.9/GJ).[2] In the near term, as argued earlier in the chapter, the low costs of locally produced biomass make these extra costs unattractive.

---

[2]   This estimate assumes a production and delivery cost of herbaceous biomass of $68 per dry metric ton based on recent RAND analysis (LaTourrette et al., 2011) and 300-mile long-distance transportation by rail at a tariff of $0.044 per metric ton-mile, inclusive of delivery charges, a nominal energy content for pellets of 17 GJ per dry metric ton and 5-percent moisture content. Since pellets are a retail home heating fuel, their price to consumers can be higher, $6.6 to $9.5 per gigajoule.

What Would Cause Biomass Markets to Grow?

A key question is this: Under what conditions would the currently small, heterogeneous markets for biomass expand into larger, regional markets? Prices and supplies of different energy sources vary regionally in the United States, including those for natural gas, gasoline and other refined petroleum products, and electricity. In these cases, constraints on infrastructure, seasonal demand, different tax codes, and air-quality regulations, among other factors, result in significant regional differences in energy markets. Given that biomass resources differ greatly by region and that transportation costs are high relative to value, for the foreseeable future, developed biomass markets will be largely regional in character.

Changes in prices, technology, and information could each lead to growth in U.S. biomass markets. Higher prices for biomass resources would have the most-direct impact on supply because biomass producers, like producers of any product, will respond by increasing production when prices rise. As mentioned earlier, current prices for woody residues are relatively low (approximately $1.9 per gigajoule, comparable to the price of coal). Higher prices could come about due to increases in demand. Policies that internalize the environmental costs of fossil energy, such as carbon taxes or cap-and-trade programs, would not affect biomass prices directly but would make bioenergy more price competitive with conventional fuels (Tharakan et al., 2005). An alternative policy is a subsidy for biomass production, such as the Biomass Crop Assistance Program (BCAP), which reduces the cost of biomass to purchasers. Programs that, like RPSs, increase the demand for renewable energy, including qualified biomass-produced energy, could lead to increased biomass use.

Technological developments that reduce production costs would make biomass more competitive with other types of energy, leading to growth in biomass markets. The cost factors for biomass include production, handling, transportation, and processing. The cost factor that is most amenable to reductions is production, principally by increasing yields of biomass energy crops. More-efficient collection and harvesting systems, especially for woody residues, are already in use in Europe and could be deployed in the United States (Van Loo and Koppejan, 2008). Transportation and handling systems could be improved slightly because they are not yet optimized for biomass. In aggregate, however, improvements aside from mass yield would have a small effect on overall supply costs. Most technologies supporting biomass are mature, and most of the costs are associated with the mechanical work required to collect, transport, and process the biomass, though not specifically tailored to the needs of combustion-based consumers.

If limited information on the part of potential biomass consumers or project financiers poses a constraint in a particular market, programs that improve information quality could spur growth. Hughes (2000) argues in favor of increased testing and demonstration programs, as well as promoting awareness of the benefits of biomass energy among consumers, policies that could foster technological development and reduce information barriers.

Hughes (2000) argues in favor of a policy that would give power plant operators assurance that their facilities would not be subjected to New Source Performance Standards as a result of upgrading plants to cofire biomass. Cantor and Rizy (1991) outline the risks associated with commercializing biomass energy in the United States and policies—including demonstration projects, loan guarantees or grants, or other reforms—that could reduce risks to producers and consumers.

One overarching limitation to expanding biomass markets is policy uncertainty, which translates into price uncertainty for producers and consumers. Many biomass resources are not valuable outside of their use to produce bioenergy. Government policies that promote biomass use directly (through quotas) or indirectly (by placing a charge on emissions of CO_2 or through subsidies) would promote more-stable demand for biomass, encouraging bioenergy production (see, e.g., de la Torre Ugarte et al., 2003).

CHAPTER EIGHT

Conclusions

Plant Operators' Experiences Cofiring Biomass

The Principal Challenge with Respect to Cofiring Biomass Is Maintaining a Consistent Fuel Supply

Plant operators reported that cofiring with biomass at up to 10 percent of total fuel energy had little effect on the performance of the boiler or on installed emission-control equipment. The lower energy content and increased moisture content of biomass relative to coal can result in a reduction in plant generating capacity, but plant operators did not cite this as a significant concern. These results are consistent with reported experience in Europe (Van Loo and Koppejan, 2008) and the United States (Tillman, 2001; Antares Group, 2009). However, most domestic experience to date concerning cofiring biomass with coal is recent, consisting of test fires or a year or two of cofiring. The potential effects that long-term cofiring (i.e. greater than five years) could have on plant components are still unknown.

One potential technical improvement that was identified, especially for boilers that burn PC, is the development of a burner specifically designed to fire biomass or mixtures of biomass and coal. Biomass storage, handling, and processing can be challenging; plant operators reported that programs that facilitate the sharing of lessons learned and best practices could be a benefit.

The most significant concern cited by the majority of interviewees was the challenge of securing a consistent supply of biomass. Suppliers tend to be small, so plants find that it is necessary to maintain relationships with several dozen suppliers to meet the fuel requirements for the plant. We did speak with one aggregator who maintains a database of biomass fuel suppliers and will charge a premium to guarantee a consistent supply of biomass.

The Choice to Cofire Biomass Depends on a Confluence of Technical and Regulatory Factors

In the absence of regulation of GHG emissions, the decision to convert a plant to cofire depends more on regulatory and policy factors than on technical factors:

- The plant operator must be able to recover the additional costs of cofiring through RECs or increases in rates.
- The ability to burn biomass must be included in the existing air permit for the plant.

Surprisingly, we did not find that the type of boiler factored significantly into the decision about whether to cofire biomass with coal: Appropriate handling and processing methods have been devised and tested to allow biomass to be used with any type of boiler. It is the aggregate of the plant's technical characteristics, cost to implement, policy, and regulatory factors that currently lead plant operators to choose to cofire biomass with coal.

Plant-Site Costs of Cofiring

Cofiring Biomass Results in Increased Capital and Operating Costs and Lost Revenues

We built a model to estimate the plant-site costs of cofiring biomass and coal at low cofire fractions (i.e., below approximately 10 percent biomass by energy content). At current prices for woody biomass (approximately $40 per dry metric ton), the additional costs associated with cofiring at 5 percent by energy are approximately $0.021 per kilowatt-hour. These costs include $0.007 per kilowatt-hour each for increased capital and nonfuel operating costs, $0.001 per kilowatt-hour for biomass fuel, and $0.005 per kilowatt-hour of lost revenue. The lost revenue is due to two factors: The plant is slightly less efficient when cofiring biomass, and the biomass requires additional parasitic electricity to process—electricity that could be sold. The costs rise linearly with the price of biomass, rising $0.006 per kilowatt-hour for each $10 increase in biomass prices: At prices for wood chips of $120 per dry metric ton, the cost of cofiring is an additional $0.069 per kilowatt-hour.

Densification of Biomass Does Not Result in Plant-Site Cost Savings

Because densified biomass (i.e., pellets) requires fewer plant-site modifications and can be commingled with coal, densification might result in significant plant-site cost savings over other biomass forms. As mentioned earlier, the additional costs of cofiring wood chips are $0.021 per kilowatt-hour at current prices of $40 per dry ton. Our analysis indicates that the delivered cost of herbaceous pellets would be $120 per dry metric ton. At that cost of biomass, the cost of cofiring at 5 percent is an additional $0.069 per kilowatt-hour.

Fixed-Price Renewable-Energy Credits Might Not Be an Effective Tool to Encourage Cofiring

Another interpretation of the cost of cofiring is the required price of a REC to recover costs associated with cofiring. For current woody biomass prices of $40 per dry metric ton, the implied price of a REC (at 5-percent cofiring) for a bus-bar electricity price of $0.0444 per kilowatt-hour is approximately $0.021 per kilowatt-hour. However, as the price of biomass rises, so does the required price of a REC. At biomass supply prices of $62 per dry metric ton, the implied price of a REC is $0.032 per kilowatt-hour, at $120 per dry metric ton, the implied price of a REC is $0.069 per kilowatt-hour. One of the plant operators we interviewed reported that he was able to receive a REC of $0.045 per kilowatt-hour, which covers costs of cofiring and associated revenue losses up to a biomass price of approximately $80 per dry metric ton. The implication of these results is that, because of the inherently varying nature of the costs, a fixed-price REC might not be an appropriate means to encourage cofiring and might be more applicable to other renewable-energy sources, such as wind, where most costs are fixed rather than variable.

Potential Biomass Demand and Logistics

The Appalachia and Northeast Regions Are Potential Biomass Importers, and the Pacific and Lake States Regions Are Potential Suppliers for the Purposes of Cofiring

Cofiring replaces a fraction of coal with biomass. If there were a widespread movement toward cofiring, regions in which a significant amount of the installed generating capacity is currently coal based could exhaust locally available resources. Conversely, a surplus of resources might exist in regions in which there was relatively little installed coal-fired electricity generating capacity. Our analysis indicates that the USDA Appalachia, Southern Plains, Northeast, and Mountain regions would likely exhaust local biomass resources under scenarios with significant development of cofiring, and the Pacific, Delta, Northern Plains, and Lake States regions could potentially be biomass suppliers.

Densification of Biomass Is Cost-Effective at Distances Greater Than 200 Miles

Densifying biomass adds between $16 and $34 per dry metric ton to the cost of biomass. However, pellets have a high bulk density and low moisture content and are easier to handle than other forms of biomass. As a result, the benefit of densification can be realized when transporting biomass long distances. Our analysis indicates that, when shipping by rail, the minimum distance at which the savings in transportation costs offset pelletization costs is approximately 225 miles for wood chips and about 200 miles for herbaceous bales. When shipping by barge, the minimum distances are 230 miles for wood chips and 160 miles for bales. Although densification provides a cost savings over raw biomass at these transportation distances, additional transportation costs are still incurred. In our examples, these additional costs were $50 per dry metric ton for wood pellets transported from Minneapolis, Minnesota, to Pittsburgh, Pennsylvania, by rail and $15 per dry metric ton for herbaceous pellets transported from Paducah, Kentucky, to southern Ohio by barge.

Greenhouse-Gas Reductions from Cofiring

Cofiring Is a Cost-Effective Means of Reducing Greenhouse-Gas Emissions

The primary current motivation for cofiring biomass with coal is to reduce the life-cycle GHG emissions associated with producing electricity. We assess cofiring biomass at input-energy fractions of 2, 5, and 10 percent of total input energy because experience to date indicates that major plant modifications are not required to cofire biomass at or below these percentages. Our analysis shows that the cost of abating GHG emissions is $21 per metric ton CO_2e at a cofire fraction of 2 percent and a biomass price of $40 per dry metric ton. The abatement costs drop as the cofire fraction increases: $16 per metric ton CO_2e for a cofire fraction of 5 percent. The cost of abating GHGs drops as the cofire fraction increases because it enables a higher utilization of the equipment installed to cofire biomass. The cost of abating GHGs rises for cofire fractions of 10 percent because additional electrical load is required to process the biomass, increasing processing costs. At a biomass supply cost of $120 per dry metric ton, approximately three times the current price of wood chips, the best estimate of cost of abating GHGs is $51 per metric ton CO_2e when cofiring at 5 percent. These figures are compared with an estimated cost of abatement of $94 per metric ton CO_2e when retrofitting subcritical PC plants for CCS (NETL, 2010). However, there is considerable uncertainty regarding the life-cycle GHG emissions of agricultural residues, resulting in estimated costs of abatement ranging from \$33 to \$100 per metric ton CO_2e.

Developing Biomass Markets

Biomass Markets for Electricity Generation Cannot Currently Support Densified Fuels

Currently, biomass energy markets in the United States comprise many small suppliers and are regionally diverse. Densified biomass could promote standardization and the integration of markets by (1) reducing plant-site costs for cofiring, (2) reducing transportation costs, and (3) increasing fuel flexibility and insulation from supply shocks. We found that propositions 1 and 2 are valid in certain circumstances and that 3 is questionable. It is true that biomass feed systems are less expensive for pellets than they are for raw biomass. For torrefied biomass, which is processed such that it has properties similar to those of coal, additional plant-site costs can be minimal. However, these differences in the costs of cofiring between densified and raw biomass are similar after taking into account the additional costs of producing a biomass pellet. Although transporting pellets long distances is less expensive than transporting raw biomass, the extra cost of manufacturing pellets results in a much higher total cost than that of using local raw biomass. Finally, the benefits of fuel flexibility do not exist in current biomass markets, which are characterized by an abundance of suppliers and an oversupply of biomass. In the absence of legislative requirements to use biomass, we expect such a situation to continue. If there were a requirement to use biomass, either as part of state RPSs or as a means of reducing life-cycle GHG emissions, that significantly increased delivered prices for local biomass, then pellets, and other densified forms of biomass, might become attractive.

Additional Details from Facility Interviews

This appendix augments the information presented in Chapter Two with some additional details from the companies and facilities that were interviewed for this study.

Allegheny Energy

Albright, West Virginia

In the past, there was an opportunity to cofire with sawdust at the Allegheny Energy Albright facility. Allegheny Energy constructed and tested the cofiring demonstration project, with the support of the DOE and NETL, from 2001 to 2002. Minimal modifications were required (e.g., installation of hopper, blower), and minor operational challenges for cofiring. For example, some initial clogging occurred in feeders not designed for sawdust, but bigger valves, quick disconnects, and adjustment of feeding screws alleviated the problem. A cofire ratio of roughly 10 percent by mass resulted in a heat rate increase of about 35 Btu per kilowatt-hour.

Permitting was a relatively complex, nine-month process. Allegheny Energy staff worked with the West Virginia Department of Environmental Protection (DEP) to find terms that would not trigger an NSR. The per-unit biomass limits (20-percent biomass cofire by weight) and the facility-wide biomass limits (60,000 tons biomass per year, on a rolling basis) were both based on the NSR analysis that was performed during this process. The West Virginia DEP also required testing to demonstrate that PM emissions would not increase because this was the pollutant of most concern under the modifications. Had Allegheny Energy continued running with biomass beyond the test period, the facility would have also had to test another six months out to verify compliance with the permit.

Biomass has not been used at the facility since 2002 due to the general high price and lack of availability of sawdust, as well as diminished financial incentives for criteria pollutant reductions. Increased fuel prices and decreased availability were related to competition for the sawdust from a nearby charcoal plant and the reduction in local sources (e.g., the shutting down of local sawmills).[1] However, in the summer of 2010, Allegheny Energy's Fuels department was completing a request-for-quote process for sawdust fuel, which would be used to consider reactivation of biomass use at Albright.

---

[1] Staff had the impression that charcoal facilities were willing to pay much more than Allegheny Energy could for sawdust, anecdotally as much as $200 per ton, although the exact price was not substantiated.

Willow Island, West Virginia

Sawdust was cofired on a daily basis more than 50 percent of the time over approximately two years at the Willow Island facility. The sawdust was blended with coal in a separate feed system, and the biomass ratio was "dialed in" and calibrated with scales to achieve 5 to 6 percent by weight. Virtually the only system changes required at the facility were related to handling. Minimal impact on performance was observed. Willow Island would not recommend use of a moving-floor conveyer because the required specialized dump trucks are expensive and hard to find. They experienced no problems with approximately 30-percent moisture levels and, in fact, appreciated the minimal dust and handling ease at this moisture level. In general, Willow Island advised good housekeeping when using sawdust. By "keeping it moving," safety issues related to combustibility can be avoided, and Willow Island experienced no incidents of spontaneous combustion during the use of sawdust.

The Willow Island facility experienced some contracting and inconsistent supply issues with the local sawdust supplier. As a result, Willow Island had begun negotiations with a cabinetmaker in Ohio to obtain "all the biomass they would ever need." However, a switch to PRB coal reduced SO_x emissions to a level that made biomass use less attractive. Willow Island is now dealing with a lower-Btu fuel even without the use of biomass. Willow Island's permit to use biomass lapsed in 2005. It is presently using the moving-floor conveyer to load some tire-derived fuel (TDF).

Dominion

At all three Dominion biomass utilization sites, the approach to biomass processing has been to contract out as much biomass trucking, processing, and prehandling as possible. For both the Pittsylvania and Altavista facilities, the staff cited air-quality regulation as the biggest issue in their experience with biomass use; they also expect this to be the worst of their problems at the new hybrid facility.[2]

Altavista

The Altavista Station was originally built next to a furniture plant to provide steam for the facility and to utilize the sawdust. The furniture mill has since shut down, and the new owner, Dominion, must now purchase biomass. The purchased biomass fuel has been mostly very fine sander dust, which is fed through pneumatic tubes. Although this fuel can, in theory, be highly flammable, Altavista has not had problems to date. It credits this to good separation procedures and a reduced sparking environment, including the systematic removal of metals (e.g., nails). Fuel acquisition has not been a problem, and the facility has not experienced any noteworthy technical issues. Fly ash required disposal in landfills due to cofiring biomass with coal.

Dominion announced in late May 2010 that it plans to shut the Altavista facility. The regional grid operator, PJM, has been asked for permission to place the Altavista Station on

---

[2] Federal New Source Performance Standards limit the facility to 1.4 lb SO_2 per megawatt-hour or 95-percent SO_2 reduction. The facility's present SO_2 emissions are below 1.4 lb per megawatt-hour. By increasing biomass use, the percentage of SO_2 *removed* from the emissions is decreased, so even though the absolute level of sulfur emissions is likely to decrease, the facility might fall out of compliance.

inactive or "cold reserve" status.[3] Long-term economic conditions would have to improve before it would make financial sense to reopen the station. Decreases in the price of natural gas and local transmission issues have made it uneconomical to keep the Altavista Station in service at this time.

Pittsylvania

The Pittsylvania Station was built for 100-percent biomass operations in 1994 and was acquired by Dominion in 2004. The facility is used for intermediate baseload, with a 70-percent capacity factor, but has greater than 90-percent availability. It has had no problems with corrosion and is able to send the biomass fly ash to be used as a soil amendment at local farms.[4]

Pittsylvania's fuel is 68- to 85-percent wood chips, with the balance as sawdust, from timber and mill residues, i.e., greenwood.[5] Average moisture content is 45 to 52 percent, and the facility notes that periods of heavy rain might cause the plant to have to derate due to open storage of fuel. It receives an average of 135 truckloads of biomass per day, with a maximum receipt capacity of 311 daily, each with an average load of 25 tons.[6] It uses approximately 1 million tons of biomass annually.[7] It has no on-site processing of biomass but does have to prescreen the fuel to remove oversized and undesirable material. There is no redundancy in conveyer feeding belts, so, when there is a fault, the plant has approximately 3 minutes to fix the problem or it must shut the boiler down. The overwhelming majority, 92 percent, of the facility's fuel comes from within a 100-mile radius in 44 counties in four states (Virginia, Maryland, North Carolina, and West Virginia). Fuel supply has not been a major issue, and Dominion sets a single price for all suppliers, which was approximately $22 per ton in 2009 and less than $18 per ton over its entire operating experience. A regional sawdust pellet facility, however, did alter the price.

Virginia City Hybrid Energy Center

The Virginia City Hybrid Energy Center, in Saint Paul, Virginia, is under construction and expects to commence commercial operations in July 2012. The permitting and design process began in 2004, and the center broke ground in 2008.

Fuel will be green sawdust and forest residues. The facility is not permitted to use post-consumer wood waste. The biomass specification is for 8 to 10 mmBtu per ton with 38 to 42 percent moisture content; dirt and bark are not expected to be problems. The facility has not yet secured suppliers but does not anticipate problems. This is based both on the Pittsylvania and Altavista experiences, which are well outside of the center's woodshed at 200 miles

---

[3] This means the unit would no longer be available for daily generation but could be brought back on-line in the future if needed.

[4] Two and three-quarters tons of ash substitute for 1 ton of lime. Dominion pays for hauling and receives no payment for the ash, but it also bears no responsibility for what happens once the ash is handed over. For example, improper spreading of warm ash has caused at least one fire on a farm, but the hauler was responsible.

[5] It requires "superior fuel quality" with low ash content of 2–3 percent, on average, due to the use of a water-cooled grate. Attempts to use storm-damaged wood led to problems due to dirt, debris, and high ash content.

[6] It takes about 13 minutes to unload a truck. Most deliveries occur between 5:00 a.m. and 7:00 p.m.

[7] The estimate varies from 0.973 to 1.045 million tons per year. "Full load" was cited as being 2,865 tons per day, and "on-site storage" for 15 days was estimated to be 35,000 to 45,000 tons of fuel.

away. An analysis by Virginia Polytechnic Institute and State University concluded that the biomass resource in the region far exceeds the facility's needs.

Initially, the facility plans to receive biomass five days per week over 10-hour shifts and will have two truck tippers on-site. Meeting a 20 percent target, however, would push this delivery schedule, requiring 125 tons delivered per hour, or 80 to 156 trucks per day requiring two 12-hour shifts staffed with a bulldozer operator. Eventually, the facility will need a 24-hour drop-off system. It will have sufficient space for 10 days of biomass storage on-site but might expand this to 15 days storage capacity. Plans are to minimize biomass processing on-site. Biomass handling will use bulldozers to push the fuel from the open storage area to the feeder. Screening will occur before the fuel is moved to a mass conveying feeding system, which will keep materials moving constantly. A gravity feeder will be used.

The Foster Wheeler boiler that the facility is using is designed for 20-percent biomass use. Biomass will be fed as a separate stream into the boiler, moving directly into the bed from all three cyclones. The owner has found that commingling wood and coal can cause plugging, so the facility will avoid this.

The facility's permit is contingent on biomass use. It must fire 5-percent biomass by 36 months after commencing commercial operations and be at 10 percent biomass by eight years. However, it may use 100-percent coal as needed initially or for short periods of time. It has designed the system to allow for this contingency.[8] The facility would not be required to meet these minimum percentages if the economics of using biomass has a significant adverse impact on ratepayers or promotes tree-cutting.[9] Waste will be stored in an on-site dry-lined landfill repository.

The facility will be obtaining RECs for biomass use that it can then sell. It expects that this financial incentive will make the biomass use cost-effective. However, provisions in the PSD air permit mean that the facility will not have to meet biomass cofire targets if doing so is not in the interest of utility ratepayers.

FirstEnergy

FirstEnergy evaluated the use of various types of biomass at its facilities. This included engineered-wood products in the form of pellets or briquettes, greenwood chips, torrefied wood pellets or briquettes, and nonbaled agricultural-based products. FirstEnergy issued a request for proposal for fuel supplies for its R. E. Burger plant. Bids were received and are currently being evaluated. In both the Bay Shore and Burger facilities, cofire testing was performed using engineered-wood pellets. Additional test firing was conducted at a boiler vendor's pilot facility.

Bay Shore

FirstEnergy's Bay Shore facility conducted biomass cofiring test burns in two of its four units. Unit 1 was recently (2000) retrofitted with a CFB boiler to accept petroleum coke from a neighboring refinery, and the other, unit 3, is a front-fired PC boiler. The cofire testing was designed to determine specific material handling issues associated with biomass fuel and to determine

---

[8]   For example, the center can take out compartments of the baghouse when firing 100-percent coal.

[9]   The language in the PSD permit reads, "Should market conditions indicate that biomass fuel has a significant ratepayer impact or promotes tree cutting, such biomass requirement shall be reduced or eliminated until market conditions correct."

the maximum amount of biomass that could be cofired with coal using the existing equipment. The facility selected a 5-percent cofire ratio based on European experience with small cofire ratios using wood pellets. By using a small percentage of pelletized biomass blended with coal, a portion of the existing coal handling systems were able to be utilized to transport the biomass fuel to the unit 1 CFB or the unit 3 existing coal pulverizers. For higher percentages of cofiring, power plants in Europe have installed parallel fuel-handling systems and hammer mill systems to process the biomass and feed it to the boiler. For the tested percentages of cofiring, no boiler problems were observed.

FirstEnergy's choice of biomass fuel type for a facility is site specific. It depends on (1) the type of existing equipment at the plant, (2) the transportation unloading systems available at the plant (e.g., barge unloading, rail unloading), and (3) the plant location, all of which affect the delivered cost of the various biomass types.

Testing on unit 1 at 5 percent by mass was conducted for one month using a single pellet source delivered by rail in covered grain hopper cars. During this period, approximately 20 rail cars of pellets were utilized. Some facility changes were required to unload and handle the biomass, but use of the biomass had virtually no impact on plant performance. The material handled and burned well, and there were no combustion-related problems. Unit 3 cofiring at 5 percent, through an individual pulverizer, achieved similar results.

R. E. Burger

FirstEnergy's R. E. Burger plant was originally constructed in the 1940s and 1950s. FirstEnergy had planned to repower units 4 and 5 to fire principally biomass as a result of a 2004 NSR lawsuit and a resulting consent decree. The consent decree required lower emissions of SO_x, NO_x, and PM than exist today. Biomass use was one way to achieve these limits. Though FirstEnergy canceled this project in late 2010, a summary of the intended project appears here.

FirstEnergy issued a request for proposal for biomass fuel supplies in early 2010 and was in the process of finalizing contracts when the project was canceled. The plant would have required approximately 1 million tons per year of biomass fuel.

Plant changes were modeled to some extent on those that have been put in place in some European facilities. A feasibility study was conducted in 2009 in which engineering needs, alternatives, and different biomass fuel options were considered. The preliminary engineering process design was finalized around mid-2010, and the order of the material handling equipment was scheduled to be completed by the end of 2010. Construction was to commence in spring 2011 with the repowered units on-line by the end of 2012. The project was estimated to cost about $200 million. There are trade-offs in costs between, for example, greenwood, which requires additional handling but no indoor storage, and engineered products, which require less processing but have more-costly storage requirements. Approximately $18 million of these costs are related to plant reliability projects, which are nonspecific to biomass use.

Biomass delivery was planned to be primarily by barge, which is how the plant received coal, and supplemented by truck delivery. A combination of existing and new material handling equipment was to be used for offloading. No truck tippers were to be used. A silo was planned to be installed on-site for storage of dry engineered-fuel products. The biomass fuels would have been handled by a combination of new conveyers and redesigned existing coal conveyers. Engineered fuels were to be processed in the existing coal pulverizers on units 4 and 5, which would have required modifications. Greenwood chips would have been combusted on a new stoker to be installed on the unit 4 existing boiler.

In the spring of 2010, test burns of engineered-wood pellets were conducted on unit 5. One of five coal mills was changed to handle 100-percent wood pellets, which represented approximately 20 percent of the total heat input to the boiler. Test results are under evaluation as of the writing of this report.

In Ohio, FirstEnergy would have received RECs for the electricity produced by biomass. The project would have been one of the options FirstEnergy used to meet the Ohio RPSs (12.5 percent renewable generation by 2025).

Florida Crystals

Florida Crystals operates an electricity generation facility with a nameplate rating of 140 million volt-amperes (MVA),[10] part of an integrated operation with one of its sugar mills, in Okeelanta, Florida. During the sugar-milling season (five months of the year), up to 80 percent of the steam produced at the plant is delivered to the mill. The plant also exports a significant amount of power: 400 to 500 gigawatt-hours (GWh) per year.

The plant was designed to fire biomass and burns almost 100 percent chipped waste wood and sugarcane waste (bagasse), in approximately a 50:50 ratio.[11] Total annual biomass use is approximately 1.5 million tons. Maintaining a consistent supply of high-quality wood fuel is always a challenge. The farthest suppliers are approximately 100 miles away, and transportation is the biggest component of the cost. The plant has a set of contracts for operation of the delivery trucks and receives approximately 100 trucks per day, with an average load of approximately 23 tons.[12]

Biomass handling is a significant issue. The various wood supply streams are mixed by rolling equipment to try to achieve a reasonably homogenous wood fuel. The moisture content of the biomass varies widely, from just a few percent for construction waste to more than 50 percent for yard trimmings. The average moisture content is about 35 percent. The plant employs about 60 people to cover three shifts in the fuel yard. They operate six front-end loaders to manage the fuel piles and to feed the boilers. The company has investigated more automated systems but has not found them to be cost-effective. The biomass fuel is transported from the yard to the boilers via conveyers and then fed into the boilers through two sets of independent feeders, one for bagasse and the second for wood fuel.

Although the plant was designed for biomass, operations have been a learning process. For example, ash alkalinity has been a problem. Within a few years of commencing operations, the plant had to upgrade the metallurgy in the boiler, especially the superheater, to reduce corrosion by replacing existing pipes and equipment with stainless steel. Ash characteristics sometimes vary, so handling can also be a challenge.

---

[10] Volt-amperes and watts have the same units, energy per unit time, but differ in their interpretation for alternating current systems. The watt rating of a power plant is always less than the volt-ampere rating and depends on the type of loads that the plant is servicing. If delivering base-load electricity to the grid, the delivered watts will be close to the volt-ampere rating.

[11] The "waste wood" consists primarily of construction waste, yard trimmings, land clearing, and forestry wood. Small amounts of natural gas are used for start-up, and the facility is also permitted to burn coal and TDF if necessary.

[12] The plant is located in a rural area and has not received resistance from the community for its operations.

To meet emission requirements, the facility has ash collectors and ESPs to maintain particulate emissions below 0.026 lb per mmBtu. The facility is also equipped with urea injection controls to keep NO_x emissions below 0.15 lb per mmBtu and with other combustion controls to limit opacity and CO emissions.

Ecostrat

Canada-based Ecostrat is one of the largest biomass aggregators in North America. It also transports biomass to Europe and Asia. It has historically provided both bulk woody biomass (e.g., greenwood chips) and densified engineered-wood products (i.e., pellets). Over the past 19 years, it has developed the largest wood fiber supplier database in North America, the Biomass Supply Network®, and a biomass contracting and financing mechanism called the Biomass Credit Wrap®. To date, typical North American purchasers have been pulp and paper companies, but, more recently, Ecostrat has also begun to work with power plants interested in biomass fuels.[13]

The Biomass Supply Network is a detailed database and mapping system with information on more than 200,000 biomass suppliers in the United States and Canada. Ecostrat collects data on available woody biomass from each of its potential suppliers, including the desired price and contract length. Direct suppliers are categorized into three virgin-biomass classes (whole tree chips including bark, forest residues, and mill residues) and two wood waste categories (postindustrial and demolition biomass).[14] For each producer, Ecostrat has information on available amount, cost, and class of biomass. The woodshed for a given project is assumed to be within a two-hour driving radius, based on currently existing roads.[15] The focus on local supply is based on the fact that, beyond these distances, the cost of the transportation can be higher than the cost of the actual biomass fuel. This is true even for densified products.[16]

Ecostrat offers a Biomass Credit Wrap service, which aggregates a guaranteed supply from the many regional sources at a negotiated price with a long-term contract (i..e, 10–15 years, with an option to extend for an additional five years). A major financial institution with investment-grade credit is the guarantor, and Ecostrat is the counterparty for all of these arrangements. This enables the biomass purchaser to obtain long-term security of price and security of supply. Not only does this simplify day-to-day operations but it might also enable a facility to more readily find financing at more-desirable rates. Additionally, long-term costs and profits are easier to predict with long-term fuel contracts.

The Biomass Credit Wrap includes a base price for wood fiber, which is marginally higher than the wood-chip spot price.[17] It also includes escalators for (1) inflation, fixed to an index; (2) regional diesel cost; (3) distance beyond base zone, when a given supplier is required to use

[13] Ecostrat notes that the size of power plant projects in general has grown in the past two years or so and that 200,000 to 1 million tons of biomass use annually is now typical. By its estimates, a 100-MW dedicated biomass facility should need 1.2 million tons of green fuel annually.

[14] This is the largest single category of suppliers.

[15] In western Pennsylvania, the radius for a 500,000-ton facility would be 60 to 100 miles. In general, the ability to use highways allows the economic radius to be expanded.

[16] Nontruck transport could change this calculation. For example, easy access to a port would change the cost ratios.

[17] This is on the order of $2 per ton.

more-distant portions of its land; and (4) stumpage.[18] Although these escalators will cause the biomass fuel supply to vary with some of the same drivers that influence the spot market, the contract protects against price increases due to speculation, as well as supply issues. Ecostrat estimates that the cost of a typical credit wrap is approximately $5 per ton.

Ecostrat contrasts the use of a Biomass Credit Wrap with the traditional biomass acquisition approach in which a biomass user works to find the largest number of suppliers within a two-hour distance of the facility. Even if the user is able to secure a long-term contract, which might be unlikely, the supplier might choose to or be forced to breach this contract for a variety of reasons, and there is no recourse for the purchaser. Even if the supply remains secure, most users transact with many suppliers. As an example, a recent 60-MW power plant project contracted with Ecostrat for 800,000 tons of green fuel. Initially, the supplier had a triple-B-minus bond rating, but, with a Biofuel Credit Wrap, it was predicted be able to achieve at triple-B-plus rating, a difference of 100 basis points or 1 percent. For a $300 million project with 100-percent debt finance, this would translate into $3 million annually.

Although Ecostrat's services might facilitate a more stable biomass market and decreased financing costs for plants, Ecostrat does not believe that lower future biomass costs are likely.[19] However, an ability to engage in long-term contracts might place electricity generators at a competitive advantage over pulp and paper plants. Additionally, as demand increases, prices are expected to rise to $40–45 per ton for greenwood. At this price, the two-hour radius of supply will no longer be an economic limit. This, in turn, will increase the attractiveness of densified biomass products. Accordingly, Ecostrat is also exploring the longer-term market possibilities for torrefied wood, which can be transported and handled much like coal, minimizing conversion costs.[20] At prices exceeding $40–45 per ton, closed-loop energy crops will begin to figure into supply.

---

[18] An increase of $0.10 per gallon in the price of diesel typically results in an increase of $0.10–0.14 per ton in the base-zone cost of biomass. The base zone is typically 0–40 miles from the project site, and the escalator is proportional to the diesel used and the distance traveled. In North Carolina, for example, the base wood cost for whole tree chips is approximately $25 per ton in this base zone. For each additional 10 miles outside of this zone, an increment of $1.10 per ton is added. In South Carolina, it is about $1.20 per ton for each additional 10 miles above the base zone. Typically, stumpage costs range between $6 and $14 per ton for land clearing, equivalent to a land rental rate.

[19] Wood suppliers might be able to invest in equipment and labor more readily if they are engaged in long-term contracts, but neither harvesting nor trucking is likely to become substantially more efficient, making price reductions improbable.

[20] For example, a barge can hold four to five times the amount of torrefied wood that a greenwood shipper can.

Supporting Information for Plant-Site Costs of Cofiring

This appendix documents the methodology underlying the calculation of the plant-site costs of cofiring, which appears in Chapter Three. To facilitate these calculations, a model of plant-site costs was built in Analytica®, a product of Lumina Decision Systems. This appendix documents the variables contained in and calculations performed by this model.

The model calculates the plant-site costs based on a set of parameters and user-determined choices. These are described in this appendix, along with the three major components to the cost calculation: methods to calculate fuel costs, capital costs, and operating costs. Key values are also listed in Chapter Three. The methods of calculating higher-order objective values, including GHG emissions, are then delineated.

All costs are in 2008 dollars. Figures in Chapter Three have been converted to 2010 dollars to be consistent with the logistical analysis.

Choice Variables and Indices

Type of Biomass
This is a user-determined choice variable that sets the type of biomass that is delivered to the plant. Options include wood chunks, wood chips, sawdust, herbaceous bales, and pellets. Combinations of these are not included.

Type of Coal
This is a user-determined choice variable that sets the type of coal used by the plant. Options include bituminous and subbituminous coal. See the coal energy content variable for more information.

Type of Boiler
This is a user-determined choice variable that sets the type of boiler at the plant. Options include stoker-fired, FB, and PC boilers.

Processing-Line Choice
This is a user-determined choice variable that sets whether the plant builds a new line for dedicated biomass processing and handling, modifies an existing coal line to process biomass, or commingles biomass and coal for processing.

System-Capacity Assumption

This is a user-defined choice variable that sets how the firing capacity and fuel requirements of the system change with a shift from coal-only firing to cofiring with biomass. The fixed-mass assumption implies that the total mass input of all fuels is constant when comparing coal firing and cofiring. The fixed–heat-input assumption implies that the total heat input of all fuels is constant when comparing coal firing and cofiring. For more details on how this choice is applied and the consequences, see the "Fuel Costs" section later in this appendix.

Low/Mid/High

This is an index that allows a three-level uncertainty range of inputs to be entered for parameter values. For some of the parameters present in the model, the literature presents a range of values. This index allows this range of possible values to be used in model calculations when appropriate. In calculations that make use of several variables indexed by low/mid/high, the calculated low values make use of all low values for these parameters when such values are indicated. Similar calculations take place for the mid and high values.

Other User-Defined Values

Boiler Rated Capacity

This is the rated capacity of the boiler to be used in cofiring. The default value is 100 MW, which is the size of one unit of the NRG Dunkirk plant discussed in Chapter Two.

Boiler-Capacity Factor

This is the fraction of a year that the boiler operates. The default value is 0.85.

Heat Rate: Coal

This is the overall heat rate for the plant when fired with coal alone. It represents the energy content of fuel (in Btu) to generate 1 kWh of net electricity.

For PC boilers, the default estimates are based on 2005 data from the NETL Coal Power Plant DataBase (NETL, 2007). The midlevel value is estimated using a weighted average of the heat rates of in-service plants with PC boilers, weighting by net annual electricity generation. The low- and high-level values are based on the same calculation but with the bottom- and top-quartile heat-rate data, respectively. Default values are 9,300, 10,200, and 12,400 Btu per kilowatt-hour for low, mid, and high, respectively.

For FB and stoker-fired boilers, there are not enough boilers in the NETL coal plant database to provide a reliable estimate of heat rates for existing plants. For FB boilers, the National Coal Council (NCC) (2004) has some estimates. Using the PC data in both the NETL and NCC sources, the NCC estimates are relatively low compared with what is observed in the current coal plant fleet; thus, the NCC estimate is used as the low-level estimate. The mid- and high-level values for FB boilers are estimated by multiplying the NCC estimate by the same factor separating the NCC value from the empirical value in the PC case. This factor is 1.10 for the mid-level value and 1.33 for the high-level value. Default values are 9,800, 10,800, and 13,000 Btu/KWh for low, mid, and high heat rates for FB boilers.

No literature value was found for the heat rate of stoker-fired boilers. Stoker-fired boilers should generally be less efficient than FB and PC boilers. Thus 11,000, 12,000, and 13,000 Btu per kilowatt-hour are used as placeholder low, mid, and high values.

Coal as Fired Energy Content

This is the energy content (higher heating value [HHV] basis) of the coal as fired. Default values are based on bituminous and subbituminous coal received in 2007–2008 (EIA, 2010a). Values are converted from Btu per pound in the source to mmBtu per ton here. Default values are 23.9 mmBtu per ton for bituminous coal and 17.4 mmBtu per ton for subbituminous coal.

Cofire Fraction

This is a user-defined choice variable indicating the fraction of biomass, on an energy basis, to be fed into the boiler. The default value is 0.05. The model assumes that cofire fractions are relatively low, so values greater than 0.15 should not be used.

Biomass Storage Capacity

This is the number of days of biomass fuel supply contained by the built storage facility. Default storage capacity for logs, chunks, chips, pellets, and bales is seven days of fuel at full-capacity firing at the specified cofiring fraction. This is within the range of storage available at interviewed plants. Because silos to store sawdust are expensive, only three days of sawdust storage are provided; this is similar to storage facilities at the plants whose representatives we interviewed for this project and consistent with the approach in McGowan (2009).

Biomass Moisture Content

This is the moisture content of the biomass as received at the plant. The default values are 0.35 for wood chunks and chips, 0.20 for sawdust, 0.15 for herbaceous bales, and 0.05 for pellets and are consistent with ranges in the literature and current experience (ORNL, 2010).

Dry Biomass Energy Content

This is the energy content of the biomass when it is dry. Though indexed by biomass form, the default values are classed only by woody (16.3 mmBtu per ton) versus herbaceous biomass (14.6 mmBtu per ton). Pellets are assigned an energy content in between the two (15 mmBtu per ton). These representative values are taken from the Biomass Energy Data Book (ORNL, 2010).

Price of Coal

This is the price of coal to be cofed into the plant. The default value of $2 per mmBtu is representative of current and projected prices from 2010 to 2019 from EIA (EIA, 2010b).

Price of Biomass

This is the price of biomass as delivered to the plant. The range of possible values reflects the range of values in the current market with the low end ($2 per mmBtu) reflecting the price of coal and the high end ($10 per mmBtu) the ceiling price of pellets in the consumer market.

Price of Electricity

The default value is the bus-bar price of electricity estimated in Crane et al. (2011) at $44.40 per megawatt-hour.

Capital Charge Rate

This is the weighted average cost of capital for building the equipment to support cofiring. The default is a relatively low rate to indicate that we expect bank financing rather than capital financing to fund the work. The default is set at 6.41 percent (Crane et al., 2011).

Amortization Period

This is the period over which capital recovery of investments occurs. The default is set at 30 years.

Capital Cost Contingency Factor

See the discussion of this variable in the "Capital Costs of Cofiring" section later in this appendix.

Subsidy for Biomass Firing

This is a user-defined choice variable indicating the magnitude (if any) of subsidies available for biomass cofiring. These also could be interpreted as the offset for biomass electricity production from a REC. The default value is $0 per megawatt-hour.

Other Data and Parameters

Additional parameters are described in the relevant sections of the model description throughout this appendix.

Heat Rate: Cofiring

The heat rate of a plant will vary slightly depending on the cofire fraction. The decrease in efficiency with cofiring is the decrease in plant efficiency due to conversion from coal-only operations to cofiring. The decrease in boiler efficiency has been found empirically by Tillman (2000) to follow the equation

$$EL = 0.0044 \times B^2 + 0.0055,$$

where EL is the efficiency loss (%) and B is the percentage biomass on a mass basis.

To calculate an adjusted heat rate for this effect, the cofiring fraction is converted to a percentage mass fraction and the efficiency loss is calculated. It is assumed that the nonboiler efficiency is on the order of 40 percent (De and Assadi, 2009). Thus, the overall decrease in efficiency (ODE) in percentage can be estimated as

$$ODE = 0.4 \times EL.$$

Note that these empirical relationships are based on wood cofiring. Cofiring with bales is likely to have a smaller efficiency impact because bales have a lower moisture content. However, this decrease in efficiency is a small value and is used for all biomass types.

If no biomass is used in firing, the efficiency loss is set at zero.

To implement these equations, the cofire fraction must be calculated on a mass basis. This is done, and converted to a percentage, according to the following expression:

$$100 \times \frac{\dfrac{\text{cofire fraction}}{\text{energy content green}}}{\dfrac{\text{cofire fraction}}{\text{energy content green}} + \dfrac{1 - \text{cofire fraction}}{\text{coal energy content}}}.$$

Once the decrease in efficiency with cofiring is calculated, it can be subtracted from the efficiency under coal-only firing to give the efficiency under cofiring. The efficiency under coal-only firing is calculated according to the following equation:

$$\text{efficiency} = \frac{1}{\text{heat rate}} \times 3,412 \text{ Btu/kWh} \times 100.$$

Once the cofiring efficiency is calculated (in percentage), it is converted back to a heat rate for cofiring according to the following equation, in which the efficiency is converted from a percentage to a fraction:

$$\text{heat rate} = \frac{1}{\dfrac{\text{efficiency}}{100}} \times 3,412 \text{ Btu/kWh}.$$

Energy Content Per Green Ton

This is the energy content for the biomass as it is received in mmBtu per ton. It is calculated according to the following expression:

$$(1 - \text{biomass moisture content}) \times \text{dry biomass energy content}.$$

Fuel Costs

In this section of the model, the amount and costs of fuel for cofiring are calculated, both for the coal and biomass components of fuel use. Key to these calculations is the system-capacity assumption, which determines the maximum amount of fuel that can be processed and fired by the plant and how this constraint changes on conversion to cofiring. If the system-capacity assumption is set to "fixed heat input," this implies that the total heat input of all fuels is constant when comparing coal firing and cofiring. In contrast, if this assumption is set to "fixed mass input," the total mass input of all fuels is constant when comparing coal firing and cofiring. Because biomass has a lower energy content than coal, more biomass mass is required to generate the same energy input as coal. Thus the "fixed mass input" assumption implies a lower level of plant gross electricity generation than the "fixed heat input" assumption.

The choice of system-capacity assumption will depend on the plant. If the plant has excess firing capacity and there is excess processing capacity or if additional processing capacity will be built, then additional fuel mass represented by cofiring biomass might not be problematic and the plant will then be able to maintain the same heat input of fuel as was used under coal-only firing, allowing for the "fixed heat input" choice. If, however, there is no additional firing or processing capacity, then the plant might not be able to fire fuel mass beyond the mass used under coal-only firing. In this case, the "fixed mass input" assumption might be more appropriate.

Thus, the fuel calculations begin by calculating fuel use in the coal-only case and then apply the chosen system-capacity assumption and cofiring ratio to calculate the amount of biomass and coal required to fire the plant at the chosen level. The fuel costs can then be calculated. The following sections describe the various nodes used in the Analytica model to perform these calculations.

Heat Input Per Hour: Coal Only

This is the heat input per hour for a coal-fired system firing at full capacity and is calculated according to the following expression:

$$\text{boiler rated capacity} \times \text{heat rate at coal-fired plant} \times 1{,}000 \text{ kWh/MWh}$$
$$\times 1 \text{ mmBtu}/1{,}000{,}000 \text{ mmBtu}.$$

Total Tons Per Hour: Coal Only

This is the mass of coal used per hour in the initial coal-only system firing at full capacity. It is calculated according to the following expression:

$$\text{heat input per hour at coal-fired plant} \times \left(\frac{1}{\text{coal energy content}} \right).$$

Heat Input Per Hour

This is the total heat input per hour from both coal and biomass under cofiring.

The value varies depending on the system-capacity assumption: If it is assumed that the total heat input remains constant on converting to biomass cofiring, the total heat input per hour is the same as the heat input per hour in the coal-only case. If it is assumed that the total fuel mass input remains constant when converted to cofiring, the calculations are more complex. Using mass and energy balances, we have a system of three equations with three unknowns: the biomass mass, the coal mass, and the total heat input.

The three equations are as follows:

1. We know that the total cofiring fuel mass (total tons per hour) must equal the fuel mass in the coal-fired system:

$$\text{biomass tons per hour} + \text{coal tons per hour} = \text{total tons per hour.} \tag{1}$$

2. We can also calculate the total heat input per hour using

$$\text{total heat input per hour} = \text{biomass tons per hour} \times (1 - \text{biomass moisture content})$$
$$\times \text{ dry biomass energy content} + \text{coal tons per hour}$$
$$\times \text{coal energy content.} \tag{2}$$

3. Finally, we can relate heat inputs to mass inputs using the chosen cofire fraction. The first term in the expression calculates the biomass tons per hour and the second term the coal tons per hour:

$$\text{cofire fraction} \times \text{total heat input per hour}$$
$$\times \left(\frac{1}{\text{dry biomass energy content}}\right) \times \left(\frac{1}{1 - \text{moisture content}}\right)$$
$$+ (1 - \text{cofire fraction}) \times \text{total heat input per hour } \times \left(\frac{1}{\text{coal energy content}}\right)$$
$$= \text{total tons per hour.} \tag{3}$$

To solve this system of equations, equation 1 is solved for coal tons per hour and substituted into equation 2. Equation 2 is then solved for biomass tons per hour and substituted into equation 3, from which total heat input per hour can be calculated.

For this node, heat input per hour is defined in the third step described above, according to the following expression (after the various substitutions have taken place):

$$\frac{\text{total tons per hour of coal-only firing}}{\left(\begin{array}{l}\text{cofire fraction} \times \left(\dfrac{1}{\text{dry biomass energy content}}\right) \times \left(\dfrac{1}{1 - \text{biomass moisture content}}\right) \\ + (1 - \text{cofire fraction}) \times \left(\dfrac{1}{\text{coal energy content}}\right)\end{array}\right)}.$$

If the system-capacity assumption is set to "fixed heat input," then the heat input is the same as that under the coal-only scenario.

Biomass Tons Per Hour
This is the number of tons of biomass that is used hourly by the plant when it is operating at full capacity. As described earlier, its value depends on whether the mass or heat input of fuel is held constant in converting to cofiring.

The calculation under the "fixed heat input" assumption is described by this expression:

$$\text{heat input per hour} \times \text{cofire fraction}$$
$$\times \frac{1}{\text{dry biomass energy content}} \times \frac{1}{1 - \text{biomass moisture content}}.$$

In the "fixed mass input case," the hourly number of tons of biomass required is determined through the system of equations described for the heat-input-per-hour node. Specifically, it is calculated according to the following expression, determined by making the necessary substitutions described earlier:

$$\frac{\text{heat input per hour} - \text{total tons per hour of coal-only firing} \times \text{coal energy content}}{(1 - \text{biomass moisture content}) \times (\text{dry biomass energy content}) - \text{coal energy content}}.$$

Coal Tons Per Hour

This is the number of tons of coal that is used hourly by the plant when it is cofiring at full capacity. As described earlier, its value depends on whether the mass or heat input of fuel is held constant in converting to cofiring.

The calculation under the "fixed heat input" assumption is described by this expression:

$$\text{heat input per hour} \times (1 - \text{cofire fraction}) \times \frac{1}{\text{coal energy content}}.$$

In the "fixed mass input case," the number of hourly tons of coal use is determined through the system of equations described for the heat-input-per-hour node. Specifically, it is calculated according to the following expression:

$$\text{total tons per hour of coal-only firing} - \text{biomass tons per hour}.$$

After the hourly values for biomass and coal are calculated, the annual fuel requirements for the plant can be determined. Then, using the prices of biomass and coal, the annual fuel costs can be calculated.

Biomass Tons Per Year

This is the annual number of tons of biomass that will be used in the plant while cofiring. It assumes that the plant operates for a fraction of the year represented by the boiler-capacity factor. It is determined by the following expression:

$$\text{biomass tons per hour} \times \text{hours per year} \times \text{boiler-capacity factor}.$$

Coal Tons Per Year

This is the annual number of tons of coal that will be used in the plant while cofiring. It assumes that the plant operates for a fraction of the year represented by the boiler-capacity factor. It is determined by the following expression:

$$\text{coal tons per hour} \times \text{hours per year} \times \text{boiler-capacity factor}.$$

Annual Biomass Fuel Cost

This is the annual cost to purchase biomass fuel under cofiring. It is calculated according to the following expression:

$$\text{biomass tons per year} \times (1 - \text{biomass moisture content})$$
$$\times \text{dry biomass energy content} \times \text{price of biomass}.$$

Annual Coal Fuel Cost

This is the annual cost of coal under cofiring. It is calculated according to the following expression:

$$\text{coal tons per year} \times \text{coal energy content} \times \text{price of coal}.$$

Annual Fuel Cost

This is the total annual cost for biomass and coal fuel and is calculated according to the following expression:

$$\text{annual biofuel cost} + \text{annual coal fuel cost}.$$

Annual Change in Fuel Cost

This is the difference in annual fuel costs between cofiring and firing coal only, with higher fuel costs under cofiring expressed as a positive value. It is calculated according to the following expression:

$$\text{annual fuel cost}$$
$$- \left(\begin{array}{l} \text{total tons per hour of coal-only firing} \times \text{hours per year} \\ \times \text{boiler-capacity factor} \times \text{coal energy content} \times \text{price of coal} \end{array} \right).$$

Capital Costs of Cofiring

This section of the model describes the costs involved in modifying and purchasing additional equipment and facilities to enable the handling and processing of biomass at the plant. For these capital costs, it is assumed that all financing occurs through debt financing at the rate given by the capital charge-rate parameter. It is also assumed that the coal portion of the plant is fully amortized and incurs no capital costs. The effects of taxation and depreciation are also neglected.

A large number of configurations are possible at the plant. For the sake of estimating costs in this model, we have taken a small, representative subset of these. We acknowledge that plants might choose to process and handle biomass through methods that are not considered here. To some extent, variation in plant-level choices is represented through the low/mid/high choice variable, which presents a range of possible price points for the relevant variables in the model.

The processing and handling equipment required is specific to both the type of biomass utilized and the type of boiler, both of which are user defined. In addition, the capital costs are associated with three major processing and handling stages through which the biomass must pass before it is suitable for firing. The first of these is a receiving and storage stage, which includes the cost of machinery to unload biomass delivery trucks at the plant site, the cost of storage facilities, and the cost of machinery to move the biomass within the storage yard and onto the processing line. The second stage is composed of initial processing for large biomass. In this stage, large biomass, such as bales of herbaceous biomass and chunks of wood, are processed to a size comparable to wood chips or pellets. In this way, it is assumed that all biomass types can be treated similarly in the third stage: final processing for firing.

Several of the equipment costs are extrapolated from estimates for various plant sizes. Linear estimates are typically used. Additional uncertainty in the capital costs is contributed by this assumption that capital costs scale linearly with the amount of biomass processed.

Some of the equipment cost parameters are listed in Table B.1. To represent costs in 2008 dollars, consistent with the rest of the model, we have used the consumer price index (CPI), a generic economy-wide deflator (Bureau of Labor Statistics [BLS], undated). In general, the equipment used to handle and process biomass is drawn from the pulp and paper industry or from farming. As a result, we might slightly overestimate capital equipment costs in some cases because of the fact that price growth is slower in the pulp and paper industry and farming than in the CPI.

Stage 1, receiving and storage, is described in the following three parts. The total cost for this stage is the sum of all of these parts, with the relevant components chosen to suit the form of biomass that is received at the plant.

Processing and Handling Stage 1, Part 1: Receipt of Biomass

The receipt-of-biomass node calculates the cost of the equipment used to transfer biomass from delivery trucks to storage. It is assumed that all biomass arrives by truck and that the facilities used to receive coal cannot also be used to receive biomass. The assumed equipment varies by the form in which the biomass is received.

Wood. For plants requiring less than 15 tons per hour of biomass, it is assumed that dump trucks are used to transport biomass to the plant and front-end loaders are used to move the biomass as required. The cost of these loaders is derived from estimates in McGowan (2009).

Table B.1
Equipment Cost Parameters and Values

Parameter	Comments	Cost (low, mid, high) in 2008 $	Reference
Truck tipper	Cost for one tipper	300,000, 800,000, 1 million	McGowan, 2009
Bale loaders, receipt	Cost in $/annual dry tons	0.41	INL, 2009
Bale loaders, transfer to line	Cost in $/annual dry tons	0.25	INL, 2009
Bale merge conveyer	For 10 ton/hour line	127,000	Antares Group, 2009
Bale infeed conveyer	For 10 ton/hour line	64,000, 85,000, 170,000	Antares Group, 2009
Moisture meter	For 10 ton/hour line	17,000	Antares Group, 2009
Bale rejector	For 10 ton/hour line	14,000	Antares Group, 2009
Destringer	For 10 ton/hour line	34,000, 41,000, 67,000	Antares Group, 2009
Debaler	For 10 ton/hour line	130,000, 138,000, 245,000	Antares Group, 2009
Debaler outfeed conveyer	For 10 ton/hour line	64,000	Antares Group, 2009
Magnet	For 10 ton/hour line	26,000, 26,000, 32,000	Antares Group, 2009
Fine hammer mill	For 10 ton/hour line	150,000, 150,000, 300,000	Antares Group, 2009
Baghouse fan	For 10 ton/hour line	7,000	Antares Group, 2009
Baghouse	For 10 ton/hour line	66,000	Antares Group, 2009
Surge bin	For 10 ton/hour line	71,000, 71,000, 92,000	Antares Group, 2009
Rotary airlocks and feeders	For 10 ton/hour line	59,000, 59,000, 70,000	Antares Group, 2009
Pneumatic transport system	For 10 ton/hour line	630,000, 630,000, 705,000	Antares Group, 2009

A linear relationship is derived from McGowan's cost and tons-processed-per-hour estimates, giving the following equation:

$$\text{front-end loader cost} = 3,960 + \text{biomass tons per hour} \times 9,000.$$

The appropriate cost for front-end loaders can then be estimated by substituting in the appropriate number of biomass tons per hour.

For plants requiring more than 15 tons per hour of biomass, it is assumed that truck tippers are used to transfer the material from the transport truck. This assumption is based on current operations according to interviews with plant operators as well as descriptions in McGowan (2009). The truck tipper cost includes both the purchase and installation cost and a receiving hopper. The low-level cost is based on estimates in McGowan (2009). The high-level cost is an estimate from interviewed plant operators. The midlevel cost is weighted toward the high-level value because installation costs are expected to be high.

The number of truck tippers required is calculated based on the required tons of biomass per hour. It is assumed that biomass arrives 14 hours per day. Based on McGowan and discussions with plant operators, it is assumed that 23 tons of wood can be carried per truck, each load using the tipper for 15 minutes. Thus, a truck tipper in use for 14 hours per day can provide for 24-hour operation of a plant at approximately 50 tons per hour:

$$23 \text{ tons/load} \times 4 \text{ loads/hour} \times 14 \text{ hours/24 hours} = 54 \text{ tons/hour}.$$

Thus, for every 50 tons per hour of biomass required, an additional truck tipper is included. The total cost for truck tippers is described by the following expression, where the Ceil function rounds up to the nearest integer, giving the number of truck tippers required:

$$\text{truck tipper cost} \times \text{Ceil}\left(\frac{\text{biomass tons per hour}}{50} \right).$$

Bales. It is assumed that bale loaders are used to unload bales from trucks and place them in storage. The capital cost estimate for these loaders is taken from INL (2009), using their estimated costs for corn stover. INL estimates the cost to purchase Caterpillar TH220-B tele-handlers to move bales, a cost it defines in terms of dollars per annual dry ton capacity. Thus, this bale-loader factor is multiplied by the annual ton capacity and multiplied by the fraction of dry mass to give the bale-loader cost. This is shown in the following expression, where the bale-loader receiving factor is the estimate in dollars per annual dry ton capacity from INL (2009):

$$\text{bale-loader receiving factor} \times \text{biomass tons per hour}$$
$$\times \left(1 - \text{biomass moisture content} \right) \times \text{hours per year}.$$

Processing and Handling Stage 1, Part 2: Storage

After the biomass is delivered to the plant, it is put into storage. It is assumed that biomass is processed on an as-needed basis from the storage location.

The amount of storage, measured in days, is a user-determined parameter. According to our interviews with plant operators, biomass storage capacity covers a short operational period, on the order of a week, because biomass can, with prolonged storage, degrade or act as a fire hazard. In addition, under cofiring, coal-only firing can be used temporarily if biomass stocks run low.

The type of storage facility, and thus the price, varies with the form of biomass used by the plant. It is assumed that wood chunks and chips are stored in open storage. Sawdust is stored in silos. Bales are stored in fully enclosed buildings as per the CVBP (Antares Group, 2009). Pellets are also stored in fully enclosed buildings due to water sensitivity.

Because sawdust has a bulk density roughly 60 percent of that of wood chips (Van Loo and Koppejan, 2008), storage-silo costs per ton of sawdust are estimated by taking the silo costs per ton of wood chips from McGowan and multiplying it by 1.67. Capital costs based on the figures in McGowan are derived by finding a linear relationship for McGowan's cost and tons-stored estimates and substituting in the appropriate number of tons to be stored, converting to 2008 dollars using the CPI. The estimate in McGowan is for three days of storage capacity, so the expression is divided by three and then multiplied by the number of days of storage capacity desired. This expression, after conversion to 2008 dollars, is as follows:

$$\frac{\left(960 + 13,600 \times \text{biomass tons per hour} \right) \times 1.67}{3} \times \text{biomass storage capacity}.$$

Both of these estimates assume a linearly increasing relationship between the amount of biomass to be stored and the cost of storage. This might overstate storage costs for large amounts of biomass.

Costs for enclosed storage buildings for pellets and bales are estimated from the CVBP case (Antares Group, 2009). A representative storage building costs $62,000 (converted to 2008 dollars from $53,000 in 2003 dollars using the CPI) and stores 520 tons of biomass. This can be scaled to the desired size using the scaling factor of 0.56 developed by Caputo et al. (2005) and used by De and Assadi (2009). The expression used to scale costs for enclosed storage buildings is as follows:

$$\text{new cost} = \$62,000 \times \left(\frac{\text{new capacity}}{\text{old capacity}} \right)^{0.56},$$

where

old capacity = 520 tons, as in the CVBP, and

new capacity = number of days of storage desired × hours per day × biomass tons per hour.

Costs to provide paved open storage for logs, chunks, and chips are estimated at $26 per ton by McGowan (2009).

Processing and Handling Stage 1, Part 3: Biomass Transfer

This is the cost of equipment to move biomass around the storage area and to transfer it onto the processing line. Again, the assumed equipment varies with biomass type. Front-end loaders are used for wood chunks and chips and pellets, as described in McGowan (2009). Bale loaders are used for bales. Because it is assumed that sawdust is stored in a silo equipped with a transfer line, no additional transfer equipment is required.

The cost for front-end loaders for pellets and wood chunk and chip transfer is estimated based on quotes in McGowan (2009). In McGowan (2009), costs are given for various plant capacities. The relationship of cost to plant capacity is not linear; at capacities below 12 tons per hour, the cost is less sensitive to capacity. For biomass requirements greater than 12 tons per hour, a linear relationship is constructed from the relevant data in McGowan. For plants using less than 12 tons per hour, a second linear relationship is derived using the data points from McGowan, 5 and 12.5 tons per hour. Substituting in the appropriate number of tons per hour into the linear relationship and converting to 2008 dollars using the CPI gives the estimated costs for front-end loaders. The relevant expressions, after conversion to 2008 dollars, are as follows:

For plants using less than 12 biomass tons/hour,

$1,722 \times$ biomass tons per hour $+ 25,800$.

For plants using more than 12 biomass tons/hour,

$5,330 \times$ biomass tons/hour $- 13,600$.

It is assumed that bale loaders are used to unload bales from trucks and place them in storage. The capital cost estimate for these loaders is taken from INL (2009), using its estimated costs for corn stover. INL (2009) estimates the cost to purchase Caterpillar TH220-B telehandlers for the purpose of transferring bales to the processing line, a cost it defines in terms of dollars per annual dry ton capacity. Thus, this bale-loader factor is multiplied by the annual ton capacity and multiplied by the fraction of dry mass to give the bale-loader cost. This is shown in the following expression, where the bale-loader preprocessing factor is the estimate in dollars per annual dry ton capacity from INL:

$$\text{bale-loader preprocessing factor} \times \text{biomass tons per hour}$$
$$\times (1 - \text{biomass moisture content}) \times \text{hours per year}.$$

Note that the cost of bale loaders to transfer biomass from storage to the processing line is different from the cost to unload trucks and transfer biomass into storage.

Processing and Handling Stage 2: Initial Processing for Large Biomass

In this stage, biomass that enters the plant as large units (chunks) is processed into smaller material, on the order of wood chips or pellets. This size reduction is applied to bales of herbaceous biomass and to wood chunks. Given the size reduction in this stage, it is assumed that all biomass types can be treated similarly in the third and final processing and handling stage. Capital costs for this second stage represent the equipment required for this initial size-reduction stage. Bales and wood chunks are treated differently, with the equipment and costs for bales based on the experience of the CVBP (Antares Group, 2009) and that for wood chunks based on descriptions in McGowan (2009). The following is a description of the cost-estimation process for each of the components.

Bales. *Bale Merge Conveyer.* This is the cost of a conveyer used to load bales into the processing and handling system. Bales are merged, sending forward one bale at a time.

The capital costs are based on the experience of the CVBP (Antares Group, 2009), a plant that was configured for approximately 10 tons per hour of biomass. Thus, it is assumed that an additional processing and handling line will be set up for each increment of 10 tons per hour. The Ceil function is used to calculate how many of these lines are required, returning the smallest integer that is greater than or equal to its argument. Thus, the following expression is used to calculate the cost, where "Bale merge cvbp" was the cost of this conveyer in the CVBP case.

$$\text{bale merge cvbp} \times \text{Ceil}\left(\frac{\text{biomass tons per hour}}{10}\right).$$

Note that this cost is based on that found in the CVBP for equipment used in its test fires. The cost of potential upgrades to this conveyer are grouped with upgrades to the bale infeed conveyer and are reflected in that node.

Bale Infeed Conveyer. This is the cost of a single-bale conveyer used to transport bales through the processing and handling system.

The capital costs are based on the experience of the CVBP (Antares Group, 2009) and is indexed over low, mid, and high estimates for this cost. The low-level cost is the cost of the unit used in the CVBP test fires. Two possible upgrades to the conveyer handling system are proposed in the CVBP documentation to help achieve commercial-level functionality. These are listed in Antares Group (2009, Appendix C). The lower-cost upgrade is added to the test-fire cost to estimate the midlevel cost, and the higher-cost upgrade is added to give the high-level cost. In both cases, the upgrade costs are converted to 2008 dollars using the CPI. Note that most of the possible upgrades to the conveyance system are grouped in this particular capital cost estimate.

The CVBP plant was configured for approximately 10 tons per hour of biomass. Thus, it is assumed that an additional processing and handling line will be set up for each increment of 10 tons per hour. The Ceil function is used to calculate how many of these lines are required, returning the smallest integer that is greater than or equal to its argument. Thus, the following expression is used to calculate the cost, where "bale infeed cvbp" is the cost of this conveyer in the CVBP case:

$$\text{bale infeed cvbp} \times \text{Ceil}\left(\frac{\text{biomass tons per hour}}{10}\right).$$

Moisture Meter. This is the cost of a meter to measure the moisture content of bales as they enter the processing line. Bales with high moisture contents are removed from the line.

The capital costs are based on the experience of the CVBP (Antares Group, 2009). Note that upgrades to the test-fire moisture meter are recommended in Appendix D of the Antares report but the cost of this replacement unit is the same as the test-fire unit's purchase price.

The CVBP plant was configured for approximately 10 tons per hour of biomass. Thus, it is assumed that an additional processing and handling line will be set up for each increment of 10 tons per hour. The Ceil function is used to calculate how many of these lines are required, returning the smallest integer that is greater than or equal to its argument. Thus, the following expression is used to calculate the cost, where "moisture meter cvbp" is the cost of this equipment in the CVBP case:

$$\text{moisture meter cvbp} \times \text{Ceil}\left(\frac{\text{biomass tons per hour}}{10}\right).$$

Bale Rejector. This is the cost of a conveyer to remove off-specification bales from the processing line.

The capital costs are based on the experience of the CVBP (Antares Group, 2009). The cost is estimated by the cost for the equipment used in the CVBP test fire. Note that upgrades to all of the conveyer systems are included in the bale infeed conveyer variable described earlier. The CVBP plant was configured for approximately 10 tons per hour of biomass. Thus, it is assumed that an additional processing and handling line will be set up for each increment of 10 tons per hour. The Ceil function is used to calculate how many of these lines are required, returning the smallest integer that is greater than or equal to its argument. Thus, the following expression is used to calculate the cost, where "bale rejector cvbp" is the cost of this conveyer in the CVBP case:

$$\text{bale rejector cvbp} \times \text{Ceil}\left(\frac{\text{biomass tons per hour}}{10}\right).$$

Destringer. This is the capital cost of the equipment used to remove the twine that binds bales.

The capital costs are based on the experience of the CVBP (Antares Group, 2009). The low-level cost is the cost of the test-fire system found in the CVBP. The other cost levels include modifications recommended for commercial operations, as listed in Appendix C in the Antares report. The midlevel cost adds costs for guards and controls. The high-level cost adds a second destringer.

The CVBP plant was configured for approximately 10 tons per hour of biomass. Thus, it is assumed that an additional processing and handling line will be set up for each increment of 10 tons per hour. The Ceil function is used to calculate how many of these lines are required, returning the smallest integer that is greater than or equal to its argument. Thus, the following expression is used to calculate the cost, where "destringer cvbp" is the cost of the destringer in the CVBP case:

$$\text{destringer cvbp} \times \text{Ceil}\left(\frac{\text{biomass tons per hour}}{10}\right).$$

Debaler. This is the cost of a hammer mill used to break bales into small pieces.

The capital costs are based on the experience of the CVBP (Antares Group, 2009). The low-level cost is the cost of the test-fire system found in the CVBP. The other cost levels include modifications recommended for commercial operations in Appendix C of the Antares report. The midlevel cost adds valves and plumbing. The high-level cost adds a second debaler to increase flexibility without providing extra capacity.

The CVBP plant was configured for approximately 10 tons per hour of biomass. Thus, it is assumed that an additional processing and handling line will be set up for each increment of 10 tons per hour. The Ceil function is used to calculate how many of these lines are required, returning the smallest integer that is greater than or equal to its argument. Thus, the following expression is used to calculate the cost, where "debaler cvbp" is the cost of the debaler in the CVBP case:

$$\text{debaler cvbp} \times \text{Ceil}\left(\frac{\text{biomass tons per hour}}{10}\right).$$

The total capital cost for the second stage of bale processing and handling is the sum of the above costs.

Wood Chunks. ***Drag Chain Conveyer.*** This is the cost of a drag chain conveyer that transfers raw wood to the processing line. Costs are derived from estimates in McGowan (2009). Capital costs are derived by finding a linear relationship for McGowan's cost and tons-processed-per-hour estimates, converting the slope and intercept values to 2008 dollars from 1982 dollars using the CPI, and substituting in the appropriate number of tons per hour into the linear relationship shown here converted into 2008 dollars:

$$biomass\ tons\ per\ hour \times 2,230 + 26,800.$$

Belt Conveyer. This is the cost of a belt conveyer to transfer biomass to processing equipment. Here, it is used to convey wood chunks through the initial processing stages. Costs are derived from estimates in McGowan (2009). Capital costs are derived by finding a linear relationship for McGowan's cost and tons-processed-per-hour estimates, converting the slope and intercept values to 2008 dollars from 1982 dollars using the CPI, and substituting the appropriate number of tons per hour into the linear expression here to arrive at the capital cost for the belt conveyer:

$$biomass\ tons\ per\ hour \times 412 + 120,000.$$

Disc Screen. This is the cost of a disc screen used in the processing of chunks of biomass. Pieces that are small enough to pass through the screen move along the handling line, whereas pieces that do not proceed to the hammer mill.

Costs are derived from estimates in McGowan (2009). Capital costs are derived by finding a linear relationship for McGowan's cost and tons-processed-per-hour estimates, converting the slope and intercept values to 2008 dollars from 1982 dollars using the CPI, and substituting the appropriate number of tons per hour into the linear relationship here to arrive at the capital cost for the disc screen:

$$biomass\ tons\ per\ hour \times 1,320 + 12,200.$$

Hammer Mill. This is the cost of a hammer mill used to reduce the size of wood chunks that do not pass through the disc screen. Costs are derived from estimates in McGowan (2009). Capital costs are derived by finding a linear relationship for McGowan's cost and tons-processed-per-hour estimates, converting the slope and intercept values to 2008 dollars from 1982 dollars using the CPI, and substituting the appropriate number of tons per hour into the linear relationship here to arrive at the capital cost for the hammer mill:

$$biomass\ tons\ per\ hour \times 2,340 + 35,200.$$

The total capital cost for the second stage of wood chunk processing and handling is the sum of these costs.

Processing and Handling Stage 3: Final Processing and Handling
Once the biomass meets size specifications, such as an appropriately sized wood chip or pellet, it can enter the final processing stage. It is assumed that, because of the homogeneity achieved in stage 2, all biomass can be treated similarly regardless of the form in which it originally entered the plant. Exceptions are noted in this section.

Two user-defined choices dominate the differences in assumed equipment and thus capital costs in this stage: boiler type and processing-line choice. The boiler types considered in this analysis are stoker-fired boilers, FB boilers, and PC boilers. Stoker-fired and FB boilers can handle relatively large fuel pieces, on the order of a wood chip or a pellet, and it is assumed that biomass entering this final processing stage is already appropriately sized to be fired in stoker boilers; thus, it is assumed that fuel needs only to be conveyed to the boiler in this third stage. In contrast, PC boilers require more–finely processed fuel, and biomass is further ground and then conveyed pneumatically to the boiler.

In addition, plants face a choice of whether to build a new processing line for the dedicated processing of biomass, to convert an existing coal line to dedicated biomass processing, or commingle biomass with coal for processing together on an existing coal line. Building a new line for the dedicated processing of biomass entails buying all new equipment for this stage of biomass processing. Making use of a commingled line or a modified line is assumed to require fewer purchases and lower capital costs. According to the experience at several cofiring plants, commingling biomass and coal together in preparation for a PC boiler is appropriate only for cofire ratios of less than 2-percent biomass by energy content (Hughes, 1998). The use of commingled lines for other boiler types is more flexible.

Processing and Handling Stage 3: Stoker-Fired and Fluidized-Bed Boilers

As described above, it is assumed that biomass entering the third stage of processing is of a suitable size to directly enter a stoker-fired or FB boiler. Thus, the only necessary equipment is a conveyer to transport the biomass to the boiler. In the case of a modified line or a commingled line where a previously established coal processing line is being used for the biomass, it is assumed that no additional capital is required to convey the biomass to the boiler; the existing equipment can be used. In the case in which a new dedicated biomass processing line is built, it is assumed that the only purchase required for this stage of processing and handling is a conveyer to deliver the biomass to the boiler. This cost is described in the next section.

Boiler Feed Conveyer. This is the cost of the conveyer that moves biomass into the boiler for stoker-fired and FB boilers.

Costs are derived from estimates in McGowan (2009). Capital costs are derived by finding a linear relationship for McGowan's cost and tons-processed-per-hour estimates, converting the slope and intercept values to 2008 dollars from 1982 dollars using the CPI, and substituting in the appropriate number of tons per hour to give the following linear expression for the conveyer cost:

$$\text{biomass tons per hour} \times 608 + 85{,}100.$$

Processing and Handling Stage 3: Pulverized-Coal Boilers

In the case of PC boilers, substantial additional processing and handling are required to reduce the biomass size and convey the smaller biomass to the boiler. The assumed necessary equipment is based primarily on the CVBP case (Antares Group, 2009), with additional sources used as described throughout this section. All of the assumed equipment for this final processing stage is indicated in this section for the new line case. The variations for the commingled and modified-line cases follow the new-line case descriptions.

New Line. *Outfeed Conveyer.* The final stage of biomass processing, in preparation for a PC boiler, begins with a conveyer to transport biomass from the previous processing stage (if any) to the fine hammer mill.

The cost is based on the cost for the outfeed conveyer at the CVBP (Antares Group, 2009). The CVBP plant was configured for approximately 10 tons per hour of biomass. Thus, it is assumed that an additional processing and handling line will be set up for each increment of 10 tons per hour. The Ceil function is used to calculate how many of these lines are required, returning the smallest integer that is greater than or equal to its argument. Thus, the following expression is used to calculate the cost, where "outfeed conveyer cvbp" is the cost of the outfeed conveyer in the CVBP case:

$$\text{outfeed conveyer cvbp} \times \text{Ceil}\left(\frac{\text{biomass tons per hour}}{10}\right).$$

Magnet. This is the cost of a magnet to screen for metal pieces before the biomass is pulverized.

The low and midlevel costs are the cost of the magnet used in the CVBP test fires (Antares Group, 2009). The mid- and high-level costs reflect suggested improvements for upgrading the CVBP system for commercial operation as noted in Appendix C of the Antares report. These costs are converted from 2006 dollars to 2008 dollars using the CPI.

The CVBP plant was configured for approximately 10 tons per hour of biomass. Thus, it is assumed that an additional processing and handling line will be set up for each increment of 10 tons per hour. The Ceil function is used to calculate how many of these lines are required, returning the smallest integer that is greater than or equal to its argument. Thus, the following expression is used to calculate the cost, where "magnet cvbp" was the cost of the magnet in the CVBP case:

$$\text{magnet cvbp} \times \text{Ceil}\left(\frac{\text{biomass tons per hour}}{10}\right).$$

Hammer Mill: Fine. This is the cost of the hammer mill used to process wood materials to the size required by a PC boiler.

The cost of this mill is based on the experience of the CVBP (Antares Group, 2009). In this case, the amount paid for the equipment for the CVBP test fire is higher than the estimated cost of an equipment upgrade. Thus, the low- and midlevel costs are the estimated costs of the hammer mills recommended for upgrade to commercial status in Antares Group (2009, Appendix C). The high-level amount is the cost for two of these hammer mills, with one of these available as a spare. Costs are converted from 2006 dollars to 2008 dollars using the CPI.

The CVBP plant was configured for approximately 10 tons per hour of biomass. Thus, it is assumed that an additional processing and handling line will be set up for each increment of 10 tons per hour. The Ceil function is used to calculate how many of these lines are required, returning the smallest integer that is greater than or equal to its argument. Thus, the following expression is used to calculate the cost, where "fine hammer mill cvbp" was the cost of the fine hammer mill in the CVBP case:

$$\text{fine hammer mill cvbp} \times \text{Ceil}\left(\frac{\text{biomass tons per hour}}{10}\right).$$

Screen. After passing through the hammer mill, the biomass is screened to ensure that it meets the size requirements. If it does not, it returns to the hammer mill. The cost of the screen is estimated using costs in McGowan (2009). Costs are derived by finding a linear relationship for McGowan's cost and tons-processed-per-hour estimates, converting the slope and intercept values to 2008 dollars from 1982 dollars using the CPI, and substituting the appropriate number of tons per hour into the following linear expression:

$$\text{biomass tons per hour} \times 1,315 + 12,200.$$

Baghouse. This is the cost of a baghouse used to separate fine particles from the larger particles so they can be conveyed separately into the surge bin.

This cost is based on the experience at the CVBP (Antares Group, 2009). The CVBP plant was configured for approximately 10 tons per hour of biomass. Thus, it is assumed that an additional processing and handling line will be set up for each increment of 10 tons per hour. The Ceil function is used to calculate how many of these lines are required, returning the smallest integer that is greater than or equal to its argument. Thus, the following expression is used to calculate the cost, where "baghouse cvbp" was the cost of the baghouse in the CVBP case:

$$\text{baghouse cvbp} \times \text{Ceil}\left(\frac{\text{biomass tons per hour}}{10}\right).$$

Baghouse Fan. This is the cost of a fan used to draw biomass from the fine hammer mill into the baghouse.

This cost is based on the experience at the CVBP (Antares Group, 2009). The CVBP plant was configured for approximately 10 tons per hour of biomass. Thus, it is assumed that an additional processing and handling line will be set up for each increment of 10 tons per hour. The Ceil function is used to calculate how many of these lines are required, returning the smallest integer that is greater than or equal to its argument. Thus, the following expression is used to calculate the cost, where "baghouse fan cvbp" was the cost of the baghouse fan in the CVBP case:

$$\text{baghouse fan cvbp} \times \text{Ceil}\left(\frac{\text{biomass tons per hour}}{10}\right).$$

Rotary Airlocks and Feeders. This is the cost of the rotary airlocks and feeders that move the processed biomass into the pneumatic transport system.

This cost is based on the experience at the CVBP (Antares Group, 2009). The low- and midlevel costs are the cost of the system used in the CVBP test fires. The high-level cost adds in the upgrade cost for purge lines. All costs are converted to 2008 dollars using the CPI.

The CVBP plant was configured for approximately 10 tons per hour of biomass. Thus, it is assumed that an additional processing and handling line will be set up for each increment of 10 tons per hour. The Ceil function is used to calculate how many of these lines are required, returning the smallest integer that is greater than or equal to its argument. Thus, the following expression is used to calculate the cost, where "airlocks feeder cvbp" was the cost of the rotary airlocks and feeders in the CVBP case:

$$\text{airlocks feeder cvbp} \times \text{Ceil}\left(\frac{\text{biomass tons per hour}}{10}\right).$$

Surge Bin. This is the cost of the bin to store pulverized biomass before transfer to the pneumatic transport system that conveys the biomass to the boiler.

This cost is based on the experience at the CVBP (Antares Group, 2009). The low and midlevel costs are approximated by the cost of the bin used by the CVBP in test fires. The high-level cost includes the costs of recommended upgrades as described in Antares Group (2009, Appendix C). These costs are converted to 2008 dollars using the CPI.

The CVBP plant was configured for approximately 10 tons per hour of biomass. Thus, it is assumed that an additional processing and handling line will be set up for each increment of 10 tons per hour. The Ceil function is used to calculate how many of these lines are required, returning the smallest integer that is greater than or equal to its argument. Thus, the following expression is used to calculate the cost, where "surge bin cvbp" was the cost of the surge bin in the CVBP case:

$$\text{surge bin cvbp} \times \text{Ceil}\left(\frac{\text{biomass tons per hour}}{10}\right).$$

Pneumatic Transport. This is the cost of a pneumatic system to transport biomass through the final stages of processing and to the boiler.

This cost is based on the experience at the CVBP (Antares Group, 2009). The midlevel cost is the cost of the system used in the CVBP test fires. The high-level cost adds in the costs for modifications to improve the system for commercial use (Antares Group, 2009, Appendix C). Two estimates for improvements are given; the lower of these two costs is used here because, if one were building the system from scratch, one would reduce costs by not building both the original system plus the improved system. It is possible that lower-priced systems could be developed if the processing and handling system were more tightly configured. We also assume the midlevel cost to be the same as the low-level cost in this case.

The CVBP plant was configured for approximately 10 tons per hour of biomass. Thus, it is assumed that an additional processing and handling line will be set up for each increment of 10 tons per hour. The Ceil function is used to calculate how many of these lines are required, returning the smallest integer that is greater than or equal to its argument. Thus, the following expression is used to calculate the cost, where "pneumatic transport cvbp" was the cost of the pneumatic transport system in the CVBP case:

$$\text{pneumatic transport cvbp} \times \text{Ceil}\left(\frac{\text{biomass tons per hour}}{10}\right).$$

It should be noted that the actual costs of a pneumatic system are unlikely to scale linearly with the fuel amount and are likely to be quite plant specific.

The total capital cost for a new, dedicated biomass processing and handling line is the sum of these costs.

Commingled Line. *Processing and Handling: Commingled Fuels.* This is the capital cost to modify an existing coal line to handle commingled coal and biomass. This is an alternative to a dedicated line for biomass processing and handling, whether a new line or a modified former coal line.

As described earlier, it is assumed that no substantial modifications to the line are required for stoker-fired and FB boilers and thus that additional costs accrue only for PC boilers. The costs are estimated using the empirical experience presented in Hughes (2000). The cost in Hughes is estimated as $50–100 per kilowatt of biomass energy generation. This cost will likely vary depending on the specific modification choices, as well as the type of biomass. The low-level estimate given here uses a capital cost of $50 per kilowatt, the midlevel estimate $75 per kilowatt, and the high-level estimate $100 per kilowatt. These values are converted to dollars per ton per hour and to 2008 dollars from 2000 dollars using the CPI.

As noted earlier, processing biomass and coal together for a PC boiler is appropriate only for cofire ratios of less than 2-percent biomass by energy content. Processing lines for other boiler types are more flexible (Hughes, 1998).

Modified Line. One final alternative processing-line choice considered in the cost model is to modify an existing coal processing line to act as a dedicated biomass processing line under cofiring. As described earlier, it is assumed that such a choice accrues no additional cost in the case of stoker-fired or FB boilers. In the case of PC boilers, the capital costs for such a case are assumed to be some combination of the equipment costs required for a new line and costs for a commingled line. A variety of approaches are possible. Here, it is assumed that, in assembling such a modified line, the plant will purchase a new magnet and hammer mill, as well as pay for additional line modifications. These additional modifications are estimated as a fraction of those required under the new-line scenario.

The costs for the magnet and fine hammer mill are assumed to be the same as those described under the new-line scenario earlier. Additional modifications are described in the next section.

Other Modifications. Aside from adding a magnet and purchasing a new hammer mill, it is assumed that other modifications will be needed to convert a coal processing line to a dedicated biomass line, modifications that are likely to be some fraction of the costs of adapting a line for commingled fuels. The relevant fraction is unknown and is estimated using a low value of 30 percent, a middle value of 50 percent, and a high value of 70 percent of the capital costs for commingled biomass. These values are provided through a commingling multiplier, and it is assumed that the range of values used covers a range of modifications that could be made by the plant.

The total capital costs for the modified-line scenario are calculated as the sum of the costs of magnet, fine hammer mill, and other modifications.

Other Capital Costs

Aside from the equipment costs associated with the form of biomass that is delivered to the plant and the type of boiler, there are other capital costs associated with biomass cofiring. These include facility and installation costs. Descriptions of these costs and the estimation strategies follow.

Facility Costs for New Equipment. When building a separate processing and handling line, a facility might not have adequate space. This is a cost estimate for modifications to an existing facility or the building of an additional facility.

It is expected that investments in a processing facility will be related to the amount of new equipment needed: Adding large amounts of equipment will require a larger facility and will reduce the likelihood of being able to modify the existing facility to include the new equipment.

It is assumed that new facility costs will scale with new equipment costs in a similar manner to how enclosed storage facility costs scale with storage capacity. Caputo et al. (2005) develop a scaling factor of 0.56 for storage facilities, based on values found in the literature.

The CVBP (Antares Group, 2009) gives a base cost of $484,000 for a new facility to process bales for a PC boiler. Thus, the costs of bale-processing equipment and equipment for processing for a PC boiler provide the base capital costs.

The facility costs for other equipment configurations are then estimated according to the following equation, as modified from Caputo et al. (2005) to suit our case:

$$\text{facility cost} = \$484,000 \times \left(\frac{\text{new equipment costs}}{\text{equipment costs for bale processing and pulverization}} \right)^{0.56}.$$

Costs Relevant to Installation Costs. These are the compiled costs used as a base to calculate installation costs. They consist of the facility costs and equipment costs for initial processing and final processing (stages 2 and 3). Note that installation costs for biomass-receiving equipment are included with the equipment costs and thus are not included here. In addition, it is assumed that costs listed for a commingled fuel line do not require additional installation, so these costs are also not included here.

Installation Costs. Installation costs are estimated at 50 percent of the equipment and facility costs represented in the variable for costs relevant to installation costs. This is consistent with the installation costs at the CVBP (Antares Group, 2009), which are approximately 54 percent of equipment and facility costs.

Total Capital Costs. The various capital costs from the three stages of the processing and handling are summed along with the facility and installation costs. They are then multiplied by a capital cost contingency factor to give total capital costs. This capital cost contingency factor is composed of an additional contingency of 25 percent that is added to the capital cost. This accounts for the low-definition design described in McGowan (2009). In the case of costs derived from the CVBP (Antares Group, 2009), the design was initially drawn together for test burns, and a commercial-level enterprise would likely require higher capital investment. This contingency factor also accounts for additional engineering and project-management costs. This contingency factor can be modified by the user.

Annual Capital Costs. This is the annual payment for capital. It is assumed that all financing occurs through debt financing at the capital charge rate. It is based on equal monthly payments made over the amortization period. Note that these costs do not take into consideration the effects of taxes and depreciation. They are calculated by the Analytica function "Pmt" given the capital charge rate, the amortization period, and the total capital costs to be paid.

Operating Costs of Cofiring

In addition to fuel and capital costs, a cofiring plant will accrue additional operating costs associated with the processing and handling of biomass. Along with maintenance and labor costs, there are costs associated with the use of energy to process and handle the biomass. In the cost

Table B.2
Operating Parameters and Values

Parameter	Brief Comments	Value	Reference
Operating costs, coal plants	$/MWh	Stoker: 5.4 FB: 7.1 PC: 5.4	Ventyx (date unknown); MIT (2007); NCC (2004)
Operating-cost parameter, biomass receipt and transfer	$/dry ton biomass	0.27	INL (2009)
Labor parameter	$/ton of biomass/million dollars in capital costs	6.5	Antares Group (2009)
Maintenance parameter	$/ton/million dollars in capital costs	Low: 0.58 Mid: 0.68 High: 0.68	Antares Group (2009); Caputo et al. (2005)
Other operating-cost parameter	$/ton/million dollars in capital costs	Low: 0.37 Mid: 0.37 High: 0.45	Antares Group (2009); Caputo et al. (2005)

NOTE: MIT = Massachusetts Institute of Technology.

Table B.3
Energy-Use Parameters and Values

Parameter	Brief Comments	Value	Reference
Parasitic load	Fraction of net generation	Stoker fired: 0.081 FB: 0.092 PC: 0.081	Ventyx (date unknown)
Energy use, biomass receipt and transfer	Btu/dry ton biomass	9,900	INL (2009)
Electricity for coarse milling	kWh/ton biomass	Chunks: 13.6 Bales, low: 10.4 Bales, mid: 12.2 Bales, high: 20.0	Van Loo and Koppejan (2008); Antares Group (2009)
Electricity for fine milling (pulverization)	kWh/ton biomass	Chunks and chips: 36.3 Sawdust, bales, pellets, low: 21 Sawdust, bales, pellets, mid: 23 Sawdust, bales, pellets, high: 30	Van Loo and Koppejan (2008); Antares Group (2009)
CVBP nonmill electricity use	kWh/ton biomass	Low: 12.7 Mid: 13.6 High: 8.1	Antares Group (2009)
Electricity for pneumatic transport	kWh/ton biomass	0.6 × CVBP nonmill electricity use	Antares Group (2009)
Electricity for baghouse	kWh/ton biomass	0.16 × CVBP nonmill electricity use	Antares Group (2009)

model, this electricity used is calculated separately from the gross electricity generated by the plant, with the electricity used considered as a cost.

Some of the operational cost parameters are indicated in Table B.2. Some of the energy-use parameters are indicated in Table B.3. For more-extensive descriptions of these values, as well as other calculations, see the details of each variable in this section.

Operating costs for the both the coal and biomass portions of the fuel use are discussed in the next section.

Operating Costs for Coal

Operating costs for coal are composed of coal-associated O&M costs, as well as the electricity cost associated with coal processing and handling. The estimation methods for these components are described in this section.

Coal Operating and Maintenance Costs. These are the O&M costs for plants firing coal only. They include all fixed and variable operating costs other than the cost of coal.

The estimates of these costs begin with total nonfuel O&M costs as modeled for coal plants by the Velocity database for operating plants in the month of February 2010 (Ventyx, date unknown). A weighted average over net generation is calculated after removing outliers (zero and negative values, as well as plants with operating costs in excess of $100 per megawatt-hour). The value is based on the weighted average over all plants and is converted from 2010 dollars to 2008 dollars using the CPI.

The vast majority of coal plants in the Velocity database use PC technology. For FB and stoker-fired plants, most are missing key data, making calculating operating costs for these boiler types infeasible based on the data from the Velocity database. Some information on operating costs for FB boilers is provided in an MIT (2007) report. The MIT authors standardize a value estimated by the NCC (2004) to meet their economic and operating assumptions, arriving at operating costs of $11.5 per megawatt-hour in 2008 dollars. However, the MIT/NCC estimates are likely higher than might be true for the existing fleet. For example, the MIT/NCC estimated operating cost for PC boilers is at the high end of what is estimated by the Velocity database model of existing plants. This is likely because the MIT study is making estimations for new plants and for plants with more-stringent environmental controls than are currently the norm. For PC plants, the MIT/NCC value is $8.7 per megawatt-hour, as opposed to the Velocity database estimate of $5.4 per megawatt-hour. Thus, the value for FB plants is estimated by taking the MIT/NCC value of $11.5 per megawatt-hour and multiplying it by a factor (5.4/8.7) to approximately convert to the Velocity standard. The value is also converted to 2008 dollars using the CPI.

Operating costs for stoker-fired boilers are not available. It is assumed that they are the same as for PC boilers.

These cost parameters are expressed in terms of dollars per megawatt-hour of net generation. They are converted to dollars per mmBtu of fuel input for further calculations in the model.

Coal Electricity Cost. This is the cost of the electricity used for the coal portion of the plant's operations. It is calculated by first determining the electricity use for the coal portion of the plant processing and handling and multiplying it by the price of electricity.

The parasitic load, or the amount of electricity used internally by coal plants, is first estimated as a fraction of the net electricity produced by the plant. It is based on modeled data from Ventyx's Velocity database for operating coal plants in February 2010 (Ventyx, date unknown). The database provides modeled estimates of net and gross generation. The estimates reported for the parasitic load fraction are

$$\frac{\text{gross generation} - \text{net generation}}{\text{net generation}}.$$

The value for PC plants is based on the modeled values for PC plants from the Ventyx database. The estimate uses the sum of net and gross generation over all PC plants.

There are few FB plants that have estimated values in the Ventyx database, but the values for these plants are relatively consistent. The estimated value presented here uses the sum of net and gross generation over all FB plants to calculate the fraction of net generation used internally as discussed earlier.

The database does not provide sufficient information for stoker-fired systems. It is assumed that these plants have the same internal electricity use as the PC systems.

The parasitic load is then converted into coal electricity use by converting it into

$$\frac{\text{MWh electricity use}}{\text{mmBtu coal energy input}}$$

according to the following expression:

$$\text{coal electricity use} = \text{parasitic load} \times \frac{1}{\text{heat rate for coal-only firing}} \times \frac{1}{\text{kWh per MWh}}$$
$$\times \text{Btu/mmBtu}.$$

The coal electricity use can then be multiplied by the price of electricity to give the coal electricity cost.

Total nonfuel coal O&M costs (per mmBtu of coal fuel use) are calculated by summing coal O&M costs and coal electricity costs.

Operating Costs for Biomass

These are the operating costs per mmBtu of biomass fuel. They include maintenance, labor, and electricity-use costs, as well as other miscellaneous costs, such as insurance. The estimation methods for these components are described in this section.

Capital Cost Base for Operating Costs. Many of the operating costs are calculated as a function of capital costs for processing and handling. These are those capital costs. Regardless of the processing-line type, the capital cost basis to calculate operating costs is the cost for new-line equipment. New-line capital costs are used because these costs include all equipment used for processing. It is assumed that operating costs vary with the types of equipment through which biomass must pass and not with whether this equipment is new, modified, or primarily a coal line.

The capital cost basis is composed of the summed capital cost for biomass processing and handling equipment. The costs of storage facilities, installation, and the contingency factor are not included. Equipment to receive biomass is not included because O&M costs are calculated separately for these components.

This capital cost base is used to aid in the calculation of labor, maintenance, and other operational costs.

Labor Cost: Biomass. This is the price of labor for the biomass component of cofiring, expressed in dollars per mmBtu biomass fuel input.

The estimation process begins by calculating the repair and maintenance cost per ton of biomass fuel per million dollars in capital costs based on information on the cost of labor in the final month of the CVBP long-term test burn (Antares Group, 2009), converted to 2008 dollars using the CPI. It is assumed that labor costs per ton of biomass are linearly related to amount of capital investment. Thus, there is a fixed estimate for labor costs per ton of biomass fuel per million dollars in capital investment.

To estimate the labor cost per mmBtu biomass fuel input, the parameter is multiplied by the capital cost basis for calculating operating costs and converted to dollars per energy unit by dividing by the green energy content by tonnage.

Note that this estimate is based on experience with bales; it is assumed that costs for other types of biomass will scale similarly. It is also assumed that labor costs per ton of biomass fuel per million dollars in capital equipment investment are constant.

Maintenance Cost: Biomass. This is the cost for repair and maintenance of the equipment related to biomass at the plant. Note that maintenance for equipment for biomass receipt at the plant is dealt with separately.

The estimation process begins by calculating the labor cost per ton of biomass fuel per million dollars in capital costs. One estimate of this cost is based on the cost of repair and maintenance in the final month of the CVBP long-term test burn (Antares Group, 2009). Here, it is assumed that repair and maintenance costs per ton of biomass are linearly related to amount of capital investment. Thus, there is a fixed estimate per ton of biomass fuel per million dollars in capital investment. To calculate this value, the repair and maintenance costs quoted in the CVBP are converted to 2008 dollars using the CPI, then divided by the number of tons processed during this period and by the capital costs (in millions of dollars) for equipment (not including storage, receiving, or installation). This value is $0.58 per ton per million dollars in capital costs.

The estimate of maintenance costs is similar to that in Caputo et al. (2005). Caputo and his colleagues estimate maintenance costs as 1.5 percent of the capital costs. Using a value of roughly 22,000 tons of biomass per year, this factor translates to $0.68 per ton per million dollars in capital investment.

Over the long term, there are likely to be larger-ticket items that need to be repaired and maintained than are represented in the CVBP estimate. Thus, the CVBP estimate is used as the low-level estimate and the Caputo et al. estimate is used for the mid- and high-level estimates.

To estimate the maintenance cost per mmBtu biomass fuel input, the estimated parameter for coal is multiplied by the capital cost base for calculating operating costs and converted to dollars per energy unit by dividing by the green energy content by tonnage.

Other Operational Costs: Biomass. These are the miscellaneous operating costs related to biomass at the plant. These costs include insurance, utilities (other than electricity), and building-lease payments.

The estimation process begins by calculating the cost per ton of biomass fuel per million dollars in capital costs. One estimate of these costs is based on the utilities and other costs (with electricity subtracted) in the final month of the CVBP long-term test burn (Antares Group,

2009, Appendix D), converted to 2008 dollars using the CPI. It is assumed that miscellaneous operating costs per ton of biomass are linearly related to the amount of capital investment. Thus, there is a fixed estimate per ton of biomass fuel per million dollars in capital investment. To calculate this value, the costs for telephone, insurance, lease, and water quoted in the CVBP are converted to 2008 dollars and divided by the number of tons processed during this period and by the capital costs (in millions), not including biomass receiving (dealt with separately) or installation capital costs. This value is $0.37 per ton per million dollars in capital costs.

This estimate is roughly similar to that in Caputo et al. (2005). Caputo and his colleagues estimate insurance and general costs as a factor of 0.01 of the capital costs. Using a value of roughly 22,000 tons of biomass per year, this factor translates to $0.45 per ton per million dollars in capital investment.

The CVBP estimate is used for the low- and midlevel estimates because it is based directly on plant experience. The Caputo et al. (2005) estimate is used for the high-level estimate.

To estimate the other operational costs per mmBtu biomass fuel input, this parameter is multiplied by the capital cost base (here including storage facilities) and converted to dollars per energy unit by dividing by the green energy content by tonnage.

Note that, unlike the other types of operational costs, the capital cost basis includes storage facility costs. Storage costs are included here because storage facilities require these other operational cost expenditures, such as insurance.

Operating Costs for Receipt and Transfer: Biomass

These are the operating costs for receiving delivery of biomass from trucks, transferring it into storage, and then moving it from storage to the processing line. These costs include repairs, maintenance, fuel, and consumables; thus, energy costs are included. Nonlabor operating costs are used because labor costs are contained in the labor parameter.

Although these costs are expected to vary depending on the methods used and the type of biomass, the costs here are estimated based on figures that INL (2009) quote for bale receipt and transfer using bale loaders. These costs are expected to be representative.

The estimate from INL is defined in terms of dollars per dry ton. It is converted to dollars per mmBtu by dividing by the dry biomass energy content in mmBtu per ton.

Biomass Electricity Costs. This is the cost of the electricity used for the biomass portion of the plant's operations. It is calculated by first determining the electricity use for processing and handling and multiplying that by the price of electricity. Fuel use for receipt and transfer is included in the variable for operating costs for receipt and transfer of biomass. Thus, electricity use for the second (initial processing of large biomass) and third (final processing and handling) stages of processing and handling are included here.

Electricity-use estimates are based primarily on the experience of the CVBP (Antares Group, 2009). In the Antares report, empirical data on energy expenditures or the share of electricity use for key pieces of equipment is documented. This information is used to estimate electricity draws for the specific equipment required given user-defined choice of boiler type and the biomass type received at the plant. The assumed equipment required by these choices is delineated under "Capital Cost Base for Operating Costs" earlier in this section. Electricity use is based on the equipment assumed for the "new processing line" case because it is assumed that electricity use will vary primarily with the processing steps and equipment required and not by whether biomass is processed on a dedicated line or commingled with coal.

Biomass electricity for preprocessing is the equivalent of the electricity required for the second stage of processing and handling, the initial processing of large biomass. It thus applies only to bales and wood chunks. It is the sum of two pieces: electricity for coarse milling and electricity for other preprocessing equipment.

Biomass electricity for processing and handling is the equivalent of the electricity required for the third stage: final processing and handling of biomass. Again, this estimate is based on the relevant equipment, given the scenario choices made by the user. Electricity use for processing and handling for a PC boiler is the sum of the electricity use of several components: electricity for pulverization, electricity for baghouse, electricity for pneumatic transport, and electricity for other PC equipment. By contrast, processing electricity for non-PC boilers comprises only the electricity draw of a boiler feed conveyer. This is described in more detail in the section on processing electricity for non-PC boilers.

Biomass Electricity: Preprocessing

Electricity for Coarse Milling. This is the electricity required to reduce the size of bales and wood chunks into pieces appropriate for further processing, a size on the scale of wood chips or pellets.

The value for wood chunks is the estimated energy consumption for breaking or chipping as listed in Van Loo and Koppejan (2008). The value in Van Loo and Koppejan is converted from kilowatt-hours per green metric ton to kilowatt-hours per short ton for use in the model.

The values for bales are taken from the experience of the CVBP (Antares Group, 2009). The midlevel estimate is the reported average power consumption of the debaler, or coarse hammer mill. The electricity use varies with moisture content; however, this relationship is nonlinear, and the relationship is difficult to parameterize. Thus, the low and high values used in the model represent low (8–9 percent) and high (20–21 percent) biomass moisture contents, respectively.

Electricity: Other Preprocessing Equipment. This is the electricity use for ancillary equipment used in the initial preprocessing of biomass. It is estimated based on a factor of the capital cost, assuming that, in general, the more equipment required to process fuel, the more electricity will be required.

The electricity use for all equipment other than the primary power draws (mills, pneumatic transport system, and baghouse) are estimated using an electricity multiplier for other equipment.

This is a multiplier used to estimate electricity use by such equipment as conveyers and lights. Because data are unavailable on electricity use for this relatively low–energy draw equipment, energy consumption is estimated based on a factor of the capital cost, assuming that, in general, the higher the cost of the equipment required to process fuel (based on new equipment cost), the more electricity will be required. The electricity draw for this equipment is relatively small, so the simplifications present in this estimation strategy should not dramatically alter the estimates of overall electricity use.

This multiplier is based on the experience of the CVBP (Antares Group, 2009). On average, 49 kWh per ton were required for bale processing and handling. Of the electricity draw used for purposes other than milling, ancillary equipment uses 24 percent of the remaining installed load and is thus estimated to constitute 24 percent of the power draw after the power use by the mills is subtracted in the case of the CVBP. Note that the proportions of electrical use are based on installed load, which is used as an estimate of the in-use load.

Once the per-ton power requirement for this ancillary equipment is calculated, the multiplier is estimated by dividing this power requirement by the capital cost of this equipment, giving a multiplier with units of

$$\frac{\text{kWh}}{\text{ton biomass} \times \$ \text{ of capital cost}}.$$

The equipment used to calculate this multiplier includes all conveyer, destringer, magnet, and other ancillary equipment; this equipment is listed in both the initial processing of bales and pulverization nodes of the capital costs.

This electricity multiplier for other equipment is multiplied by the relevant equipment costs: nonmilling capital for preprocessing. These are the capital costs for the equipment required for initial processing, not including milling equipment. Multiplying the relevant capital costs by the multiplier gives the estimate of electricity for other preprocessing equipment.

Chariton Valley Biomass Project Nonmill Electricity Use. The estimates of ancillary equipment power usage are based on this figure. It is the electricity used for processing and handling baled biomass at the CVBP (Antares Group, 2009) aside from electricity used for milling. The Antares report gives low, average, and high values for total electricity used in processing and handling, as well as the low, average, and high values for the equipment that has the highest power draw: the two types of mills (for coarse milling and pulverization). At each of the high, mid, and low levels, this nonmill electricity use is the difference between total power use and that used by the two mills. Note that the midlevel is greater than the low, which is greater than the high. This is because, in the CVBP electricity-use data, in the high-level case, the mills use a disproportionately high share of the electricity.

The total biomass electricity for preprocessing is the sum of electricity for coarse milling and electricity for other preprocessing equipment.

Biomass Electricity: Processing and Handling for the Boiler. Estimates for the electricity use for this stage of processing depend greatly on the type of boiler at the plant site. Estimates in preparation for both non-PC and PC boilers are described in this section.

Processing Electricity for Non–Pulverized Coal Boilers. In the case of stoker-fired and FB boilers, electricity use for this third processing and handling stage consists solely of the electricity estimate for the boiler feed conveyer. The capital cost for this conveyer is multiplied by the electricity multiplier for other equipment (described earlier) to give the electricity-use estimate, in a similar fashion to the estimation of electricity for other preprocessing equipment described earlier.

Estimating processing electricity for PC boilers is a more complex calculation because there are more pieces of equipment involved. The description follows.

Electricity for Pulverization. This is the electricity required to reduce the size of biomass fuel for use in a PC boiler in units of kilowatt-hours per ton biomass.

The electricity demand in the case of wood chips and chunks is the estimated energy consumption to pulverize biomass as listed in Van Loo and Koppejan (2008). These values are converted from kilowatt-hours per tonne to kilowatt-hours per short ton for use in the model.

The values for bales are taken from the experience of the CVBP (Antares Group, 2009). The midlevel estimate is the average power consumption of the "eliminator" hammer mill. The electricity use varies with moisture content; however, this relationship is nonlinear, and the relationship is difficult to parameterize. Thus in addition to the midlevel value, low and high values are given here, representing low (8–9 percent) and high (20–21 percent) moisture content, respectively.

Because pellets are relatively dry, they are assigned the same (lower) values as bales. Because sawdust is already relatively fine, it is also assigned these lower values.

Electricity for the Baghouse. This is the electricity required for a baghouse in the processing and handling line in kilowatt-hours per ton biomass.

It is estimated based on power use values from the experience of the CVBP (Antares Group, 2009). The Antares report gives low, average, and high values for total electricity used in processing and handling, as well as the low, average, and high values for the equipment that has the highest power draw: the two types of mills (for coarse milling and pulverization). Of the electricity draw used for purposes other than milling, baghouse fans constitute 16 percent of the installed load and are thus calculated as 16 percent of the power draw after the power use by the two mills is subtracted. Note that the relative use by the baghouse fans is based on installed load; installed load is used as an estimate of the in-use load.

Electricity for Pneumatic Transport. This is the electricity required for a pneumatic transport system for biomass fuel in kilowatt-hours per ton biomass. A pneumatic transport system is assumed for plants with a PC boiler.

This electricity demand is estimated based on power-use values from the experience of the CVBP with bale processing (Antares Group, 2009). The Antares report gives low, average, and high values for total electricity used in processing and handling, as well as the low, average, and high values for the equipment that has the highest power draw: the two types of mills (for coarse milling and fine milling). Of the electricity draw used for purposes other than milling, blowers and airlocks for the pneumatic system constitute 60 percent of the installed load and are thus calculated as 60 percent of the power draw after the power use by the mills is subtracted. Note that the relative use by the pneumatic system is based on installed load, which is used as an estimate of the in-use load.

Electricity: Other Pulverized-Coal Equipment. This is the estimate of electricity consumption of ancillary equipment used to prepare biomass for use in a PC boiler.

The electricity use for ancillary equipment (equipment other than mills, pneumatic transport, and baghouse) is estimated based on a factor of the capital cost, assuming that, in general, the more equipment required to process fuel, the more electricity will be required. Thus, as in the other equipment cases described earlier, this electricity use is estimated by multiplying the capital cost for this ancillary equipment by the electricity multiplier for other equipment, described earlier. In this case, ancillary equipment includes the outfeed conveyer, magnet, screen, and surge bin.

Electricity use for this third stage, in the case of a PC boiler, is the sum of electricity for pulverization, electricity for the baghouse, electricity for pneumatic transport, and electricity for other PC equipment.

The estimated electricity use from the second and third processing stages are summed to give the per-ton electricity demand for biomass processing. This is multiplied by the price of electricity to give the electricity cost per ton biomass and then divided by the energy content per green ton to give the cost of electricity per mmBtu biomass.

Total Operational Costs

The total nonfuel biomass operational costs (in dollars per mmBtu) are the sum of operating costs for receipt and transfer, labor cost for biomass, maintenance cost for biomass, other operational costs, and cost of electricity per mmBtu biomass.

Annual coal operating costs and annual biomass operating costs are calculated by taking coal tons per year and biomass tons per year, respectively, converting to energy units by dividing by the energy content, and multiplying by the appropriate operating cost.

The total annual operating costs are then the sum of annual coal operating costs and annual biomass operating costs. The annual change in operating costs (as opposed to the case of firing coal only) is the difference between operating costs under cofiring and operating costs with 100-percent coal use and is calculated using the following expression:

$$\text{annual operating costs} - \left(\begin{array}{l} \text{total tons per hour coal-only firing} \\ \times \text{hours per year} \times \text{boiler capacity factor} \\ \times \text{coal energy content} \times \text{total nonfuel coal O\&M costs} \end{array} \right).$$

Higher-Order Objectives

Using the estimates for fuel costs, capital costs, and operating costs, some key objective values can be calculated for use in evaluating cofiring scenarios. These higher-order objectives are described in this section, along with other high-order scenario considerations.

Total Annual Cost

This is the total annual cost under cofiring. It includes fuel costs, amortized capital costs, and operational costs.

Note that electrical costs are included as an operational cost. In practice, the electricity used to operate the plant is likely to be generated within the plant and thus simply lead to a decrease in the net electricity that can be sold on the market.

Change in Annual Cost

This is the difference between the total annual cost of cofiring and the annual cost of firing with coal. It includes fuel costs, amortized capital costs, and operational costs. A positive value implies that costs under cofiring are greater than costs under coal firing.

Note that electrical costs are included as an operational cost. In practice, the electricity used to operate the plant is likely to be generated within the plant and thus simply lead to a decrease in the net electricity that can be sold on the market.

Gross Annual Electricity Generation: Cofiring (megawatt-hours per year)

This is the gross amount of electricity generated by the plant under cofiring with biomass. If the system capacity is based on a fixed heat input assumption (heat input under cofiring is the same as under coal-only firing), this will be approximately the same as the value for coal-only firing. However, if there is a fixed mass input assumption in place, then the electricity value under cofiring is lower than the coal-only value because biomass has a lower energy content per ton. The value is calculated according to the following expression:

$$\text{heat input per hour} \times \left(\frac{1}{\text{heat rate under cofiring}} \right)$$

$$\times \text{Btu per mmBtu} \times \frac{1}{\text{kWh per MWh}}$$

$$\times \text{boiler capacity factor} \times \text{hours per year.}$$

Net Annual Power Generation: Biomass (megawatt-hours per year)

This is the net annual power generation from biomass sources. It is calculated by subtracting the annual energy demand for biomass (for processing and handling) from the gross annual electricity generated from biomass. This gross annual electricity generated from biomass sources is calculated by multiplying the gross annual electricity generation from cofiring by the cofiring fraction.

Annual Electricity Value: Coal Firing Only

This is the annual value of electricity generated by the plant under coal-only firing.

Note that this node represents the value of all electricity generated, not just the electricity that is sold on the market. The costs of electricity to process and handle fuel are noted under operational costs. The net value of the electricity generated would subtract these processing and handling electrical requirements.

Annual Electricity Value: Cofiring

This is the annual value of gross electricity generated by the plant under cofiring with biomass. If system capacity is based on a fixed heat input assumption (heat input under cofiring is the same as under coal-only firing), this will be approximately the same as the value for coal-only firing. However, if there is a fixed mass input assumption in place (fuel mass under cofiring is the same as under coal-only firing), then the electricity value under cofiring is lower than the coal-only value because biomass has a lower energy content per ton.

Note that this node represents the value of the gross electricity generated. The costs of electricity to process and handle fuel are noted under operational costs. The net value of the electricity generated would subtract these processing and handling energy requirements.

Direct Costs of Cofiring

This is the cost of producing a unit of cofired electricity. It is assumed that capital expenses are associated only with cofiring and that all capital costs associated with the coal plant are fully amortized.

It is calculated by dividing total annual costs by gross annual electricity generation from cofiring. To convert to dollars per kilowatt-hour, the value is also divided by 1,000 kWh per megawatt-hour.

Direct Costs of Firing Biomass

This is the direct cost of producing electricity with biomass via cofiring. It is defined as the total costs of cofiring divided by the net generation attributed to biomass (net annual power generation from biomass).

Subsidies for Biomass Firing

The model includes the possibility of incorporating a user-defined subsidy for biomass cofiring. The subsidy amount is then the net power generated from biomass multiplied by the biomass subsidy per energy unit.

Annual Profits: Cofiring

These are the estimated annual profits for a plant that is cofiring. It is defined through the following expression:

annual electricity value from cofiring + subsidies for biomass firing − total annual cost.

Change in Annual Profits

This is the difference between annual profits under cofiring and annual profits when firing all coal. A negative value implies that profits under cofiring are lower than profits under coal firing. It is defined according to the following expression:

annual electricity value from cofiring + subsidies for biomass firing

−annual electricity value from coal firing − change in annual cost.

Implied Renewable-Energy Credit Price

This is the price that must be offered for a REC on a dollars-per-kilowatt-hour basis for the plant to recover the costs and lost revenues associated with cofiring biomass. The value is defined by the following expression:

$$\frac{-\text{change in annual profits}}{\text{net annual power generation from biomass} \times \text{kWh per MWh}}.$$

State Summaries of Biomass Use and Potential Demand

Existing Biomass and Cofiring Power Plants

Existing dedicated biomass power plants in the United States are typically concentrated in the pulp and paper industry and have capacities less than 100 MW. Biomass power plants experienced a period of rapid construction in the 1980s, growing from a capacity of 280 MW in 1980 to nearly 1,500 MW in 1990 (ORNL, 2010). A U.S. total of 2,310 MW of biomass power plants was characterized in 2006 in the Biomass Energy Data Book (ORNL, 2010), as listed in Table C.1.

Table C.1
Existing Biomass Power Plants

State	Plant	Capacity (MW)	Heat Rate (Btu/kWh)	Cogeneration Facility	On-Line Year
Ala.	Ala. Pine Pulp	32.09	15,826	Yes	1991
Ariz.	APS Biomass I	2.85	8,911	No	2006
Ark.	Century Flooring Co.	1.70	15,826	Yes	1980
Ark.	Potlatch Southern Wood Products	10.00	15,826	Yes	1991
Ark.	STEC-S LLC	2.00	10,265	Yes	1997
Calif.	Pacific Lumber	7.50	15,826	Yes	1938
Calif.	Diamond Walnut	4.20	15,826	Yes	1981
Calif.	Wheelabrator Martell	15.00	15,826	Yes	1985
Calif.	Pacific Oroville Power	8.25	20,081	No	1985
Calif.	Pacific Oroville Power	8.25	20,081	No	1985
Calif.	Mt. Lassen Power	10.50	19,607	No	1985
Calif.	Sierra Pacific Susanville	12.60	15,826	Yes	1985
Calif.	Collins Pine Project	9.80	15,826	Yes	1985
Calif.	Burney Mountain Power	9.75	18,938	No	1985
Calif.	Sierra Power	7.00	15,826	Yes	1985
Calif.	Ultrapower Chinese Station	19.80	20,111	No	1985

Table C.1—Continued

State	Plant	Capacity (MW)	Heat Rate (Btu/kWh)	Cogeneration Facility	On-Line Year
Calif.	Fairhaven Power	17.30	21,020	No	1986
Calif.	Sierra Pacific Quincy Facility	14.50	15,826	Yes	1986
Calif.	Sierra Pacific Quincy Facility	14.50	15,826	Yes	1986
Calif.	Sierra Pacific Burney Facility	18.00	15,826	Yes	1986
Calif.	Wheelabrator Shasta	17.30	19,254	No	1987
Calif.	Wheelabrator Shasta	17.30	19,254	No	1987
Calif.	Wheelabrator Shasta	17.30	19,254	No	1987
Calif.	Rio Bravo Fresno	24.30	18,456	No	1988
Calif.	Pacific Lumber	8.67	15,826	Yes	1988
Calif.	Pacific Lumber	8.67	15,826	Yes	1988
Calif.	Pacific Lumber	8.67	15,826	Yes	1988
Calif.	Wadham Energy	25.50	12,637	No	1989
Calif.	AES Mendota	25.00	17,874	No	1989
Calif.	HL Power	30.00	14,944	No	1989
Calif.	Rio Bravo Rocklin	24.40	16,645	No	1989
Calif.	Burney Forest Products	15.50	16,350	Yes	1989
Calif.	Burney Forest Products	15.50	16,350	Yes	1989
Calif.	Sierra Pacific Loyalton Facility	14.00	15,826	Yes	1989
Calif.	Woodland Biomass Power Ltd.	25.00	15,302	No	1989
Calif.	Delano Energy	27.00	17,237	No	1990
Calif.	Tracy Biomass	16.46	17,342	No	1990
Calif.	Mecca Plant	23.50	14,158	No	1991
Calif.	Mecca Plant	23.50	14,158	No	1991
Calif.	Delano Energy	22.00	17,237	No	1993
Calif.	Sierra Pacific Lincoln Facility	5.60	15,826	Yes	1997
Calif.	Sierra Pacific Lincoln Facility	5.60	15,826	Yes	1997
Calif.	Sierra Pacific Anderson Facility	4.00	15,826	Yes	1999
Calif.	Wheelabrator Shasta	3.50	19,254	No	2000

Table C.1—Continued

State	Plant	Capacity (MW)	Heat Rate (Btu/kWh)	Cogeneration Facility	On-Line Year
Calif.	Sierra Pacific Lincoln Facility	18.00	15,826	Yes	2004
Calif.	Puente Hills Energy Recovery	8.00	8,911	No	2005
Fla.	Bryant Sugar House	6.63	15,826	Yes	1962
Fla.	Bryant Sugar House	6.63	15,826	Yes	1962
Fla.	Bryant Sugar House	6.63	15,826	Yes	1962
Fla.	Bryant Sugar House	6.63	15,826	Yes	1962
Fla.	DG Telogia Power	12.50	21,020	No	1986
Fla.	Jefferson Power LLC	7.50	16,258	No	1990
Fla.	Ridge Generating Station	47.10	21,020	No	1994
Fla.	Okeelanta Cogeneration	24.97	13,600	Yes	1996
Fla.	Okeelanta Cogeneration	24.97	13,600	Yes	1996
Fla.	Okeelanta Cogeneration	24.97	13,600	Yes	1996
Fla.	Buckeye Fla.	25.00	8,911	No	2006
Ga.	Port Wentworth	21.60	15,826	Yes	1991
Idaho	Plummer Forest Products	5.77	15,000	Yes	1982
Idaho	Tamarack Energy Partnership	5.80	9,650	Yes	1983
Ky.	Cox Waste to Energy	3.00	15,826	Yes	1995
Ky.	Cox Waste to Energy	0.30	15,826	Yes	2002
La.	Agrilectric Power Partners Ltd.	10.90	17,327	No	1984
La.	Agrilectric Power Partners Ltd.	1.30	17,327	No	1995
Maine	East Millinocket Mill	19.04	15,826	Yes	1954
Maine	Somerset Plant	34.23	15,826	Yes	1976
Maine	Forster Strong Mill	0.35	15,826	Yes	1980
Maine	S. D. Warren Somerset	26.875	15,826.23	No	1982
Maine	Wheelabrator Sherman Energy Facility	21.00	11,987	Yes	1986
Maine	Boralex Fort Fairfield	31.00	21,020	No	1987
Maine	Indeck West Enfield Energy Center	25.60	21,020	No	1987
Maine	Indeck Jonesboro Energy Center	26.80	9,650	No	1987
Maine	Greenville Steam	16.10	13,337	No	1988

Table C.1—Continued

State	Plant	Capacity (MW)	Heat Rate (Btu/kWh)	Cogeneration Facility	On-Line Year
Maine	Boralex Stratton Energy	45.70	19,601	No	1989
Maine	Worcester Energy	13.00	14,500	No	1989
Maine	Somerset Plant	42.63	15,826	Yes	1990
Maine	Boralex Beaver Livermore Falls	34.70	14,309	No	1992
Maine	Forster Strong Mill	0.50	15,826	Yes	2004
Maine	Worcester Energy	24.56	8,911	No	2005
Mass.	Pinetree Power Fitchburg	17.00	15,673	No	1992
Mass.	Ware Biomass Cogen	7.79	15,826	Yes	2003
Mass.	Ware Cogeneration	4.09	8,911	Yes	2006
Mich.	Central Mich. University	0.95	15,826	Yes	1987
Mich.	Hillman Power LLC	17.80	15,655	No	1987
Mich.	Viking Energy of McBain	16.00	15,982	No	1988
Mich.	Viking Energy of Lincoln	16.00	13,646	No	1989
Mich.	Grayling Generating Station	36.20	14,597	No	1992
Mich.	Cadillac Renewable Energy	36.80	15,470	No	1993
Mich.	Genesee Power Station LP	35.00	21,020	No	1995
Minn.	Rapids Energy Center	11.02	10,079	Yes	1969
Minn.	Rapids Energy Center	11.02	10,079	Yes	1969
Minn.	M. L. Hibbard	15.30	14,500	Yes	1988
Minn.	M. L. Hibbard	33.30	14,500	Yes	1988
Minn.	Central Minn. Ethanol	0.95	8,911	No	2006
Minn.	Fibrominn Biomass Power Plant	55.00	8,911	No	2007
N.H.	Berlin Gorham	5.00	15,826	No	1948
N.H.	Schiller	47.20	12,788	No	1955
N.H.	Pinetree Power	15.00	15,033	No	1986
N.H.	Pinetree Power Tamworth	20.00	14,972	No	1987
N.H.	Bridgewater Power LP	16.00	14,232	No	1987
N.H.	Hemphill Power and Light	14.13	14,605	No	1987
N.H.	Whitefield Power and Light	14.50	13,025	No	1988
N.H.	Schiller Biomass Con	47.50	8,911	No	2006

Table C.1—Continued

State	Plant	Capacity (MW)	Heat Rate (Btu/ kWh)	Cogeneration Facility	On-Line Year
N.Y.	American Ref-Fuel of Niagara	9.00	15,826	Yes	1980
N.Y.	Lyonsdale Biomass LLC	19.00	13,230	Yes	1992
N.Y.	Boralex Chateaugay Power Station	18.00	15,094	No	1993
N.C.	Craven County Wood Energy LP	45.00	12,622	No	1990
Ohio	Sauder Power Plant	3.60	14,900	Yes	1993
Ohio	Sauder Power Plant	3.60	14,900	Yes	1993
Ore.	Medford Operation	3.10	15,826	Yes	1956
Ore.	Medford Operation	4.40	15,826	Yes	1965
Ore.	Biomass One LP	8.50	19,236	Yes	1985
Ore.	Biomass One LP	14.00	14,427	Yes	1985
Ore.	Co-Gen LLC	6.98	11,987	Yes	1986
Ore.	Co-Gen II LLC	6.98	11,987	Yes	1987
Pa.	Koopers Susquehanna Plant	11.50	9,650	Yes	1988
Pa.	Viking Energy of Northumberland	16.00	13,500	Yes	1988
S.C.	Stone Container Florence Mill	7.63	15,826	Yes	1963
Texas	Snider Industries	5.00	15,826	Yes	1983
Vt.	J. C. McNeil	52.00	21,020	No	1984
Vt.	Ryegate Power Station	20.00	21,020	No	1992
Vt.	Blue Spruce Farm Ana	0.26	8,911	No	2005
Va.	Stone Container Hopewell Mill	20.35	15,826	Yes	1980
Va.	Multitrade of Pittsylvania LP	26.55	13,541	No	1994
Va.	Multitrade of Pittsylvania LP	26.55	13,541	No	1994
Va.	Multitrade of Pittsylvania LP	26.55	13,541	No	1994
Va.	Scott Wood	0.80	15,826	No	2003
Va.	Scott Wood	2.60	15,826	No	2003
Wash.	Kettle Falls Generating Station	50.00	11,860	No	1983
Wash.	Everett Cogen	36.00	19,000	Yes	1996

Table C.1—Continued

State	Plant	Capacity (MW)	Heat Rate (Btu/ kWh)	Cogeneration Facility	On-Line Year
Wash.	Colville Indian Power and Veneer	5.00	15,826	No	2002
Wash.	Colville Indian Power and Veneer	7.50	15,826	No	2002
Wash.	Sierra Pacific Aberdeen	16.00	15,826	Yes	2003
Wis.	French Island	14.00	10,400	No	1940
Wis.	French Island	14.00	10,400	No	1940
Wis.	Bay Front	22.00	16,190	No	1952
Wis.	Bay Front	22.00	18,720	No	1954
Wis.	Minergy Neenah	6.50	15,826	Yes	1999
Total		2,310			

SOURCE: ORNL (2010).

Near-term biomass expansion to produce electricity might occur via coal cofiring. The EIA Renewable Energy Annual (EIA, 2010c) lists coal power plants with biomass cofiring capabilities. A large coal power plant typically has several (two to four) coal boilers, and cofiring is generally initiated in one or two of the boilers. This results in a total U.S. cofiring capacity (5,080 MW) that is less than total plant capacity (8,121 MW), as detailed in Table C.2. By matching power plants from the Renewable Energy Annual with data from NETL's Coal Power Plant Database (NETL, 2007), boiler type for cofiring units (based on data availability) are also listed in Table C.2. When more than one boiler is present at the power plant, all technologies are listed. Cofiring occurs across all major boiler types: PC, FB, and stoker fired.

Table C.2
2007 Net Summer Capacity at Power Plants with Cofiring Capability

State	Plant Name	Boiler Type	Biomass or Coal Cofiring Capacity (MW)	Total Plant Capacity (MW)
Ala.	Mobile Energy Services LLC	Uncategorized	91	91
Ala.	Georgia Pacific Naheola Mill	Uncategorized	31	78
Ala.	International Paper Prattville Mill	Uncategorized	49	90
Ark.	Ashdown	Rear firing	157	157
Ariz.	H. Wilson Sundt Generating Station	Front firing	173	559
Del.	Edge Moor	Tangential firing	252	710
Fla.	International Paper Pensacola	Uncategorized	83	83
Fla.	Jefferson Smurfit Fernandina Beach	Uncategorized	74	128
Fla.	Stone Container Panama City Mill	Uncategorized	20	34

Table C.2—Continued

State	Plant Name	Boiler Type	Biomass or Coal Cofiring Capacity (MW)	Total Plant Capacity (MW)
Ga.	Georgia Pacific Cedar Springs	Rear firing	101	101
Ga.	International Paper Augusta Mill	Uncategorized	85	85
Ga.	SP Newsprint	Uncategorized	45	82
Hawaii	Hawaiian Comm and Sugar Puunene Mill	Uncategorized	46	62
Iowa	Ames Electric Services Power Plant	Uncategorized	109	109
Iowa	Archer Daniels Midland Clinton	Uncategorized	180	211
Iowa	University of Iowa Main Power Plant	Uncategorized	21	23
Ky.	H. L. Spurlock	Opposed/tangential/ FB firing	659	1,609
La.	International Paper Louisiana Mill	Uncategorized	59	59
Md.	Luke Mill	Uncategorized	65	65
Maine	Rumford Cogeneration	FB firing	103	103
Maine	S. D. Warren Westbrook	Uncategorized	15	81
Mich.	Decorative Panels International	Uncategorized	8	8
Mich.	Escanaba Paper Company	Uncategorized	81	103
Mich.	S. D. Warren Muskegon	Uncategorized	51	51
Mich.	TES Filer City Station	Uncategorized	70	70
Minn.	Rapids Energy Center	Uncategorized	27	28
Minn.	M. L. Hibbard	Uncategorized	73	123
Mo.	University of Missouri Columbia	Uncategorized	6	91
Miss.	Weyerhaeuser Columbus Miss.	Uncategorized	123	123
N.C.	Coastal Carolina Clean Power	Uncategorized	44	44
N.C.	Corn Products Winston Salem	Uncategorized	8	8
N.C.	Domtar Paper Co. LLC Plymouth N.C.	Uncategorized	162	162
N.C.	Primary Energy Roxboro	Uncategorized	68	68
N.Y.	AES Greenidge LLC	Front firing	113	163
N.Y.	AES Hickling LLC	Uncategorized	70	70
N.Y.	AES Jennison LLC	Uncategorized	60	60
N.Y.	Black River Generation	Uncategorized	56	56
N.Y.	WPS Power Niagara	Uncategorized	56	56
Pa.	Johnsonburg Mill	Uncategorized	54	54

Table C.2—Continued

State	Plant Name	Boiler Type	Biomass or Coal Cofiring Capacity (MW)	Total Plant Capacity (MW)
Pa.	P. H. Glatfelter	Front firing	6	110
S.C.	International Paper Eastover Facility	Tangential firing	48	110
S.C.	Stone Container Florence Mill	Opposed firing	79	108
S.C.	Cogen South	Uncategorized	99	99
Utah	Desert Power LP	Uncategorized	43	135
Va.	Bassett Table	Uncategorized	2	2
Va.	Georgia Pacific Big Island	Uncategorized	8	8
Va.	International Paper Franklin Mill	Uncategorized	97	155
Va.	Covington Facility	Uncategorized	105	105
Va.	Virginia City Hybrid Energy Center	FB firing	668	668
Wash.	Steam plant	Uncategorized	50	50
Wis.	Fox Valley Energy Center	Uncategorized	7	7
Wis.	Blount Street	Front firing	100	188
Wis.	Manitowoc	Spreader stoker/FB firing	10	213
Wis.	Mosinee Paper	Uncategorized	20	23
Wis.	Biron Mill	Uncategorized	22	62
Wis.	Whiting Mill	Uncategorized	4	4
Wis.	Wisconsin Rapids Pulp Mill	Uncategorized	72	72
Wis.	Niagara Mill	Uncategorized	12	25
Wis.	Bay Front	Uncategorized	40	68
Wis.	Waupun Correctional Central Heating Plant	Uncategorized	2	2
Wis.	University of Wis. Madison Charter Street Plant	Uncategorized	10	10
Wis.	International Paper Kaukauna Mill	Uncategorized	33	45
Total			5,080	8,121

SOURCES: EIA (2010c); NETL (2007).

Coal Demanded for Electric Power

An estimate of the potential demand locations for biomass cofiring can be inferred from current coal demand. Coal demand for electric power is estimated by state and aggregated to the USDA region level. Coal demand in 2008, average energy content of delivered coal by state, and coal-fired net generation in the electric power sector in each state are estimated by EIA (EIA, 2010a, 2010d) and summarized in Table C.3. To illustrate the potential energy needed to be supplied by biomass for cofiring, 1, 2, 5, and 10 percent of existing coal energy demanded are listed in Table C.4.

Table C.3
2008 Electric Power Sector Coal Demand and Generation by State

State	USDA Region	Coal Generation Electric Power 2008 (TWh)	Electric Power Coal Receipts 2008 (million metric tons)	Average Heat Value (GJ per metric ton)	Total Coal Energy Demanded for Electric Power 2008 (PJ)
Ky.	Appalachia	91.6	37.6	26.8	1,008
N.C.	Appalachia	75.8	28.5	28.5	811
Tenn.	Appalachia	57.1	26.1	25.8	673
Va.	Appalachia	31.8	14.1	29.1	409
W.Va.	Appalachia	89.1	34.7	27.7	961
Ill.	Corn Belt	96.6	54.9	20.7	1,135
Ind.	Corn Belt	122.0	55.4	24.4	1,351
Iowa	Corn Belt	40.4	25.2	20.0	505
Mo.	Corn Belt	73.5	40.6	20.6	835
Ohio	Corn Belt	130.7	53.1	26.6	1,414
Ark.	Delta	26.1	14.2	20.3	289
La.	Delta	24.1	14.0	19.0	266
Miss.	Delta	16.7	8.8	21.6	190
Mich.	Lake States	69.9	34.7	23.0	799
Minn.	Lake States	31.8	18.0	20.7	373
Wis.	Lake States	41.7	24.1	21.0	506
Conn.	Northeast	4.4	1.8	23.8	44
Del.	Northeast	5.3	2.1	29.0	62
Maine	Northeast	0.4	0.2	30.2	7
Md.	Northeast	27.2	10.1	28.8	291
Mass.	Northeast	10.6	4.2	26.8	114
N.H.	Northeast	3.5	1.3	30.0	40
N.J.	Northeast	9.0	4.1	28.1	114
N.Y.	Northeast	19.2	8.6	26.2	226
Pa.	Northeast	117.6	51.7	25.8	1,334
R.I.	Northeast	0.0	0.0	N/A	0
Vt.	Northeast	0.0	0.0	N/A	0

Table C.3—Continued

State	USDA Region	Coal Generation Electric Power 2008 (TWh)	Electric Power Coal Receipts 2008 (million metric tons)	Average Heat Value (GJ per metric ton)	Total Coal Energy Demanded for Electric Power 2008 (PJ)
Kan.	Northern Plains	34.0	19.5	19.9	388
Neb.	Northern Plains	21.5	13.3	19.8	263
N.D.	Northern Plains	29.7	22.8	15.5	354
S.D.	Northern Plains	3.7	2.0	19.5	40
Okla.	Southern Plains	36.3	21.1	20.2	426
Texas	Southern Plains	147.1	93.4	18.0	1,686
Ala.	Southeast	74.6	33.2	24.8	823
Fla.	Southeast	64.8	26.3	27.7	730
Ga.	Southeast	85.5	36.0	25.5	917
S.C.	Southeast	41.5	14.4	28.9	418
Ariz.	Mountain	43.8	21.2	22.9	485
Colo.	Mountain	34.8	17.2	22.8	392
Idaho	Mountain	0.1	0.2	23.1	4
Mont.	Mountain	18.3	11.2	19.4	217
Nev.	Mountain	7.8	3.6	24.8	89
N.M.	Mountain	27.0	14.0	21.3	298
Utah	Mountain	38.0	16.5	25.7	423
Wyo.	Mountain	43.8	25.3	20.4	517
Calif.	Pacific	2.3	1.6	27.1	44
Ore.	Pacific	4.0	2.4	19.4	47
Wash.	Pacific	8.8	5.2	19.5	102
Alaska	N/A	0.6	0.8	20.2	17
D.C.	N/A				
Hawaii	N/A	1.6	0.6	24.8	15
U.S. total		1,985.8	970.4		22,452
U.S. total minus Alaska and Hawaii		1,983.5	969.0		22,419

SOURCES: EIA (2010a, 2010d).
NOTE: PJ = petajoule (10^{15} joules).

Table C.4
1, 2, 5, and 10 Percent of 2008 Electric Power Sector Coal Energy Demand by State

State	USDA Region	1% of Coal Input Energy (PJ)	2% of Coal Input Energy (PJ)	5% of Coal Input Energy (PJ)	10% of Coal Input Energy (PJ)
Ky.	Appalachia	10.1	20.2	50.4	100.8
N.C.	Appalachia	8.1	16.2	40.6	81.1
Tenn.	Appalachia	6.7	13.5	33.7	67.3
Va.	Appalachia	4.1	8.2	20.4	40.9
W.Va.	Appalachia	9.6	19.2	48.1	96.1
Ill.	Corn Belt	11.4	22.7	56.8	113.5
Ind.	Corn Belt	13.5	27.0	67.6	135.1
Iowa	Corn Belt	5.0	10.1	25.2	50.5
Mo.	Corn Belt	8.4	16.7	41.8	83.5
Ohio	Corn Belt	14.1	28.3	70.7	141.4
Ark.	Delta	2.9	5.8	14.4	28.9
La.	Delta	2.7	5.3	13.3	26.6
Miss.	Delta	1.9	3.8	9.5	19.0
Mich.	Lake States	8.0	16.0	40.0	79.9
Minn.	Lake States	3.7	7.5	18.7	37.3
Wis.	Lake States	5.1	10.1	25.3	50.6
Conn.	Northeast	0.4	0.9	2.2	4.4
Del.	Northeast	0.6	1.2	3.1	6.2
Maine	Northeast	0.1	0.1	0.3	0.7
Md.	Northeast	2.9	5.8	14.6	29.1
Mass.	Northeast	1.1	2.3	5.7	11.4
N.H.	Northeast	0.4	0.8	2.0	4.0
N.J.	Northeast	1.1	2.3	5.7	11.4
N.Y.	Northeast	2.3	4.5	11.3	22.6
Pa.	Northeast	13.3	26.7	66.7	133.4
R.I.	Northeast	0.0	0.0	0.0	0.0
Vt.	Northeast	0.0	0.0	0.0	0.0
Kan.	Northern Plains	3.9	7.8	19.4	38.8
Neb.	Northern Plains	2.6	5.3	13.1	26.3
N.D.	Northern Plains	3.5	7.1	17.7	35.4
S.D.	Northern Plains	0.4	0.8	2.0	4.0
Okla.	Southern Plains	4.3	8.5	21.3	42.6

Table C.4—Continued

State	USDA Region	1% of Coal Input Energy (PJ)	2% of Coal Input Energy (PJ)	5% of Coal Input Energy (PJ)	10% of Coal Input Energy (PJ)
Texas	Southern Plains	16.9	33.7	84.3	168.6
Ala.	Southeast	8.2	16.5	41.2	82.3
Fla.	Southeast	7.3	14.6	36.5	73.0
Ga.	Southeast	9.2	18.3	45.8	91.7
S.C.	Southeast	4.2	8.4	20.9	41.8
Ariz.	Mountain	4.8	9.7	24.2	48.5
Colo.	Mountain	3.9	7.8	19.6	39.2
Idaho	Mountain	0.0	0.1	0.2	0.4
Mont.	Mountain	2.2	4.3	10.9	21.7
Nev.	Mountain	0.9	1.8	4.5	8.9
N.M.	Mountain	3.0	6.0	14.9	29.8
Utah	Mountain	4.2	8.5	21.2	42.3
Wyo.	Mountain	5.2	10.3	25.8	51.7
Calif.	Pacific	0.4	0.9	2.2	4.4
Ore.	Pacific	0.5	0.9	2.3	4.7
Wash.	Pacific	1.0	2.0	5.1	10.2
Alaska	N/A	0.2	0.3	0.8	1.7
D.C.	N/A	0.0	0.0	0.0	0.0
Hawaii	N/A	0.2	0.3	0.8	1.5
U.S. total		224.5	449.0	1,122.6	2,245.2
U.S. total minus Alaska and Hawaii		224.2	448.4	1,121.0	2,241.9

SOURCES: EIA (2010a, 2010d).

Estimated Biomass Residues by State

We use a county-level estimation of biomass resources by NREL that was completed with 2007 biomass residue data (Milbrandt, 2005). State-level data are presented in Table C.5. Secondary mill residues, which comprise less than 5 percent of total mill residues, have been combined in the table with primary mill residues. A regional representation of forest and mill residues is presented in Figure C.1.

The total estimate used here, 300 million dry metric tons, includes solely forest, mill, and crop residues and does not include the 61 million to 84 million dry metric tons of dedicated energy crops that potentially could be grown on CRP farmland (Milbrandt, 2005). Additionally, since there are no existing coal-fired power plants in Rhode Island or Vermont, these states will require biomass for cofiring with coal but will provide biomass supply to the Northeast

Table C.5
2007 Estimated Biomass Residues

State	USDA Region	Forest Residues (1,000 dry metric tons)	Primary and Secondary Mill Residue (1,000 dry metric tons)	Crop Residues (1,000 dry metric tons)	Total Biomass Residues (1,000 dry metric tons)
Ky.	Appalachia	2,213	1,101	2,086	5,400
N.C.	Appalachia	4,366	3,673	1,819	9,858
Tenn.	Appalachia	1,461	1,481	1,528	4,470
Va.	Appalachia	3,046	2,026	678	5,750
W.Va.	Appalachia	1,143	647	27	1,818
Ill.	Corn Belt	728	299	20,636	21,663
Ind.	Corn Belt	814	639	10,221	11,674
Iowa	Corn Belt	223	163	22,005	22,392
Mo.	Corn Belt	1,813	921	6,472	9,207
Ohio	Corn Belt	507	377	7,041	7,925
Ark.	Delta	3,334	3,729	4,512	11,576
La.	Delta	4,506	3,165	3,458	11,130
Miss.	Delta	4,867	4,524	2,050	11,441
Mich.	Lake States	1,587	1,547	3,500	6,633
Minn.	Lake States	2,635	1,096	12,611	16,342
Wis.	Lake States	3,351	1,444	3,962	8,757
Conn.	Northeast	11	57	0	67
Del.	Northeast	43	23	279	346
Maine	Northeast	3,009	394	0	3,403
Md.	Northeast	239	197	731	1,167
Mass.	Northeast	96	143	0	239
N.H.	Northeast	404	268	0	672
N.J.	Northeast	11	59	118	188
N.Y.	Northeast	1,096	1,038	599	2,733
Pa.	Northeast	1,507	1,346	1,231	4,084
R.I.	Northeast	2	17	0	19
Vt.	Northeast	261	86	0	347
Kan.	Northern Plains	123	37	9,521	9,681
Neb.	Northern Plains	54	47	13,147	13,248
N.D.	Northern Plains	26	6	6,657	6,690
S.D.	Northern Plains	121	179	6,544	6,844

Table C.5—Continued

State	USDA Region	Forest Residues (1,000 dry metric tons)	Primary and Secondary Mill Residue (1,000 dry metric tons)	Crop Residues (1,000 dry metric tons)	Total Biomass Residues (1,000 dry metric tons)
Okla.	Southern Plains	727	588	1,747	3,063
Texas	Southern Plains	2,195	3,444	5,527	11,166
Ala.	Southeast	3,656	4,700	437	8,793
Fla.	Southeast	2,176	1,826	2,446	6,449
Ga.	Southeast	5,274	4,844	1,153	11,270
S.C.	Southeast	2,846	1,944	547	5,337
Ariz.	Mountain	42	125	253	420
Colo.	Mountain	41	140	1,812	1,994
Idaho	Mountain	675	2,031	1,940	4,646
Mont.	Mountain	651	1,382	1,932	3,965
Nev.	Mountain	4	15	9	28
N.M.	Mountain	46	112	161	318
Utah	Mountain	17	54	80	151
Wyo.	Mountain	57	203	102	362
Calif.	Pacific	1,631	3,516	1,548	6,695
Ore.	Pacific	3,421	6,952	656	11,029
Wash.	Pacific	2,962	4,866	1,714	9,542
Alaska	N/A	300	65	0	364
D.C.	N/A		0		
Hawaii	N/A	0	9	302	311
U.S. total		70,319	67,546	163,800	301,666
U.S. total minus Alaska and Hawaii		70,020	67,472	163,498	300,990

SOURCE: Milbrandt (2005).

USDA region. This analysis ignores some cofiring with natural gas and activities in Vermont in which forestry residues are used for heating applications.

NREL includes in its resource estimate agricultural residues from corn, wheat, soybeans, cotton, sorghum, barley, oats, rice, rye, canola, beans, peas, peanuts, potatoes, safflower, sunflower, sugarcane, and flaxseed. NREL assumes that 35 percent of total residues can be harvested for use as biomass energy (Milbrandt, 2005).

Figure C.1
Forest and Primary and Secondary Mill Residue Potential by Region

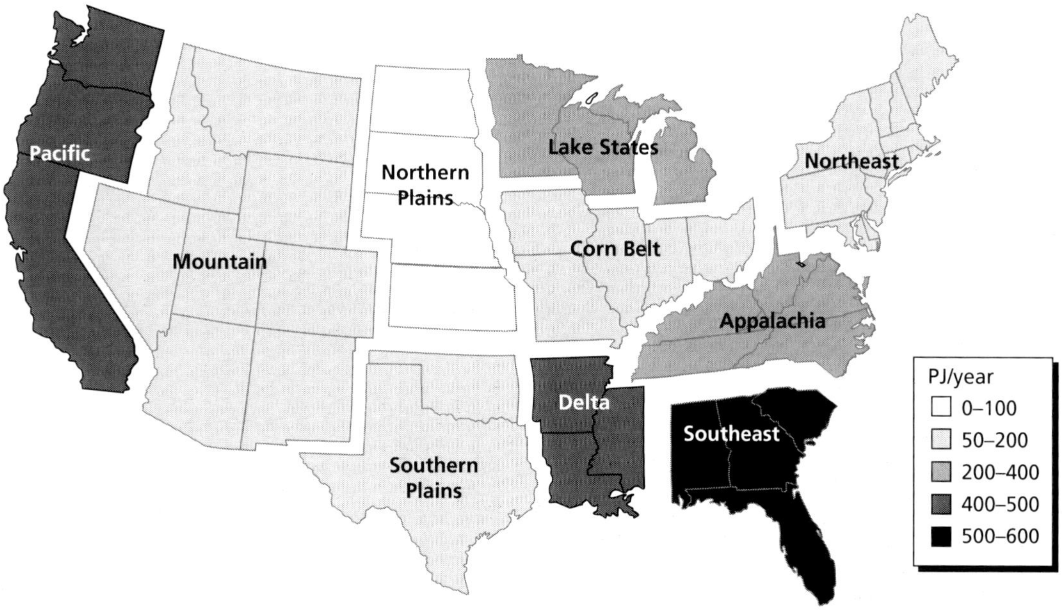

SOURCE: Milbrandt (2005).
RAND *TR-984-C.1*

Estimated Energy from Biomass Residues by State

Using an average energy content of 17.0 GJ per dry metric ton for herbaceous biomass and 19.0 GJ per dry metric ton for woody biomass, total annual energy content of biomass residues by state is estimated in Table C.6.

Table C.6
Estimated Energy from Biomass Residues

State	USDA Region	Energy Available from Forest Residues (PJ/year)	Energy Available from Primary and Secondary Mill Residues (PJ/year)	Energy Available from Crop Residues (PJ/year)	Total Biomass Energy Available (PJ/year)
Ky.	Appalachia	42.0	20.9	35.4	98.3
N.C.	Appalachia	82.8	69.6	30.9	183.3
Tenn.	Appalachia	27.7	28.1	26.0	81.7
Va.	Appalachia	57.8	38.4	11.5	107.7
W.Va.	Appalachia	21.7	12.3	0.5	34.4
Ill.	Corn Belt	13.8	5.7	350.4	369.9
Ind.	Corn Belt	15.4	12.1	173.6	201.1
Iowa	Corn Belt	4.2	3.1	373.7	381.0
Mo.	Corn Belt	34.4	17.5	109.9	161.8

Table C.6—Continued

State	USDA Region	Energy Available from Forest Residues (PJ/year)	Energy Available from Primary and Secondary Mill Residues (PJ/year)	Energy Available from Crop Residues (PJ/year)	Total Biomass Energy Available (PJ/year)
Ohio	Corn Belt	9.6	7.2	119.6	136.3
Ark.	Delta	63.2	70.7	76.6	210.6
La.	Delta	85.4	60.0	58.7	204.2
Miss.	Delta	92.3	85.8	34.8	212.9
Mich.	Lake States	30.1	29.3	59.4	118.8
Minn.	Lake States	50.0	20.8	214.2	284.9
Wis.	Lake States	63.5	27.4	67.3	158.2
Conn.	Northeast	0.2	1.1	0.0	1.3
Del.	Northeast	0.8	0.4	4.7	6.0
Maine	Northeast	57.1	7.5	0.0	64.5
Md.	Northeast	4.5	3.7	12.4	20.7
Mass.	Northeast	1.8	2.7	0.0	4.5
N.H.	Northeast	7.7	5.1	0.0	12.7
N.J.	Northeast	0.2	1.1	2.0	3.3
N.Y.	Northeast	20.8	19.7	10.2	50.6
Pa.	Northeast	28.6	25.5	20.9	75.0
R.I.	Northeast	0.0	0.3	0.0	0.4
Vt.	Northeast	4.9	1.6	0.0	6.6
Kan.	Northern Plains	2.3	0.7	161.7	164.7
Neb.	Northern Plains	1.0	0.9	223.3	225.2
N.D.	Northern Plains	0.5	0.1	113.1	113.7
S.D.	Northern Plains	2.3	3.4	111.1	116.8
Okla.	Southern Plains	13.8	11.2	29.7	54.6
Texas	Southern Plains	41.6	65.3	93.9	200.8
Ala.	Southeast	69.3	89.1	7.4	165.8
Fla.	Southeast	41.3	34.6	41.5	117.4
Ga.	Southeast	100.0	91.8	19.6	211.4
S.C.	Southeast	53.9	36.9	9.3	100.1
Ariz.	Mountain	0.8	2.4	4.3	7.5
Colo.	Mountain	0.8	2.7	30.8	34.2
Idaho	Mountain	12.8	38.5	33.0	84.3
Mont.	Mountain	12.3	26.2	32.8	71.4

Table C.6—Continued

State	USDA Region	Energy Available from Forest Residues (PJ/year)	Energy Available from Primary and Secondary Mill Residues (PJ/year)	Energy Available from Crop Residues (PJ/year)	Total Biomass Energy Available (PJ/year)
Nev.	Mountain	0.1	0.3	0.1	0.5
N.M.	Mountain	0.9	2.1	2.7	5.7
Utah	Mountain	0.3	1.0	1.4	2.7
Wyo.	Mountain	1.1	3.8	1.7	6.7
Calif.	Pacific	30.9	66.7	26.3	123.9
Ore.	Pacific	64.9	131.8	11.1	207.8
Wash.	Pacific	56.2	92.3	29.1	177.5
Alaska	N/A	5.7	1.2	0.0	6.9
D.C.	N/A	0.0	0.0	0.0	0.0
Hawaii	N/A	0.0	0.2	5.1	5.3
U.S. total		1,333.2	1,280.7	2,781.7	5,395.6
U.S. total minus Alaska and Hawaii		1,327.6	1,279.3	2,776.6	5,383.4

SOURCE: Milbrandt (2005).

Table C.7 shows the percentage of available biomass residues in each region that would be required to meet 1, 2, 5, and 10 percent of that region's coal energy demanded for electric power.

Table C.7
Fraction of Regional Forest, Mill, and Crop Residues Required to Displace 1, 2, 5, and 10 Percent of Electric Power Coal Demand

USDA Region	Fraction of Regional Available Biomass Needed to Displace 1% of Coal Input Energy	Fraction of Regional Available Biomass Needed to Displace 2% of Coal Input Energy	Fraction of Regional Available Biomass Needed to Displace 5% of Coal Input Energy	Fraction of Regional Available Biomass Needed to Displace 10% of Coal Input Energy
Mountain	11.4	22.8	57.0	113.9
Northeast	9.1	18.2	45.4	90.8
Southern Plains	8.3	16.5	41.3	82.7
Appalachia	7.6	15.3	38.2	76.4
Southeast	4.9	9.7	24.3	48.6
Corn Belt	4.2	8.4	21.0	41.9
Lake States	3.0	6.0	14.9	29.9
Northern Plains	1.7	3.4	8.4	16.8
Delta	1.2	2.4	5.9	11.9
Pacific	0.4	0.8	1.9	3.8
Total U.S.	4.2	8.3	20.8	41.6

APPENDIX D

Logistics Analysis Documentation

This appendix documents the cost assumptions used in the logistics analysis. Cost elements are reported for producing biomass; transportation by truck, rail, and barge; handling and transshipment between modes; processing; and delivery. The costs have been derived to best represent the supply scenarios discussed in Chapter Five.

Biomass Production Cost

Biomass production cost refers to the "farm gate" cost of producing biomass. It comprises the cost of agricultural inputs, including seed, irrigation, fertilization, and labor, among others, and the opportunity cost of using the land for producing biomass energy rather than some other potential use.

Densification Costs

One option to facilitate the transport of biomass is to densify it. Either bales or woody biomass can be densified. Several alternative techniques exist for densification, including briquettes, "bripells," and pellets; they differ in the degree of processing and final size. We consider only pellets in this analysis because they are the industry standard. The fundamental processes are similar for the alternative approaches, and all should yield similar results.

Our estimate of densification costs is based on that of Mani et al. (2006). Capital costs are estimated by beginning with the equipment estimate in Mani et al. (2006, Table 1). We assume a slightly larger facility, with a pellet production rate of 9.1 metric tons per hour (10 short tons per hour) and an average capacity factor of 0.85. We escalate costs for procuring and installing all installed capital equipment using a scale factor of 0.6. To account for the low-definition design of Mani et al. (2006), we add an additional contingency of 25 percent. Noninstalled equipment, such as vehicles and land, are not escalated. Since the pellet production is for an industrial consumer, we remove the packaging unit from the cost estimate. We convert 2004 to 2010 dollars using first-quarter to first-quarter implicit price deflators for gross domestic product as compiled by BEA (2010). The annual cost of capital is 6.41 percent.

Operating costs are based on Mani et al. (2006, Table 2), omitting the costs of drying, which are included in a separate calculation. Because there are few opportunities for the exchange of heat, the scaling factor used to escalate nonfeedstock operating costs is 1.0.

We build four cases, two for herbaceous biomass and two for woody biomass.

135

- Case 1: herbaceous biomass. Because it is possible to harvest herbaceous biomass, such as SG or corn stover, with a moisture content of 15–20 percent, a separate drying step is not required, and these plant capital and operating costs are not applied to herbaceous biomass cases.
- Case 2: herbaceous biomass with ash removal. The Show Me Energy Cooperative (Flick, 2009) claims to have a proprietary method for removing ash and alkali metals from the pellets it produces from herbaceous biomass. The ability to do this is a benefit because it reduces the potential for corrosion that can result from firing herbaceous biomass. For the purpose of this analysis, we assume that this process is highly efficient, removing only ash from the herbaceous biomass and resulting in a low-ash pellet with slightly higher energy content per unit mass. According to the Biomass Energy Data Book (ORNL, 2010, Table B.1), the ash content of corn stover ranges from 9.8 to 13.5 percent and the ash content of SG ranges from 2.8 to 7.5 percent. We assume that 7 percent of the total mass is removed as ash. We assume that the additional equipment and installation costs are $375,000 and that the operating cost of removing ash is $5.00 per metric ton.
- Case 3: woody biomass with drying provided by natural gas. In the woody biomass cases, we include equipment and installation charges for dryers. We assume that the biomass needs to be dried from 35 percent to 10 percent moisture. Natural gas provides the heat for drying and costs $7 per gigajoule. We assume the efficiency of the dryer to be 80 percent and of the natural gas heater to be 80 percent.
- Case 4: woody biomass with drying provided by biomass. In this case, a portion of the woody biomass is used as fuel to dry the remaining biomass. We assume capital and installation costs as in case 3 but reduce efficiency of the wood heater to 70 percent.

We assume that the pellet inherits the heat content of the feedstock, adjusted for moisture content and, in case 2, for ash removal. The final moisture content of the pellets is assumed to be 5 percent.

The resulting costs of densification are summarized in Table D.1 for a nominal case in which the cost of the biomass feedstock is $4.00 per gigajoule. The cost of the feedstock has a small effect on the cost of densification in case 4, in which it is also used for drying. Namely, a $1.00 change in the feedstock cost (on a per-gigajoule basis) results in a $0.10 change in the nonfeedstock operating costs.

Storage Costs

We assume that the harvested herbaceous biomass is baled into large rectangular dimensions of 1.2 m by 0.9 m by 2.4 m. To apply to a range of biomass types, we assume a nominal bulk density of herbaceous biomass to be 160 kg per cubic meter, with a range of 150 kg per cubic meter to 170 kg per cubic meter. This range of bulk density is inclusive of bulk densities for corn stover and SG cited by ORNL (2010), Sokhansanj et al. (2002), and Antares Group (2009). We assume a nominal moisture content of 15 percent.

We assume that, consistently with standard practice, herbaceous biomass is stored prior to use (Leesley, 2009). The cost of storage is the sum of the costs of building and operating the storage barn and loading and unloading the bales from the flatbed trailer. As part of the CVBP, a series of storage sheds was constructed to store bales of biomass in anticipation of

Table D.1
Costs of Densification for Herbaceous and Woody Biomass

Cost	Case 1: Herbaceous Biomass		Case 2: Herbaceous Biomass with Ash Removal		Case 3: Woody Biomass, Natural Gas Drying		Case 4: Woody Biomass, Biomass-Fired Drying	
	$/metric ton	$/GJ	$/metric ton	$/GJ	$/metric ton	$/GJ	$/metric ton	$/GJ
Capital cost	3.8	0.23	4.2	0.24	6.0	0.33	6.0	0.33
Nonfeedstock operating cost	11.7	0.72	16.7	0.96	27	1.47	24	1.32
Total cost	16	0.96	21	1.2	33	1.8	30	1.7

SOURCE: Mani et al. (2006); ORNL (2010); BEA (2010).

NOTE: Feedstock cost is assumed to be $4.00/GJ. Feedstock energy content is 17 GJ/dry metric ton for herbaceous biomass and 19 GJ/dry metric ton for woody biomass. Costs are for pellets, which are assumed to have a moisture content of 5 percent.

burning. The typical cost of construction of these sheds was approximately $97 per square meter, which we adopt as the most likely value (Antares Group, 2009).[1] We assume a nominal size for a storage shed of 2,300 m² and a storage capacity of 7,500 bales (Antares Group, 2009). Storage sheds are assumed to occupy 0.8 hectare (ha) with a rental rate of $200 per hectare; the ownership and operating costs of the storage shed are assumed to be 12 percent of the construction costs per year (Duffy, 2008). Under these assumptions, the cost of storing herbaceous biomass is $18 per dry metric ton.

We use the estimate of Holmgren, Casavant, and Jesusp (2007, Table 6) for the cost of stacking bales, which is $0.77 per dry metric ton.

Transportation and Handling Costs

Truck Transportation Costs

Biomass trucking costs consist of a fixed cost for loading and unloading and a variable cost of transport as a function of distance. Loading and unloading costs are derived from Mahmudi and Flynn (2006), relying on prior studies by Kumar, Cameron, and Flynn (2004, 2005). To adjust the estimate of Mahmudi and Flynn (2006), we convert from 2000 to 2010 dollars and adjust moisture contents to be specific with our nominal cases of 15 percent for herbaceous biomass and 35 percent for woody biomass. The combined loading and unloading cost then becomes $5.90 per dry metric ton for bales and $4.80 per dry metric ton for wood chips.

We assume that transportation costs for pellets are similar to those of transporting grain. Specifically, similar equipment and techniques are used to load, transport, and unload grain; therefore, quoted rates for these activities are also applicable to biomass pellets. Specifically, the Iowa Farm Custom Rate Survey (Edwards and Johanns, 2011) reports the rate for augering grain to be $0.066 per bushel. Converting to metric units and adjusting for a nominal moisture content of 5 percent, this rate becomes $2.74 per dry metric ton. We assume this handling

[1] Costs are reported in first-quarter 2010 dollars and were converted from 2009 dollars using the implicit price deflator for gross national product (BEA, 2010).

charge to also include an unloading operation, which would entail opening gates on the grain trailer to allow the grain to flow out.

For the distance-variable cost of transporting by truck, we rely on several sources. Using the estimate of Mahmudi and Flynn (2006), we estimate the variable cost of transporting straw bales with a moisture content of 15 percent to be $0.16 per dry metric ton-kilometer. Solomon (2010) reports that the average distance-variable cost of transporting wood chips by truck is $0.12 per dry metric ton-kilometer assuming a moisture content of 35 percent. For pellets, we apply the average grain transport rate of $0.07 per dry metric ton-kilometer, assuming a moisture content of 5 percent.

Rail Transportation Costs

Like those for truck transport, rail transport costs comprise fixed costs for loading and unloading biomass and a variable cost associated with transporting the biomass a certain distance. The loading and unloading costs for rail are those associated with capital and labor at a transshipment facility (assuming that, initially, all biomass has to be collected by truck) and at the energy facility. Mahmudi and Flynn (2006, Table 2) estimate theses costs, which we modify for our purposes. Namely, we exclude the costs of purchasing the railcars because the rates that we quote for rail transport assume the use of carrier-owned equipment (CSX, undated [b]), apply a capital charge rate of 6.41 percent amortized over 30 years, and convert the estimates to 2010 dollars. The resulting estimates for transshipment to rail and unloading at the energy facility are $4.65 per dry metric ton for bales and $2.68 per dry metric ton for wood chips, assuming a nominal 15-percent moisture content for bales and 35-percent moisture content for wood chips. For pellets, we assume the same loading and unloading cost as for wood chips but adjust for the reduced moisture content, resulting in an estimated loading and unloading cost of $1.83 per dry metric ton.

To estimate the distance-variable costs for rail, we estimate capacities of common railcars that would be used to transport biomass by rail, then refer to recent quoted rates (by car) for routes throughout the United States. We assume that bales would be transported on 19 m (62 ft.) bulkhead flatcars, wood chips in 164 m³ (5,800 ft³) wood chip hopper cars, and pellets in 135 m³ (4,750 ft³) covered grain hopper cars.[2] The capacity of the bulkhead flatcar is approximately 60 1.2 m by 0.9 m by 2.4 m bales, with a mass of 22 dry metric tons. If we assume a bulk density of 140 kg per cubic meter for wood chips (at 35-percent moisture), the wood chip hopper has a capacity of 15 dry metric tons. If we assume a bulk density of 600 kg per cubic meter for pellets (at 5-percent moisture), the covered grain hopper has a capacity of 77 dry metric tons. Bulk density estimates are from Sokhansanj and Fenton (2006, Table 4).

Rail rates are estimated from published current carrier rates for unit trains using carrier-owned cars. Table D.2 summarizes these rates and data sources.

Barge Transportation Costs

Biomass handling costs for barge freight were assumed to be the same as rail freight (see previous section). The estimates for barge loading and unloading at the energy facility are $4.65 per dry metric ton for bales and $2.68 per dry metric ton for wood chips, assuming a nominal 15-percent moisture content for bales and 35-percent moisture content for wood chips. For

---

2   For more information on rail car types, see CSX (undated [a]).

Table D.2
Rail Routes and Tariffs Used to Estimate Shipping Rates for Biomass Energy Sources

Biomass Type	Route	Distance (km)	Tariff ($/car)	Tariff ($/dry metric ton/km)	Tariff Basis
Bales	Evansville, Ind., to Rochester, N.Y.	1,175	2,084	0.08	CSX 1191
	Omaha, Neb., to Casper, Wyo.	1,014	2,620	0.12	BNSF 01191
Wood chips	Burlington, Vt., to Atlanta, Ga.	1,931	4,628	0.16	CSX 98087
	Okanogan, Wash., to Casper, Wyo.	1,743	3,417	0.13	BNSF 2411715
Pellets	Evansville, Ind., to Rochester, N.Y.	1,175	3,103	0.03	CSX 92342
	Omaha, Neb., to Casper, Wyo.	1,014	3,019	0.04	BNSF 0115971

SOURCES: CSX (undated [b]); BNSF (undated).

NOTE: Distances were derived using Google Maps for off-highway routes. Rail tariffs are for unit trains employing carrier-owned cars. Bale rates are those for hay, CSX code 1191. Wood-chip rates are those for "hogged fuel, bark and mulch," BNSF code 111394. Pellet rates are those for grains shipped in covered hopper cars, CSX tariff codes 92342, 9305, and 4306, depending on destination. Rates are quoted from April 2010.

pellets, we assume the same loading and unloading cost as for wood chips but adjust for the reduced moisture content, resulting in an estimated loading and unloading cost of $1.83 per dry metric ton.

Barge freight costs vary considerably depending on supply, demand, route, fuel prices, and time of year. Additionally, barge operators will attempt to maximize barge utilization and will price shipments based on the potential availability of paid return cargo. To estimate the distance-variable cost of transporting biomass by barge, we use published average weekly Mississippi River barge rates for transporting agricultural goods (Agricultural Marketing Service [AMS], 2011). AMS, part of USDA, presents barge rates from New Orleans, Louisiana, to St. Louis, Missouri, as percentage of the base tariff, $3.99 per ton. The percentages vary from 300 to 423 percent for the five-year average, and we use 400 percent as a conservative estimate. Therefore, under these assumptions, the transport of a ton of barge freight traveling the 1,743 river km (1,083 river miles) from New Orleans to St. Louis costs $15.96.

We estimate barge capacity by using nominal biomass bulk density parameters utilized earlier for truck and rail estimates (ORNL, 2010) applied to standard jumbo covered hopper barges with a capacity of 1,784 m³ and 1,600 tons (Coosa-Alabama River Improvement Association [CARIA], undated). Because of the differences in densities, a greater mass of pellets can be shipped in each barge. Derived nominal distance-variable costs for transporting biomass by barge are listed in Table D.3. The two derived rates are listed as a range, which is not necessarily inclusive of all possible rates.

Biomass Logistics Scenario Parameters

The biomass supply scenarios discussed in Chapter Five utilize the parameters listed in Table D.4 to estimate the costs and impacts of biomass sourcing.

Table D.3
Distance-Variable Costs for Transporting Biomass by Barge Freight

Biomass Type	Moisture Content (%)	Distance-Variable Cost Range ($/dry metric ton-km, $/dry ton-mi)
Herbaceous biomass (bales)	15	0.06–0.09, 0.10–0.14
Woody biomass (wood chips)	35	0.09–0.16, 0.14–0.26
Densified biomass (pellets)	5	0.01–0.02, 0.01–0.03

SOURCE: AMS (2011).

NOTE: Costs are reported in 2010 dollars. Figures are reported to no more than two significant figures.

Table D.4
Biomass Logistics Parameters

Parameters	Units	Baseline	Low	High
Energy content woody biomass	GJ/dry metric ton	19	18.6	21.1
Energy content herbaceous biomass	GJ/dry metric ton	17	16.1	19.1
Energy content wood pellet	GJ/dry metric ton	19	18.6	19.6
Energy content herbaceous pellet	GJ/dry metric ton	17	16.6	17.6
Energy content herbaceous pellet with alkali removed	GJ/dry metric ton	18.3	17.9	18.9
Truck local collection radius	km	125	100	150
Truck local collection tortuosity	Constant	1.8	1.3	3.0
Truck local collection total travel	km	150	87	300
Truck external collection radius	km	125	100	150
Truck external collection tortuosity	Constant	1.8	1.3	3.0
Truck external collection total travel	km	150	87	300
Long-haul rail shipment distance	km	1,450	475	2,400
Long-haul barge shipment distance	km	1,050	475	800
Long-haul truck shipment distance	km	325	150	1,492

Many options exist for handling methods and transport mode depending on biomass type and decisions regarding densification. Our analysis estimated costs and impacts across a wide range of options, with the results presented in Chapter Five the best representative of the supply scenarios discussed. Table D.5 indicates the cost categories that are included in the sourcing scenarios in Chapter Five. Table D.5 also includes additional cost elements not considered in Chapter Five.

Table D.6 presents logistics cost subtotals based on aggregated cost categories and parameters summarized in Tables E.4 and E.5 in Appendix E.

Table D.5
Biomass Logistics Scenarios

Inputs	Local Wood	Local Bales	External Wood	External Wood Pellets	External Bales	External Herbaceous Pellets
Chapter Five sourcing scenario	1, 2		2	2		3
Local raw wood cost	x					
Local raw bales cost		x				
External raw wood cost			x	x		
External raw bales cost					x	x
Load local collection (wood)	x					
Load local collection (bales)		x				
Truck collection transportation (wood)	x					
Truck collection transportation (bales)		x				
Unload raw bales from truck to storage (local)		x				
Stack bales in storage (local)		x				
Bale storage (local)		x				
Load raw bales from storage (local)		x				
Load external collection for truck (wood)			x	x		
Load external collection for truck (bales)					x	x
External truck collection transportation (wood)			x	x		
External truck collection transportation (bales)					x	x
Unload raw wood to storage or depot (external)			x	x		
Unload raw bales to storage or depot (external)					x	x
Stack bales in storage (external)					x	x
Storage (external)					x	x
Load raw wood from storage or depot for transport (external)			x	x		
Load raw bales from storage or depot for transport (external)					x	x
Unload raw to external pellet plant (wood)				x		

142 Near-Term Opportunities for Integrating Biomass into the U.S. Electricity Supply: Technical Considerations

Table D.5—Continued

Inputs	Local Wood	Local Bales	External Wood	External Wood Pellets	External Bales	External Herbaceous Pellets
Unload raw to external pellet plant (bales)						x
Densification (external: wood)				x		
Densification (external: bales)						x
Load external rail car (wood)			x			
Load external rail car (bales)						
Load external rail car (pellets)				x		
Load external barge (wood)						
Load external barge (bales)					x	
Load external barge (pellets)						x
Load external truck (wood)						
Load external truck (bales)						
Load external truck (pellets)						
Rail shipment from external to power plant (wood)			x			
Rail shipment from external to power plant (bales)						
Rail shipment from external to power plant (pellets)				x		
Barge shipment from external to power plant (wood)						
Barge shipment from external to power plant (bales)					x	
Barge shipment from external to power plant (pellets)						x
Truck shipment from external to power plant (wood)						
Truck shipment from external to power plant (bales)						
Truck shipment from external to power plant (pellets)						
Unload rail locally at power plant (wood)			x			
Unload rail locally at power plant (bales)						
Unload rail locally at power plant (pellets)				x		
Unload barge locally at power plant (wood)						

Table D.5—Continued

Inputs	Local Wood	Local Bales	External Wood	External Wood Pellets	External Bales	External Herbaceous Pellets
Unload barge locally at power plant (bales)					x	
Unload barge locally at power plant (pellets)						x
Unload truck locally at power plant (wood)	x					
Unload truck locally at power plant (bales)			x			
Unload truck locally at power plant (pellets)						

Table D.6
Biomass Logistics Scenario Costs

Subtotals	Local Wood	Local Bales	External Wood	External Wood Pellets	External Bales	External Bale Pellets
Biomass feedstock cost	17.65	26.15	17.65	17.65	26.15	26.15
Local handling	2.40	9.62	1.34	0.44	2.33	0.44
Local transportation	17.39	28.62	—	—	—	—
Local storage	—	18.39	—	—	—	—
External handling	—	—	8.54	10.99	11.94	13.95
External transportation	—	—	17.39	17.39	28.62	28.62
External storage	—	—	—	—	18.39	18.39
External densification	—	—	—	31.31	—	16.27
Long-haul transport	—	—	190.21	49.95	75.89	14.99
Total cost for delivered metric ton	39.84	85.72	235.12	127.74	163.31	118.82
Logistics cost for delivered MG	22.19	59.57	217.48	110.09	137.16	92.67
Total cost for delivered GJ	2.10	5.04	12.37	6.72	9.61	6.99
Logistics cost for delivered GJ	1.17	3.50	11.45	5.79	8.07	5.45

Calculation of Net Greenhouse-Gas Emissions from Biomass Cofiring

Introduction

Net GHG emissions for a given biomass feedstock depend on several factors that might or might not be known in advance of the actual biomass acquisition process and might or might not be within the control of a power producer. Accordingly, it is important to explore a broad range of plausible biomass feedstock procurement scenarios and the implications of different assumptions before embarking on a biomass cofiring decision intended to significantly reduce GHG emissions relative to coal-only electricity generation. Under some scenarios, emissions might be only marginally reduced, if at all, relative to coal-only combustion.

Calculations of net emissions saved for biomass-based energy production include both upstream GHG emissions—emissions associated with the production, transport, and processing of biomass—and use-phase emissions—which, in the case of biomass, are the plant-site emissions due to the assumption of net-zero emissions of the biomass combustion itself. Also included are the corresponding avoided emissions from the coal that the biomass displaces in cofire applications—emissions from mining, processing, transport, combustion, and plant-site energy use. Here, we describe how the various components of these net emissions were determined. We also explore some parameters that influence uncertainty in biomass emissions. Although it is important to consider this full range of possible GHG emission scenarios, in the end, we focus on the emissions associated with the representative near-term logistics scenarios outlined in Chapter Five and present the GHG emissions on which the analysis in Chapter Six is based.

Biomass Production Emissions

Production emissions for biomass feedstocks include all GHG emissions from cultivating and harvesting a biomass feedstock. This includes chemical inputs and any net CO_2 emissions associated with soil and root carbon gains or losses resulting from direct land-use changes induced in the cultivation of the feedstock. Under many scenarios, these emissions dominate the upstream portion of the emissions. The production emission values we have used are based on the CUBE model.[1]

---

[1] The values herein are based on CUBE 2.0. CUBE 1.0 became available from NETL in March 2010 (undated). CUBE 2.0 is expected to become available in late 2011 and corrects some calculation errors identified in CUBE 1.0.

Production emissions for biomass feedstocks can be highly scenario dependent.[2] Perhaps the most important factor determining these emissions is geographic location of the cultivation site for the biomass. This is because both the region, which determines important aggregate factors (such as soil type and climate), and the baseline ecosystem, which determines the preexisting levels of soil and root carbon prior to biomass feedstock cultivation strongly influence the net changes associated with biomass cultivation. This point is illustrated in Table E.1 for three herbaceous biomass feedstocks (SG; mixed prairie biomass [MPB]; and stover), as well as one

Table E.1
Production Greenhouse-Gas Emissions from the Calculating Uncertainty in Biomass Emissions Model: Impact of Biomass Cultivation Location, Four Regions on Four Baseline Ecosystems

USDA Region	Biomass Feedstock	Production Emissions by Baseline Ecosystem, kg CO_2e/metric ton dry biomass			
		Row Crops	CRP	Pasture/Grasses	Forest
Appalachia	SG	−1,240	−611	116	−847
	MPB	−3,700	−1,960	51.9	−2,610
	Stover	929	929	929	929
	Forest residue	N/A	N/A	N/A	72.3
Corn Belt	SG	−2,030	−553	119	−1,940
	MPB	−5,020	−1,540	51.9	−4,800
	Stover	662	662	662	662
	Forest residue	N/A	N/A	N/A	44.6
Lake States	SG	−4,660	1,870	143	2,370
	MPB	−5,020	1,880	51.9	2,410
	Stover	782	782	782	782
	Forest residue	N/A	N/A	N/A	44.6
Northeast	SG	−3,600	−424	129	−2,070
	MPB	−5,740	−807	−51.9	−3,360
	Stover	1,230	1,230	1,230	1,230
	Forest residue	N/A	N/A	N/A	48.9

NOTE: In the CUBE model, mill residue is viewed as a pure residue, so GHG emissions associated with feedstock production are assumed to be zero under all scenarios. The values in this table are based on emission levels obtained in years 2–5 following conversion from the land use defined by the baseline ecosystem. In subsequent years, the contribution to emissions from direct land-use change emissions will be lower. In the case of stover, the scenario is further defined as one in which GHG emissions assigned to stover are only those marginal additional emissions associated with stover collection (i.e., the marginal production allocation scenario). In other words, stover is treated as a residue rather than as a crop in its own right.

---

[2] There is also considerable variability within a given scenario. We illustrate the impact of uncertainty in GHG emissions by considering a range of scenarios in detail herein; the final values in Tables E.9, E.10, and E.12 and used in the analysis in Chapter Six additionally include data uncertainty within these scenarios. The issue of uncertainty in GHG emissions is explored more fully in Johnson et al. (2011).

woody biomass feedstock (forest residue).[3] The baseline ecosystems considered in the CUBE model are (1) row crops, (2) CRP lands, (3) pasture or grasslands, and (4) forests.

Production emissions for a given feedstock also vary over time after the land is converted to cultivation of the biomass energy crop. This is due primarily to aboveground biomass changes in the first year and the declining rate of change in root and soil carbon, which equilibrate over approximately ten and 100 years, respectively. Table E.2 illustrates this point for three biomass feedstocks assumed to be grown in the Corn Belt region.

Another important source of uncertainty in GHG emissions results from assumptions made regarding the allocation of emissions across coproducts.[4] In this analysis, this allocation decision is relevant to forest and mill residues, which are both treated as nonprimary products in the CUBE model. The only production emissions for forest residues are related to harvest-

Table E.2
Production Greenhouse-Gas Emissions from the Calculating Uncertainty in Biomass Emissions Model: Impact of Time Since Land-Use Conversion for Herbaceous Feedstocks Grown in the Corn Belt Region on Four Baseline Ecosystems

Time Since Conversion	Biomass Feedstock	Production Emissions by Baseline Ecosystem, kg CO_2e/metric ton dry biomass			
		Row Crops	CRP	Pasture/Grasses	Forest
Year 1	SG	−2,030	250	508	19,000
	MPB	−5,020	361	971	44,700
	Stover	662	662	662	662
Years 2–5[a]	SG	−2,030	−553	119	−1,940
	MPB	−5,020	−1,540	51.9	−4,800
	Stover	662	662	662	662
Years 6–10	SG	−123	122	119	153
	MPB	−520	59.9	51.9	132
	Stover	662	662	662	662
Years 11–20	SG	−54.3	57.6	119	−71.0
	MPB	−357	−93.2	−51.9	−397
	Stover	52.4	52.4	52.4	52.4
Years 21–100	SG	86.6	108	119	83.4
	MPB	−24.9	24.7	51.9	−32.2
	Stover	52.4	52.4	52.4	52.4

NOTE: As earlier, for the case of stover, the scenario is further defined as one in which GHG emissions assigned to stover are only those marginal additional emissions associated with stover use (i.e., the marginal production allocation scenario). In other words, stover is treated as a residue rather than as a crop in its own right.
[a] Values for years 2–5 are the same as those presented in Table E.1.

---

[3] To determine all of the values in this appendix illustrating scenario uncertainty, all parameter values have been set to "mean" or "most likely" and the model was run in boundary analysis mode.

[4] Alternatively, this might be considered model uncertainty rather than scenario uncertainty.

ing, and mill residues are treated as a pure residue with no associated farming or production emissions. Stover emissions in the CUBE model are very dependent on allocation choice, as well as on assumptions regarding the impact that stover removal can have on soil carbon levels.[5] Table E.3 shows the effects of both of these assumptions.

Although it is important to consider this full range of potential net GHG emissions—which range from –5,740 to 44,700 kg CO_2e per dry metric ton biomass in the examples presented in Tables E.1–E.3—it is also instructive to focus on the most-likely scenarios for a given electricity generating facility. Based on the considerations detailed in Chapters Four and Five, a subset of regions and feedstocks are considered in this analysis, as summarized in Table E.4. The GHG values in Table E.4 represent emissions for the first five years following conversion of the specified baseline ecosystem to the biomass feedstock of interest, excluding any aboveground biomass changes.[6] Over a 30-year facility lifetime, the magnitude of many of these emission scenarios will decrease, assuming that the facility continues to source the same type of biomass from the same types of sites. Feedstocks are assumed to be obtained from the Northeast, Lake States, or Corn Belt region, with wood chips coming from the Northeast, wood pellets coming from the Lake States, and SG and stover pellets from the Corn Belt.

Biomass Handling, Processing, and Transport Emissions

Although the biomass production emissions described in the previous section often dominate total upstream GHG emissions of biomass feedstocks, other upstream processes (such as handling, processing, transporting, and storage) are also potential GHG sources. In this section, we describe how these were determined for this analysis and summarize the values used.

Direct emissions associated with loading and unloading are determined primarily by the amount of fuel or electricity used to operate the handling equipment and will vary with the types of biomass and relevant transport modes. For example, in this analysis, we assume that pellets are handled as dry grain would be, with a grain auger (see Appendix D and Edwards and Johanns, 2011). If this were performed by a 8.9 kW (12 hp) auger that can handle about 140 metric tons of biomass per hour, about 0.0685 kWh of electricity would be required per dry metric ton of biomass.[7] Resulting emissions of GHGs are on the order of 0.055 kg CO_2e per dry metric ton biomass.[8] This would correspond to about 0.1 percent of the biomass production emissions of the scenario with the lowest total net production emissions (see Table E.4). In most cases, it would be a much smaller fraction of emissions than this. Note

---

[5] The values calculated by the CUBE model are all based on the assumption that, when stover is removed for use as an energy feedstock in its own right, only 25 percent of the stover is harvested, and the balance remains on the field at the end of the harvest cycle. This is thought to avoid adverse impacts, such as excessive soil carbon loss and erosion.

[6] This is an especially important distinction in the case of forest baseline ecosystems, where aboveground biomass can be significant. Exclusion of aboveground biomass in net GHG calculations is equivalent to assuming that this biomass has been purposefully used and is either not contributing to net GHGs (e.g., biomass is turned into furniture) or is accounted for elsewhere (e.g., biomass was turned into fuel and associated GHGs are credited or debited separately).

[7] The specifications for the example from which these figures are derived are for 5,000–6,000 bushels per hour (Harvest International, undated). Assuming that corn is 56 lb per bushel and is 15.5 percent moisture, or 42.27 bushels per dry ton, this auger could move about 130 dry tons of grain per hour. One hp is roughly equivalent to 750 W.

[8] One kWh of electricity produces about 0.8 kg CO_2e, based on values in Greenhouse Gases, Regulated Emissions, and Energy Use in Transportation (GREET) 1.8.

Table E.3
Production Greenhouse-Gas Emissions from the Calculating Uncertainty in Biomass Emissions Model: Impact of Allocation and Soil Carbon Penalty Assumptions on Components of Production Emissions for Corn Stover for One Region-Baseline Ecosystem Scenario

Assumptions for Soil Carbon Penalty and Allocation	Production Emissions by Production Stage, kg CO$_2$e/metric ton dry biomass					
	Farming	Chemicals	Chemical Transport	Direct Land-Use Change	N$_2$O Emissions[a]	Total
Soil carbon penalty; marginal allocation[b]	0	30.9	1.08	610	20.4	662
Soil carbon penalty; mass-based allocation[c]	47.8	62.4	2.01	3,470	31.4	3,610
No soil carbon penalty; marginal allocation	0	30.9	1.08	0	20.4	52.4
No soil carbon penalty; mass-based allocation	47.8	62.4	2.01	3,360	31.4	3,500

NOTE: N$_2$O = nitrous oxide. The values in this table are based on a scenario defined by three assumptions for cultivation of corn biomass feedstocks: (1) grown in the Corn Belt region of the United States, (2) grown on former pasture or grassland, (3) emission levels are in years 2–5 following conversion to this land use. In subsequent years, direct land-use change emissions will be lower.

[a] N$_2$O emissions include both direct and indirect emissions from volatilization of excess nitrogen fertilizer.

[b] The final row of this table provides values for the case considered and carried forward in this analysis. This is also the default case in the CUBE 2.0 model.

[c] This is one value for the alternate stover case shown in Table E.4.

too that, even in a case in which production emissions were net zero, loading emissions of this magnitude would be less than 1 percent of the lowest processing and transport emission combinations considered in this analysis.[9] Other loading and unloading processes can be similarly estimated and result in similarly small emissions of GHGs. Consequently, we assume in this analysis that, although the *costs* of loading and unloading biomass are significant, the GHG emissions associated with these processes are not. We similarly assume that emissions associated with storage activities and infrastructure are negligible.

Processing biomass will also result in GHG emissions. The amount of these emissions depends on the ultimate desired form of biomass. The values we assume for this analysis are summarized in Table E.5. Three nonpellet woody biomass forms are included in the plant-site cost analysis: chunks, chips, and sawdust. In this analysis, we assume that a chipper, which processes 29.25 dry metric tons (32.2 dry tons) per hour, consumes 37 liters (9.77 gallons) of diesel per hour, which means that fuel use for chipping is 1.26 liters per dry metric ton

---

[9]   The model chipper is a Morbark 30/36A whole tree chipper fitted with a 325 hp diesel engine with a specific fuel consumption of 0.03 gallons per horsepower-hour. Additionally, in some cases, the small emissions that would be attributed to the loading process are actually included in the processing emissions. For example, when processing wood into chips, the blowing mechanism of the chipper itself often serves to load the chips onto a chip van or truck.

Table E.4
Production Emissions from the Calculating Uncertainty in Biomass Emissions Model: Scenarios Most Relevant to This Analysis

USDA Region	Biomass Feedstock	Production Emissions by Baseline Ecosystem, kg CO_2e/metric ton dry biomass			
		Row Crops	CRP	Pasture/Grasses	Forest
Northeast	SG	−3,600	−424	129	−2,070
	MPB	−5,740	−807	51.9	−3,360
	Forest residue	N/A	N/A	N/A	48.9[a]
	Mill residue	N/A	N/A	N/A	0
Lake States	SG	−4,660	1,870	143	2,370
	MPB	−5,020	1,880	51.9	2,410
	Forest residue	N/A	N/A	N/A	44.6[a]
Corn Belt	SG	−2,030[b]	−553[b]	119[b]	−1,940[b]
	MPB	−5,020	−1,540	51.9	−4,800
	Stover	662[b]	662[b]	662[b]	662[b]
	Stover, alternate[c]	255	2,560	3,610	400
	Forest residue	N/A	N/A	N/A	44.6

NOTE: The values in this table are based on emission levels obtained in years 2–5 following conversion from the land use defined by the baseline ecosystem. For the primary case of stover, the scenario is further defined as one in which GHG emissions assigned to stover are only those marginal additional emissions associated with stover use (i.e., the marginal production allocation scenario). In other words, stover is treated as a residue rather than as a crop in its own right.

[a] These exact values are carried forward in Table E.9 as the middle values for forest residue production emissions. Additional inclusion of data uncertainty provides the minimum and maximum values in Table E.9.

[b] This case is carried forward in the analysis and is used for the tallies in Table E.9. However, with inclusion of data uncertainty, the minimum, middle, and maximum values do not necessarily correspond to the exact values in this table.

[c] The alternate scenario also includes the soil carbon penalty for removal of stover, but it and all other emissions are split between stover and grain as a mass-based allocation between the two coproducts.

(0.303 gallons per dry ton).[10] If this chipper must be moved, on average, 160 km (100 miles) to a given chipping site, an additional 0.718 liters per dry metric ton (0.172 gallons per dry ton) of diesel fuel will be required.[11] The total fuel use per unit of wood chips is then 1.98 liters per dry metric ton (0.475 gallon per dry ton), and the GHG emissions associated with this diesel use are 6.52 kg CO_2e per dry metric ton. If the process of chunking wood is assumed to use 50 percent of the diesel that chipping required, this implies total emissions of 4.44 kg CO_2e per dry metric ton of wood chunks. The third nondensified woody fuel in this analysis, sawdust, is assumed to be obtained as mill residue and therefore has no associated processing emissions.

---

[10] The fuel-use rate is based on a throughput of 45 green metric tons per hour and 35-percent moisture content.

[11] Assuming 1.91 km per liter (4.5 miles per gallon) to haul the chipper 320 km (200 miles) roundtrip, the daily fuel consumption will be 168 liters (44.4 gallons). Further, assuming an eight-hour workday, 234 dry metric tons (258 dry tons) of chips will be produced each day.

Table E.5
Processing Emissions

Feedstock	Form	Processing Emissions, kg CO_2e/dry metric ton biomass[a]
Woody: forest residue	Chunks	4.44
	Chips	6.52[b]
	Pellets	319[b]
Woody: mill residue	Sawdust	0
	Pellets	175
Herbaceous: all	Bales	49.1[b]
	Pellets	222[b]
Mixed: forest residue: herbaceous, 50:50	Pellets	271
Mixed: mill residue: herbaceous, 50:50	Pellets	199

SOURCE: Total diesel emissions, direct and upstream = 3.294 kg CO_2e/ liter diesel, based on 95.0 kg CO_2e/mmBtu lower heating value (LHV) and 5.512 mmBtu/barrel (bbl) (NETL, 2008).

[a] The weight difference between dry biomass and the actual final form of the various feedstock fuels varies. For example, chips are 35-percent moisture, and pellets are 5-percent moisture.

[b] Value carried forward.

Both corn stover and perennial grasses (i.e., SG and MPB) are assumed to be gathered and transported as bales. In this analysis, we rely on the estimates from the CVBP for baling and stacking (Antares Group, 2009). We calculate associated emission values to be 17.5 and 31.6 kg CO_2e per dry ton biomass, respectively.[12]

In this analysis, pellets are assumed to be made from either woody biomass (i.e., derived from forest or mill residues) or herbaceous (i.e., SG, MPB, or stover) feedstocks. Here, we determine the emissions associated with single-sourced pellets first and then calculate the emissions associated with the mixed-feedstock pellets. Emissions from chopping, grinding, and pelletizing are assumed to be the same regardless of the feedstock, with the exception of mill residues, which will not require the hammer-mill processing prior to pelletization. This processing requires an energy input of 956 MJ per metric ton pelletized biomass for nonsawdust biomass (Sokhansanj and Fenton, 2006).[13] Assuming that this processing is performed using electricity with a fuel mix that reflects the average U.S. electricity portfolio implies emissions of 211 kg CO_2e per metric ton pellet biomass, or 222 kg CO_2e per dry metric ton.[14] As noted, mill residue is assumed to be in the form of sawdust and therefore not to require all initial sizing steps.

[12] The CVBP report (Antares Group, 2009) assumes emissions of 139.7 and 252.7 lb CO_2e per acre for baling and stacking, respectively. We further assume an herbaceous crop yield of approximately 4 dry tons per acre.

[13] The energy input required to produce pellets is estimated to be 956 MJ per metric ton, assuming that artificial drying is not required.

[14] The average emissions of U.S. electricity are approximately 0.794 kg per kWh (Wang, Wu, and Elgowainy, 2007).

Because these emissions are not incurred, total emissions for sawdust pelletization are lower, at 175 kg CO_2e per dry metric ton pellets.[15]

The initial moisture content, and the resulting required predrying, distinguishes pelletizing of forest residues from herbaceous biomass types, which are assumed to be 35- and 15-percent moisture, respectively. The herbaceous feedstocks are assumed to require no further drying before sizing and pelletizing, the final moisture level of pellets being achieved via the heating required by the pelletizing process itself. Mill residue sawdust is similarly assumed to require no predrying. On the other hand, predrying is required by woody feedstocks and leads to increased GHG emissions. Assuming that drying is performed using natural gas, the process requires 1.4 GJ per metric ton pellet biomass.[16] This is equivalent to 97.2 kg CO_2e per dry metric ton pellets, and these additional emissions are added to the other nondrying pelletizing emissions to obtain a value of 319 kg CO_2e per dry metric ton pellets.[17]

Transport GHG emissions depend both on the mode of transport and the distance over which the biomass is moved. Emissions associated with each of the three modes of transport considered in this analysis—truck, rail, and barge—were calculated based on the total GHG emissions from diesel fuel use divided by the ton-miles per gallon associated with each mode. Tables E.6–E.8 list the calculated per-ton-mile emissions from each of the three forms of transport included in this analysis. These are further converted to emissions per metric ton of biomass as received and to emissions per dry metric ton, depending on the distance shipped and the biomass form, as specified in Tables E.6–E.8.

Table E.6
Transport Parameters: Emissions and Distances, by Transport Mode

Transport Mode	Transport Emissions, kg CO_2e/metric ton-km
Barge, inland waterways	0.0148
Railroad	0.0207
Truck	0.0551

Table E.7
Transport Parameters: Emissions and Distances, by Transport Mode and Distance

Transport Mode (Distance, km)	Transport Emissions, kg CO_2e/metric ton
Barge, inland waterways (1,050)	15.5
Railroad (1,450)	30.0
Truck (84; 150; 300)	4.63; 8.27; 16.5

---

[15] According to Sokhansanj and Fenton (2006), the assumption is that sizing emissions contribute 21 percent of the total nondrying emissions of the pelletization process.

[16] This is equivalent to case 3 for densification considered in Appendix D. This value is less than the assumption in Sokhansanj and Fenton (2006), 2,440 MJ per metric ton, but is also based on lower initial moisture content.

[17] Derived from the information in GREET's "Fuel Specs" worksheet, the direct emissions of CO_2 from combustion of natural gas are 56.3 kg CO_2 per GJ (59.4 kg CO_2 per mmBtu); based on the GREET "NG" [natural gas] worksheet, upstream emissions are 9.7 kg CO_2e per GJ (10.2 kg CO_2e per mmBtu).

Table E.8
Transport Parameters: Emissions and Distances, by Biomass Form, Transport Mode, and Distance

Biomass Form; Transport Mode (Distance, km)	Transport Emissions, kg CO_2e/dry metric ton
Pellets via barge, inland waterways (1,050)	16.4
Pellets via railroad (1,450)	31.6
Chips via truck (84; 150; 300)	7.12; 12.7; 25.4
Bales via truck (84; 150; 300)	5.45; 9.72; 19.4
Sawdust via truck (84; 150; 300)	5.79; 10.3; 20.7

SOURCES: Total diesel emissions, direct and upstream: 12.47 kg CO_2e/gallon diesel, based on 95.0 kg CO_2e/mmBtu LHV and 5.512 mmBtu/bbl (NETL, 2008). Ton-miles per gallon for barge, rail, and truck: 576, 413, and 155, respectively (Kruse et al., 2009).

Total Biomass Emissions

Based on the GHG emission estimates described in the previous two sections, total net GHGs associated with biomass use can be calculated for the three scenarios considered in Chapter Five. For each scenario, consideration of different combinations of plausible biomass feedstock types and forms, as well as a range of assumptions regarding the region, baseline ecosystems, and allocation choices, allows low, mid-range, and high expected emissions to be estimated. In all of the cases, we characterize the life-cycle GHG emissions of the marginal economic unit of biomass—that is, the biomass that is the most expensive and assumed to be transported the farthest.

Scenario 1 is based on a facility located in western Pennsylvania that acquires only local biomass from within a given collection radius. The biomass feedstock is exclusively locally obtained wood chips, so the emissions will vary systematically based only on the transport distance required and not by differences in feedstock type and form or type of land on which the feedstock is grown. Expected GHG emissions associated with scenario 1 are listed in Table E.9. The final emission values that are carried forward into the results, i.e., the values used for the analysis in Chapter Six, are in noted in Table E.10.

Scenario 2 again is based on a western Pennsylvania cofire facility, but, in this scenario, biomass is obtained both locally and imported from outside of the region. The external biomass is assumed to be wood pellets transported by rail from the Lake States region. As shown in Chapter Five, pellets are more economical than raw wood chips when transporting biomass over this distance.[18] In scenario 2, the local fuel is wood chips and the external fuel is wood pellets. We assume that 75 percent of the input biomass energy comes from the local wood chips and 25 percent of the input biomass energy from the external pellets. The emissions for local wood chips are the same as they were in scenario 1. In this analysis, emissions associated with producing and delivering pellets depend on forest residue production emissions, transportation emissions both to the pelletization facility and long distance by rail and on chipping and pelletization emissions. The emissions in Table E.9 vary based only on the assumed truck

---

[18] The analysis in Chapter Five does not include any costs associated with changes in net GHG emissions when using biomass relative to coal-only operations, either positive or negative. Those considerations are made in Chapter Six based on the emissions calculated in this appendix.

Table E.9
Total Potential Greenhouse-Gas Emissions for All Individual Biomass Types and Forms Included in the Scenarios in This Analysis, Metric Tons

| Scenario | Description of Biomass Type(s) in Scenario | Total Emissions by Biomass Type, kg CO_2e/metric ton biomass | | |
		Low	Mid	High
1	Local Northeast wood chips	52.4	68.1	97.9
2	Local Northeast wood chips	52.4	68.1	97.9
	External Lake States wood pellets via rail	400	414	443
3	External Corn Belt SG pellets via barge	−2,440	−825	432
	External Corn Belt stover pellets via barge	925	960	1,090

NOTE: The values in this table, which carry forward to the analysis in Chapter Six, include data uncertainty in addition to the scenario uncertainty presented in detail in earlier sections of this appendix. This additional variability can be important but is generally much smaller in magnitude than scenario-related variation.

Table E.10
Total Potential Greenhouse-Gas Emissions for All Individual Biomass Types and Forms Included in the Scenarios in This Analysis, Gigajoules

| Scenario | Description of Biomass Scenario | Total Emissions by Biomass Type, kg CO_2e/GJ | | |
		Low	Mid	High
1	Local Northeast wood chips	2.76[a]	3.58[a]	5.16[a]
2	Local Northeast wood chips	2.76	3.58	5.16
	External Lake States wood pellets via rail	21.0	21.8	23.3
	75% woodchips, 25% wood pellets	7.33[a]	8.14[a]	9.69[a]
3	External Corn Belt SG pellets via barge	−143	−48.5	25.4
	External Corn Belt stover pellets via barge	54.4	56.4	64.1
	Mixed SG and corn stover pellets	−44.4[a]	3.97[a]	44.8[a]

[a] Value used for the analysis in Chapter Six.

distance required to move the biomass to the external pelletization facility. The final values from Table E.10 that carry forward (i.e., are used in the calculations for Table E.12 and Chapter Six) are noted.

Scenario 3 is based on a power facility located on the Ohio River that accepts biomass from external centralized biomass processing facilities via barge. Based on the economics of long-distance shipping as described in Chapter Five, all of this biomass is assumed to be delivered as pellets.[19] In scenario 3, biomass is assumed to be 50 percent SG pellets sourced from the

---

[19] This is again assuming the exclusion of any costs associated with GHGs.

Corn Belt and 50 percent corn stover pellets also sourced from the Corn Belt. GHG emissions associated with all of these scenarios are summarized in Table E.9, where the values noted are again used for the analysis in Chapter Six.

Coal Emissions

The net life-cycle GHG emissions embodied in coal fuel feedstock will include both upstream emissions related to mining and transport of the coal to the energy facility and those associated with combustion. Coal-mining emissions depend on the type of coal and include methane released during the mining process. The upstream values for bituminous coal are based on an NETL life-cycle analysis of an integrated gasification combined cycle (IGCC) plant (NETL, 2009a).[20] Subbituminous upstream emissions are based on an NETL life-cycle analysis of PRB mining and transport (NETL, 2009b).[21] Combustion emissions are calculated based on the carbon content and heating values of the respective coal types (Air Force Research Lab [AFRL], 2010; NETL, 2009b). All embodied coal emissions are summarized in Table E.11.

Table E.11
Coal Emissions

Emission Source	Bituminous Coal Emissions (kg CO_2e/GJ HHV)	Subbituminous Coal Emissions (kg CO_2e/GJ HHV)
Coal mining and transport	8.74	1.14
Coal combustion	86.2	124
Net emissions	95.0	125

SOURCES: NETL (2009a, 2009b); AFRL (2010).

Net Change in Fuel Greenhouse-Gas Emissions

To calculate the net change in GHG emissions embodied in the fuels that are associated with cofiring biomass with coal relative to coal-only combustion, we use the total GHG emissions of the various types and forms of biomass, as summarized in Table E.10, and make the following further assumptions:

- Biomass cofiring will be 2 percent, 5 percent, or 10 percent by energy content. We assume that the emissions from biomass sourcing are the same for the three cofire fractions.
- Mid-values for emissions from Table E.9 will be used as the expected values.
- For scenario 2, we assume that the biomass source is 75 percent wood chips and 25 percent wood-derived pellets.
- For scenario 3, we assume the herbaceous pellets are 50 percent each SG and stover.

---

[20] Mining and transport emission values for Illinois No. 6 coal were taken from Tables 2-1 and 2-4, respectively.

[21] Mining and transport emission values for PRB coal were taken from Tables 3-5 and 4-1, respectively.

The difference between the net biomass emissions and coal emissions is used to calculate the net change in emissions per kilowatt-hour. To do this, we use derived heat rates for cofiring as described in Appendix B for cofire fractions of 2 percent, 5 percent, and 10 percent. The net changes in life-cycle emissions relative to subbituminous coal-only electricity, which are noted in Table E.12, are the values used in the analysis in Chapter Six.

Plant-Site Emissions

In addition to the GHGs embodied in the fuel feedstocks themselves, which, as noted, include production, processing, transport, and combustion and were estimated as detailed in this appendix, there are also changes in net emissions associated with plant-process modifications that occur as a result of substituting biomass for coal. These translate into changes in the amount of diesel and electricity use per kilowatt-hour of electricity produced at the plant. The plant-site emissions are then based on diesel and electricity GHG emission values noted earlier—namely, (1) total diesel emissions, both direct and upstream, are 3.294 kg CO_2e per liter diesel, based on 95.0 kg CO_2e per mmBtu LHV and 5.512 mmBtu per barrel (NETL, 2008), and (2) total average emissions of U.S. electricity are approximately 0.794 kg per kilowatt-hour (Wang, Wu, and Elgowainy, 2007). The plant-site emissions are calculated within the model and are added to the net biomass fuel-associated emissions (i.e., the values in Table E.9), minus the net avoided emissions from coal (i.e., the values in Table E.12). The total emissions associated with the specific cofire ratios considered in this analysis are given in Table 6.1 in Chapter Six.

Table E.12
Change in Feedstock-Related Greenhouse-Gas Emissions Using Biomass Relative to Coal

| Scenario | Net Biomass Fuel Emissions (kg CO_2e/GJ) (from Table E.9) | | | Type of Coal | Change in Fuel Emissions Relative to Coal Only (kg CO_2e/GJ) | | |
	Low	Mid	High		Low Biomass GHGs	Mid Biomass GHGs	High Biomass GHGs
1	2.76	3.58	5.16	Bituminous	−92.2	−91.4	−89.8
				Subbituminous	−122[a]	−121[a]	−120[a]
2	7.33	8.14	9.69	Bituminous	−87.7	−86.9	−85.3
				Subbituminous	−118[a]	−117[a]	−115[a]
3	−44.4	3.97	44.8	Bituminous	−139	−91.0	−50.2
				Subbituminous	−169[a]	−121[a]	−80.2[a]

[a] Value carried forward to analysis in Chapter Six.

References

AFRL—*See* Air Force Research Lab.

Agricultural Marketing Service, U.S. Department of Agriculture, "Agricultural Transportation: Average Weekly Mississippi River Barge Rates," modified January 10, 2011. As of July 20, 2010:
http://www.ams.usda.gov/AMSv1.0/ams.fetchTemplateData.do?template=TemplateR&navID=AgriculturalTransportation&leftNav=AgriculturalTransportation&page=ATAverageWeeklyMSRiverBargeRates&description=%20Average%20Weekly%20Mississippi%20River%20Barge%20Rates&acct=transmodes

Air Force Research Lab, "Life Cycle Greenhouse Gas Analysis of Advanced Jet Propulsion Fuels: Fischer-Tropsch Based SPK-1 Case Study," Wright-Patterson Air Force Base, Ohio: U.S. Air Force, working final draft, 2010.

Alstom Power, "Co-Firing Biomass with Coal," 2008.

Andrews, Susan S., *Crop Residue Removal for Biomass Energy Production: Effects on Soils and Recommendations*, Washington, D.C.: U.S. Department of Agriculture, updated February 22, 2006. As of August 11, 2010:
http://soils.usda.gov/sqi/management/files/agforum_residue_white_paper.pdf

Antares Group, *Final Project Technical Report: Chariton Valley Biomass Project*, Landover, Md., May 2009. As of June 6, 2011:
http://www.iowaswitchgrass.com/__docs/pdf/Reports/CVBP%20Final%20Report.pdf

Antares Group and Parsons Power, *Utility Coal-Biomass Co-Firing Plant Opportunities and Conceptual Assessments*, December 13, 1996. As of June 6, 2011:
http://www.nrbp.org/pdfs/pub12.pdf

ASTM International, *Standard Specification for Coal Fly Ash and Raw or Calcined Natural Pozzolan for Use in Concrete*, Standard C618-08a, undated. As of June 8, 2011:
http://www.astm.org/Standards/C618.htm

BLS—*See* Bureau of Labor Statistics.

Bravender, Robin, "Biomass Industry Sees 'Chilling Message' in EPA's Greenhouse Gas Emissions Rule," *New York Times*, May 17, 2010. As of June 6, 2011:
http://www.nytimes.com/gwire/2010/05/14/14greenwire-biomass-industry-sees-chilling-message-in-epas-60072.html

Bureau of Economic Analysis, "Implicit Price Deflators for Gross Domestic Product," *National Economic Accounts*, Table 1.1.9, updated May 27, 2010. As of June 16, 2010:
http://www.bea.gov/national/nipaweb/TableView.asp?SelectedTable=13&Freq=Qtr&FirstYear=2009&LastYear=2011

Bureau of Labor Statistics, "Consumer Price Index," undated. As of May 31, 2010:
http://www.bls.gov/cpi/

Burlington Northern Santa Fe Railroad, "BNSF Railprices: Point and Click," undated. As of June 17, 2010:
http://www.bnsf.com/bnsf.was6/rp/RPLinkDisplayController

Cantor, R. A., and C. G. Rizy, "Biomass Energy: Exploring the Risks of Commercialization in the United States of America," *Bioresource Technology*, Vol. 35, No. 1, 1991, pp. 1–13.

Caputo, Antonio C., Mario Palumbo, Pacifico M. Pelagagge, and Federica Scacchia, "Economics of Biomass Energy Utilization in Combustion and Gasification Plants: Effects of Logistic Variables," *Biomass and Bioenergy*, Vol. 28, No. 1, January 2005, pp. 35–51.

Coosa-Alabama River Improvement Association, "Barges and Tugboats," undated. As of July 20, 2010: http://www.caria.org/barges_tugboats.html

Crane, Keith, Aimee E. Curtright, David S. Ortiz, Constantine Samaras, and Nicholas Burger, "The Economic Costs of Reducing Greenhouse Gas Emissions Under a U.S. National Renewable Electricity Mandate," *Energy Policy*, Vol. 39, No. 5, May 2011, pp. 2730–2739.

CSX, "Which Kind of Railcar Is Right?" undated (a).

———, "Price Look-Up," undated (b). As of June 17, 2010: http://shipcsx.com/public/ec.shipcsxpublic/Main?module=public.pricing

Curtright, Aimee E., Henry H. Willis, David R. Johnson, David S. Ortiz, Nicholas Burger, and Constantine Samaras, "Calculating Uncertainty in Biomass Emissions Model, Version 1.0 (CUBE 1.0)," March 1, 2010.

De, S., and M. Assadi, "Impact of Cofiring Biomass with Coal in Power Plants: A Techno-Economic Assessment," *Biomass and Bioenergy*, Vol. 33, No. 2, February 2009, pp. 283–293.

De la Torre Ugarte, Daniel, Marie E. Walsh, Hosein Shapouri, and Stephen P. Slinsky, *The Economic Impacts of Bioenergy Crop Production on U.S. Agriculture*, Washington, D.C.: U.S. Department of Agriculture, Office of the Chief Economist, Office of Energy Policy and New Uses, February 2003. As of June 23, 2011: http://www.usda.gov/oce/reports/energy/AER816Bi.pdf

Duffy, Mike, "Estimated Costs for Production, Storage and Transportation of Switchgrass," Ames, Iowa: Iowa State University Extension, file A1-22, February 2008. As of March 7, 2010: http://www.extension.iastate.edu/agdm/crops/html/a1-22.html

Economic Research Service, U.S. Department of Agriculture, "Farm Income: USDA Production Regions," updated October 21, 2008. As of June 1, 2011: http://www.ers.usda.gov/data/farmincome/USDA-Production-regions.htm

Edwards, William, and Ann Johanns, "2011 Iowa Farm Custom Rate Survey," Ames, Iowa: Iowa State University, revised March 2011. As of June 17, 2010: http://www.extension.iastate.edu/agdm/crops/pdf/a3-10.pdf

EIA—*See* Energy Information Administration.

Electric Power Research Institute, "Pneumatic Transport of Pulverized Wood Pellets," Palo Alto, Calif., September 30, 2010.

Energy Information Administration, U.S. Department of Energy, *Annual Energy Review 2008*, DOE/EIA-0384(2008), June 2009. As of August 4, 2010: http://www.eia.gov/FTPROOT/multifuel/038408.pdf

———, *Cost and Quality of Fuels for Electric Plants 2007 and 2008*, DOE/EIA-0191(2008), January 2010a. As of August 4, 2010: http://www.eia.gov/FTPROOT/electricity/cqa2008.pdf

———, *Annual Energy Outlook 2010*, May 2010b. As of June 10, 2011: http://www.eia.gov/oiaf/archive/aeo10/index.html

———, *Renewable Energy Annual 2008 Edition*, August 2010c. As of August 4, 2010: http://www.eia.gov/cneaf/solar.renewables/page/rea_data/rea_sum.html

———, "1990–2008 Net Generation by State by Type of Producer by Energy Source," *Electric Power Annual with Data for 2008*, Washington, D.C., November 23, 2010d. As of August 4, 2010: http://www.eia.doe.gov/cneaf/electricity/epa/generation_state.xls

EPA—*See* U.S. Environmental Protection Agency.

ERS—*See* Economic Research Service.

Fargione, Joseph, Jason Hill, David Tilman, Stephen Polasky, and Peter Hawthorne, "Land Clearing and the Biofuel Carbon Debt," *Science*, Vol. 319, No. 5867, February 29, 2008, pp. 1235–1238.

Flick, Steve, chair of the board, Show Me Energy Cooperative, personal communication with Tom LaTourrette, RAND Corporation, August 7, 2009.

Harvest International, "T-Series Auger Features," undated. As of July 30, 2010:
http://www.harvestauger.com/t-series-auger.php

Hill, Jason, Erik Nelson, David Tilman, Stephen Polasky, and Douglas Tiffany, "Environmental, Economic, and Energetic Costs and Benefits of Biodiesel and Ethanol Biofuels," *Proceedings of the National Academy of Sciences of the United States of America*, Vol. 103, No. 30, July 25, 2006, pp. 11206–11210.

Holmgren, Mark, Ken Casavant, and Eric L. Jessup, *Review of Transportation Costs for Alternative Fuels*, Pullman, Wash.: Washington State University School of Economic Sciences, Strategic Freight Transportation Analysis Research Report 25, December 2007. As of June 6, 2011:
http://www.sos.wa.gov/library/docs/dot/Report25_TransCostsAltFuels_2008_004943.pdf

Hughes, Evan, "Utility Coal-Biomass Cofiring Tests," *Proceedings of the Advanced Coal-Based Power and Environmental Systems Conference*, U.S. Department of Energy National Energy Technology Laboratory, paper 4.2, 1998.

———, "Biomass Cofiring: Economics, Policy and Opportunities," *Biomass and Bioenergy*, Vol. 19, No. 6, December 2000, pp. 457–465.

Idaho National Laboratory, "Uniform-Format Feedstock Supply System Design for Lignocellulosic Biomass," INL/EXT-08-14752 Revision 0, Idaho Falls, Idaho. March 2009.

INL—*See* Idaho National Laboratory.

Johnson, David R., Henry H. Willis, Aimee E. Curtright, Constantine Samaras, and Timothy Skone, "Incorporating Uncertainty Analysis into Life Cycle Estimates of Greenhouse Gas Emissions from Biomass Production," *Biomass and Bioenergy*, Vol. 35, No. 7, July 2011, pp. 2619–2626.

Kruse, James C., Annie Protopapas, Leslie E. Olson, and David H. Bierling, *A Modal Comparison of Domestic Freight Transportation Effects on the General Public*, U.S. Department of Transportation Maritime Administration and National Waterways Foundation, December 2007, amended March 2009. As of June 7, 2011:
http://www.nationalwaterwaysfoundation.org/study/public%20study.pdf

Kumar, Amit, Jay B. Cameron, and Peter C. Flynn, "Pipeline Transport of Biomass," *Applied Biochemistry and Biotechnology*, Vol. 113, No. 1–3, March 2004, pp. 27–39.

———, "Pipeline Transport and Simultaneous Saccharification of Corn Stover," *Bioresource Technology*, Vol. 96, No. 7, May 2005, pp. 819–829.

LaTourrette, Tom, David S. Ortiz, Eileen Hlavka, Nicholas Burger, and Gary Cecchine, *Supplying Biomass to Power Plants: A Model of the Costs of Utilizing Agricultural Biomass in Cofired Power Plants*, Santa Monica, Calif.: RAND Corporation, TR-876-DOE, 2011. As of June 6, 2011:
http://www.rand.org/pubs/technical_reports/TR876.html

Leesley, Rick, personal communication with Tom LaTourrette, RAND Corporation, July 23, 2009.

Mahmudi, Hamed, and Peter C. Flynn, "Rail vs Truck Transport of Biomass," *Applied Biochemistry and Biotechnology*, Vol. 129, No. 1–3, March 2006, pp. 88–103.

Mani, S., S. Sokhansanj, X. Bi, and A. Turhollow, "Economics of Producing Fuel Pellets from Biomass," *Applied Engineering in Agriculture*, Vol. 22, No. 3, 2006, pp. 421–426.

Manomet Center for Conservation Sciences, *Biomass Sustainability and Carbon Policy Study*, Brunswick, Maine, June 2010.

Massachusetts Institute of Technology, *The Future of Coal: Options for a Carbon-Constrained World*, Boston, Mass., 2007. As of June 6, 2011:
http://web.mit.edu/coal/The_Future_of_Coal.pdf

McGowan, Thomas F., ed., *Biomass and Alternate Fuel Systems: An Engineering and Economic Guide*, Hoboken, N.J.: John Wiley and Sons, 2009.

McKendry, Peter, "Energy Production from Biomass (Part 1): Overview of Biomass," *Bioresource Technology*, Vol. 83, No. 1, May 2002, pp. 37–46.

Milbrandt, A., *A Geographic Perspective on the Current Biomass Resource Availability in the United States*, Washington, D.C.: U.S. Department of Energy, NREL/TP-560-39181, December 2005. As of June 6, 2011: http://www.osti.gov/servlets/purl/861485-eVMQig/

MIT—*See* Massachusetts Institute of Technology.

National Coal Council, *Opportunities to Expedite the Construction of New Coal-Based Power Plants*, Washington, D.C., 2004.

National Energy Technology Laboratory, "Energy Analyses—Model; Calculating Uncertainty in Biomass Emissions, Version 1.0 (CUBE 1.0)," undated. As of June 13, 2011: http://www.netl.doe.gov/energy-analyses/cube_model.html

———, "NETL Coal Plant Database," as of 2007.

———, *Development of Baseline Data and Analysis of Life Cycle Greenhouse Gas Emissions of Petroleum-Based Fuels*, DOE/NETL-2009/1346, November 26, 2008. As of June 6, 2011: http://www.netl.doe.gov/energy-analyses/pubs/NETL%20LCA%20Petroleum-based%20Fuels%20Nov%20 2008.pdf

———, *Life Cycle Analysis: Integrated Gasification Combined Cycle (IGCC) Power Plant*, DOE/NETL-403/110209, draft, 2009a.

———, *Life Cycle Analysis: Powder River Basin Coal Mining and Train Transport*, Subtask 41817.403.01.14, Activity 3), draft, 2009b.

———, *Affordable, Low-Carbon Diesel Fuel from Domestic Coal and Biomass*, Pittsburgh, Pa.: U.S. Department of Energy, January 2009c.

———, "Cost and Performance Baseline for Fossil Energy Plants," Pittsburgh, Pa.: U.S. Department of Energy, 2010.

NCC—*See* National Coal Council.

NETL—*See* National Energy Technology Laboratory.

North American Electric Reliability Corporation, *2010 Special Reliability Scenario Assessment: Resource Adequacy Impacts of Potential U.S. Environmental Regulations*, Princeton, N.J., October 2010. As of June 6, 2011: http://www.nerc.com/files/EPA_Scenario_Final.pdf

Oak Ridge National Laboratory Center for Transportation Analysis, *Biomass Energy Data Book, Edition 2*, Oak Ridge, Tenn., 2010.

ORNL—*See* Oak Ridge National Laboratory.

Rösch, Christine, and Martin Kaltschmitt, "Energy from Biomass: Do Non-Technical Barriers Prevent an Increased Use?" *Biomass and Bioenergy*, Vol. 16, No. 5, May 1999, pp. 347–356.

Searchinger, Timothy, Ralph Heimlich, R. A. Houghton, Fengxia Dong, Amani Elobeid, Jacinto Fabiosa, Simla Tokgoz, Dermot Hayes, and Tun-Hsiang Yu, "Use of U.S. Croplands for Biofuels Increases Greenhouse Gases Through Emissions from Land-Use Change," *Science*, Vol. 319, No. 5867, February 29, 2008, pp. 1238–1240.

Sokhansanj, Shahab, and Jim Fenton, *Cost Benefit of Biomass Supply and Pre-Processing*, Kingston, Ont.: BIOCAP Canada, March 2006. As of July 30, 2010: http://www.biocap.ca/rif/report/Sokhansanj_S.pdf

Sokhansanj, Shahab, Anthony Turhollow, Janet Cushman, and John Cundiff, "Engineering Aspects of Collecting Corn Stover for Bioenergy," *Biomass and Bioenergy*, Vol. 3, No. 5, November 2002, pp. 347–355.

Solomon, Jordan, personal communication with Nicholas Burger, David Ortiz, and Constantine Samaras, RAND Corporation, June 11, 2010.

Tennessee Valley Authority, "Coal-Fired Power Plant," undated. As of May 26, 2011:
http://www.tva.gov/power/coalart.htm

Tharakan, Pradeep J., Timothy A. Volk, Christopher A. Lindsey, Lawrence P. Abrahamson, and Edwin H. White, "Evaluating the Impact of Three Incentive Programs on the Economics of Cofiring Willow Biomass with Coal in New York State," *Energy Policy*, Vol. 33, No. 3, February 2005, pp. 337–347.

Tillman, David A., "Biomass Cofiring: The Technology, the Experience, the Combustion Consequences," *Biomass and Bioenergy*, Vol. 19, No. 6, December 2000, pp. 365–384.

———, *Final Report: EPRI-USDOE Cooperative Agreement: Cofiring Biomass with Coal*, Clinton, N.J.: Foster Wheeler, September 2001. As of July 29, 2010:
http://www.osti.gov/energycitations/servlets/purl/794284-R0SmnT/native/794284.pdf

Tilman, David, Jason Hill, and Clarence Lehman, "Carbon-Negative Biofuels from Low-Input High-Diversity Grassland Biomass," *Science*, Vol. 314, No. 5805, December 2006, pp. 1598–1600.

Trømborg, Erik, Torjus Folsland Bolkesjø, and Birger Solberg, "Biomass Market and Trade in Norway: Status and Future Prospects," *Biomass and Bioenergy*, Vol. 32, No. 8, August 2008, pp. 660–671.

University of Missouri Extension, "Large Round Balers," revised March 1987. As of July 30, 2010:
http://extension.missouri.edu/publications/DisplayPub.aspx?P=G1250

U.S. Environmental Protection Agency, "Proposed Transport Rule Would Reduce Interstate Transport of Ozone and Fine Particle Pollution," Washington, D.C., c. July 2010a. As of June 7, 2011:
http://www.epa.gov/airtransport/pdfs/FactsheetTR7-6-10.pdf

———, "Fact Sheet—Proposed Rule: Prevention of Significant Deterioration and Title V Greenhouse Gas Tailoring Rule," Washington, D.C., updated November 10, 2010b.

———, "National Emission Standards for Hazardous Air Pollutants from Coal- and Oil-Fired Electric Utility Steam Generating Units and Standards of Performance for Fossil-Fuel–Fired Electric Utility, Industrial-Commercial-Institutional, and Small Industrial-Commercial-Institutional Steam Generating Units: A Proposed Rule by the Environmental Protection Agency on May 3, 2011," *Federal Register*, Vol. 76, May 3, 2011a, pp. 24976–25147. As of June 23, 2011:
http://federalregister.gov/a/2011-7237

———, "Cross-State Air Pollution Rule (CSAPR)," last updated July 11, 2011b. As of July 18, 2011:
http://www.epa.gov/crossstaterule/index.html

Van Loo, Sjaak, and Jaap Koppejan, eds., *The Handbook of Biomass Combustion and Co-Firing*, London: Earthscan, 2008.

Ventyx, "The Velocity Suite," date unknown.

Wahlund, Bertil, Jinyue Yan, and Mats Westermark, "Increasing Biomass Utilisation in Energy Systems: A Comparative Study of CO_2 Reduction and Cost for Different Bioenergy Processing Options," *Biomass and Bioenergy*, Vol. 26, No. 6, June 2004, pp. 531–544.

Wang, Michael, May M. Wu, and Amgad Elgowainy, "GREET 1.8 Fuel-Cycle Model for Transportation Fuels and Vehicle Technologies," Argonne, Ill.: Argonne National Laboratory, 2007.

Wiltsee, G., *Lessons Learned from Existing Biomass Power Plants*, Golden, Colo.: National Renewable Energy Laboratory, NREL/SR-570-26946, February 2000. As of July 29, 2010:
http://www.nrel.gov/docs/fy00osti/26946.pdf